The Reading Room
Saint Martin in the Fields Church
3110 ASHFORD DUNWOODY ROAD •ATLANTA, GEORGIA 30319 •404/261-4292

Kairos
and Logos

Kairos
and Logos

Studies in
the Roots and Implications
of Tillich's Theology

edited by
JOHN J. CAREY

MERCER

ISBN 0-86554-106-X

All books published by Mercer University Press are produced
on acid-free paper that exceeds the minimum standards set by the
National Historical Publications and Records Commission.

Library of Congress Cataloging in Publication Data:

Kairos and logos.

Includes bibliographical references.
1. Tillich, Paul, 1886-1965—Addresses, essays, lectures.
I. Carey, John Jesse.
BX4827.T53K33   1984   230'.092'4   84-6738
ISBN 0-86554-106-X (alk. paper)   '

Contents

Part I
Tillich and the Western Philosophical Tradition:
Critical Assessments of
His Roots, Debts and Perspectives

Dedication

This book is dedicated to:

RENATE ALBRECHT

Editor of Tillich's *Gesammelte Werke*

GERTRAUT STÖBER

Curator of the Tillich Archive, Göttingen, Germany

in appreciation for their work in recording,
editing, and guiding into publication
the previously unpublished materials
of Paul Tillich.

Preface

The publication of this volume has been a project of the North American Paul Tillich Society, which was founded in Chicago in October, 1975 following two national consultations on Tillich Studies sponsored by the American Academy of Religion. The Society has worked with the European Tillich Gesellschaft (founded in 1960) to encourage creative theological scholarship consistent with Tillich's wide ranges of interest. A number of the studies published in this volume were initially presented for discussion at the national meeting of the Society in 1975, 1976, and 1977.

I am indebted to Professor James Luther Adams for his sagacious counsel on several points as this volume began to take shape, and to Professors Jack Boozer of Emory University and Franklin Sherman of the Lutheran School of Theology in Chicago for their assistance as members of the Publications Committee of the North American Paul Tillich Society.

Juliana Klein and Linda Loyd of the Department of Religion at Florida State University patiently and accurately typed and retyped the manuscript, and retained their good spirits over many months through many revisions and details. Without their help this manuscript would never have seen the light of day.

The Society gratefully acknowledges a grant from the Sarah Campbell Blaffer Foundation of Houston, Texas, which facilitated the publication of the volume.

Tallahassee, Florida   *John J. Carey*
June 7, 1978

Preface
to the Second Printing

The North American Paul Tillich Society is pleased to have this volume reprinted by Mercer University Press. The limited funds of the Society restricted the advertisement and circulation of the 1978 edition, and we are grateful for this opportunity to make the work available to a broader community of scholars. This book now stands as volume 1 in the NAPTS—Mercer University Series on Paul Tillich Studies; volume 2 is the companion work entitled *Theonomy and Autonomy: Studies in Tillich's Engagement with Modern Culture* (1984). We anticipate additional joint publications in this series.

I have used this occasion to make several editorial changes in the original text and to update the "Notes in Contributors" section. Special thanks go to Dr. Watson E. Mills, director of the Mercer University Press, for his early interest in this project, and to Ms. India Fuller, whose editorial skills at the Press helped to bring this project to fruition.

Tallahassee, Florida   *John J. Carey*
February 21, 1984

Editor's Introduction

There is no such thing as a "safe" theology. All theology which is earnest is also dangerous. It is an act of adoration fraught with the risk of blasphemy.

Expository Times, 64:11,
in an editorial memorializing Paul Tillich.

The above words are an appropriate testimony to the vision and boldness of Paul Tillich's theological endeavors. The studies found in this volume are tributes to Tillich's continued influence in Christian theology, and are attempts to clarify the intertwining of philosophical, theological, and cultural facets in Tillich's thought. Because Tillich was such a "boundary" thinker, who probed the fields of philosophy, theology, and culture in both their European and American contexts, his legacy to a succeeding generation has been rich and diffuse. The thirteen years since his death have given us time to assess better his roots and distinctive viewpoints, and the recently published biography of Tillich by Wilhelm and Marian Pauck has brought to a wider public a perspective of Tillich's life and intellectual development.[1] Although Tillich cannot be said to have founded a "school" of theological inquiry which is identifiable by viewpoint or methodology, his creative and dialectical way of looking at problems has influenced numerous scholars in Europe, the United States and Canada, and his works continue to be a source of exegetical probing for Protestant and Roman Catholic scholars alike.[2]

It is surprising that, given Tillich's stature and influence, there has been no single volume in the past twenty-five years which comprehensively reappraised his thought and its implications for the contemporary theological scene. There have been, of course, many dissertations and recent monographs which have illumined particular facets of Tillich's thought,[3] but no work in English has attempted a broad-gauge assessment of Tillich's work since the long-outdated Kegley and Bretall volume of 1952, *The Theology of Paul Tillich* (New York: The Macmillan Company). The festschrift for Tillich edited by Walter Leibrecht in 1959 entitled *Religion and Culture* (New York: Harper and Row) was an impressive profes-

---

[1]*Paul Tillich: His Life and Thought*, vol. 1 (New York: Harper and Row, 1976).

[2]Thor Hall, in his *Directory of Systematic Theologians in North America* (Council on the Study of Religion and the University of Tennessee at Chattanooga, 1977), requested the 554 respondents to his questionnaire to indicate which theologian(s) they would regard as a "Major Mentor." Tillich was the most frequently cited thinker (123 designations), leading Thomas Aquinas (87), Karl Rahner (78), Karl Barth (76), St. Augustine (51), and John Calvin (47).

[3]*The Journal of Presbyterian History*, vol. 53, no. 2 (Summer 1975), lists fifty-three doctoral dissertations done on Tillich in the United States and Canada from 1965-1972 alone. Frau Gertraut Stöber has informed me that the Tillich Archive in Göttingen has copies of forty-five European doctoral dissertations on Tillich, twenty-one of which have been written by Protestants, and twenty-four of which have been written by Roman Catholics. In addition to these studies, some representative recent monographs would include Leonard Wheat, *Paul Tillich's Dialectical Humanism: Unmasking the God Above God* (Baltimore: Johns Hopkins Press, 1970); Eberhard Amelung, *Die Gestalt der Liebe: Paul Tillich's Theologie der Kultur* (Gutersloher Verlagshaus Gerd Mohn, 1972); Wayne W. Mahan, *Tillich's System* (San Antonio: Trinity University Press, 1974); Jean-Claude Petit, *La Philosophie de la Religion de Paul Tillich, Genese et Evolution: La Period Allemande 1919-1933* (Montreal: Fides, 1974); Alistair M. MacLeod, *Paul Tillich: An Essay on the Role of Ontology in His Philosophical Theology* (London: Allen and Unwin, 1974); Robert W. Schrader, *The Nature of Theological Argument: A Study of Paul Tillich* (Missoula MT: Scholars Press, 1975); Ronald Modras, *Paul Tillich's Theology of the Church: A Catholic Appraisal* (Detroit: Wayne State University Press, 1976); and John R. Stumme, *Socialism in Theological Perspective: A Study of Paul Tillich, 1918-1933* (Missoula MT: Scholars Press, 1978).

sional tribute to Tillich but (save for Leibrecht's Introduction and the articles by Gustave Weigel and Erich Przywara) was not edifying as to the roots or implications of his thought. The volume edited by Thomas F. O'Meara, O. P., and Donald M. Weisser, O. P., *Paul Tillich in Catholic Thought* (Chicago: Priory Press, 1964) was a noteworthy anthology of how Catholic thinkers had appropriated Tillich's thought, but much of the Catholic perspective mirrored in that volume is pre-Vatican II, and the volume has a heavy concentration on revelation, which was, of course, just one aspect of Tillich's thought. The five articles in the special issue of *Religion in Life* (Winter, 1966), which were subsequently printed separately by Abingdon Press as *Paul Tillich: Retrospect and Future* (1966), were all thoughtful assessments of Tillich, but the brevity of the articles limited their importance for a later theological generation. The North American Paul Tillich Society published a volume entitled *Tillich Studies: 1975* in conjunction with the founding meeting of the Society, but the limited scope of that volume (it concentrated on Tillich's understanding of politics) could not do justice to the many ways that Tillich's influence is still felt. I hope that this present volume, therefore, will fill a long-needed gap in the exploration of the philosophical, theological, and cultural dimensions of Tillich's thought.

I

With regard to Tillich's roots in the Western philosophical tradition, this volume contains studies exploring his interaction with Schelling, Kant and Hegel, along with two studies (by Robert Scharlemann and Roy D. Morrison II) which consider problem areas in Tillich's philosophy of religion. Although it has been frequently said that Tillich owed much to Schelling, that relationship was unclear for most English-speaking scholars for many years both because much of Schelling's work had never been translated into English and because Tillich's two dissertations on Schelling were never translated.[4] English-speaking scholars are now able to follow Tillich's studies of Schelling more precisely because of the recent trans-

---

[4]One of the few attempts in the English-speaking world to probe Tillich's appropriation of Schelling was Günther Sommer's *The Significance of the Late Philosophy of Schelling for the Formation and Interpretation of the Thought of Paul Tillich* (unpublished Ph.D. dissertation, Duke University, 1960).

lation of the Schelling dissertations by Victor Nuovo.[5] It seems appropriate, therefore, that this volume begin with Jerome Stone's essay that
succinctly explores this important root of Tillich's thought. Tillich, it will
be noted, was not uncritical in his appropriation of Schelling, but a number
of concepts found in Schelling shaped Tillich's philosophical assumptions
for the rest of his life. Roy D. Morrison II, in his analysis of Tillich's engagement with naturalism, points out how Schelling influenced Tillich's
doctrine of natural evolution, and furthermore showed Tillich how the concept of being could be incorporated into an understanding of nature.

Victor Nuovo's contribution to this volume takes seriously Tillich's own
capacity for intellectual growth and self-criticism, and critically compares
Tillich's notion of theonomy with Kant's call for a religion based on autonomous reason. Given Tillich's ties with German idealism, a study of his
thought informed by Kantian insights is both timely and clarifying—even if
Nuovo does finally side with Kant!

The most technical piece of writing in the present volume is the essay
by Robert Scharlemann on the question of truth in Tillich's philosophy of
religion. This study picks up an elusive problem in some of Tillich's early
writings on the philosophy of religion, probing both the paradoxical nature
of religious truth and Tillich's notion of the "conquest" (*Uberwindung*) of
the concept of religion. Scharlemann's article was first presented as a paper to the Paul Tillich Gesellschaft at its 1976 meeting at Hofgeismar.

Roy Morrison examines the relationship between idealism and naturalism in Tillich's thought—a point of considerable dispute among those
who have sought to find an appropriate niche for Tillich in the history of
Western philosophy. Morrison argues that Tillich, via dialectical reasoning, incorporates this voluntaristic form of naturalism into his ontology,
thus yoking nature and idea, thinking and being, into a mystical unity. Morrison's analysis clarifies why Tillich several times described his philosophical position as a self-transcending or "ecstatic" naturalism, and how
Tillich sought to avoid the pitfalls of reductionism so often associated with
naturalism.

---

[5]The dissertations are *The Construction of the History of Religion in Schelling's Positive
Philosophy: Its Presuppositions and Principles* (1910); and *Mysticism and Guilt-Conscious-
ness in Schelling's Philosophical Development* (1912). Both were published by the Bucknell
University Press in 1974.

II

Primarily because of the changed theological climate since Tillich's death, his work in systematic theology has not been studied or cited as much as one would have anticipated fifteen years ago. Although the first volume of his *Systematic Theology* did not appear until 1951, the recent Pauck biography clarifies that Tillich had an interest in developing his thought in a systematic manner as early as the 1920s. In his contribution to this volume, Paul Wiebe sees the roots of Tillich's becoming a systematic theologian in his 1923 work, *Das System der Wissenschaften*, and describes two periods in Tillich's intellectual life (designated as Tillich I and Tillich II) based on the transition from philosophical/scientific interests to those of a more theological focus. John Clayton furthers the probe of Tillich as a theologian by examining Tillich's famous "method of correlation." Clayton points out that the "questioning" and "answering" schema found in that method actually has much earlier roots, and grows out of Tillich's engagements with Barth and other dialectical theologians in the 1920s. At a time when Tillich scholarship has tended to emphasize Tillich's political and cultural interests as the dominant motifs of his early career, these essays serve as a corrective and put his theological concerns in proper focus.

Joel Smith turns his attention to one of the vexing problems in Tillich's theology: the relationship between human freedom and divine creativity in the fall of man. The difficulties of that topic, of course, have filled many a theological tome, and Smith is clearly not satisfied with Tillich's solution that "God fulfills creation by directing human freedom to actualize itself in an estranged existence." On the whole Smith feels that Tillich's approach to theodicy is too abstract, and thus not satisfying nor persuasive for contemporary persons. Smith's paper was initially presented for discussion at the 1977 meeting of the North American Paul Tillich Society in San Francisco.

Eberhard Amelung's essay, while showing engagement with Tillich's concept of "life" (a theme, by the way, that has seldom been explored by Tillich scholars), moves beyond exegesis to probe the implications and adequacy of Tillich's thought on this problem for the present situation. Amelung is concerned about the social fabric of modern life, and he sees a problem in Tillich's tendency to stress the importance of the integrated self in his ethics. Behind Amelung's essay, although not addressed directly by

him, lies the criticism that in his later years Tillich retreated from his earlier social and political interests and became preoccupied with the "centered" self. That criticism, in turn, implies a transition in Tillich from
philosophical to psychological and/or ethical concerns. Amelung's essay
was initially presented to the North American Paul Tillich Society at its
founding meeting in Chicago of 1975.

III

The bulk of the studies in this volume, however, deal with Tillich's theology of culture. The past decade would suggest that it is in this area that
Tillich has most influenced a later theological generation, despite the fact
that our generation now sees problems pertaining to religion and culture
that Tillich did not see. (Black theology and feminist theology are cases in
point.) Three of America's well-known theologians of culture—Tom F.
Driver of Union Seminary in New York, Harvey Cox of the Harvard Divinity School, and Richard L. Rubenstein of Florida State University—have
acknowledged in print their indebtedness to Tillich.[6] The essays contained
here probe both the roots and implications of Tillich's understanding of culture. John Heywood Thomas, England's foremost Tillich scholar, has been
doing impressive studies of Tillich's approach to culture for a number of
years, and emphasizes in his contribution to this volume the influences
that Hegel had on Tillich's concept of culture. Thomas gives particular attention to the impact of Hegel's essay on "The Spirit of Christianity." Tillich's debt to Hegel is underscored by Thomas as opposed to the oft-cited
other influence of post-World War I politics or the aesthetic impact of German Expressionism. The difficulties in giving too much weight to Tillich
as a Hegelian, however, are pointed out by Robert R. N. Ross in his reply
to Professor Thomas. Ross would give more emphasis to the KAIROS
theme in Tillich's thought, arguing that the KAIROS concept establishes
that Tillich was not Hegelian. This exchange sharpens the dialectical way
that Tillich used the terms, KAIROS and LOGOS, and shows why both exis-
tentialists and essentialists have been drawn to Tillich.

---

[6]See Driver's article, "Form and Energy: An Argument with Paul Tillich," *Union Sem-
inary Quarterly Review*, vol. 31, no. 2 (Winter 1976): 102-12; Cox, *Seduction of the Spirit*
(New York: Simon and Schuster, 1973) 262-67; and Rubenstein's *Power Struggle* (New
York: Charles Scribner's Sons, 1974) 154-64.

The contemporary relevance of Tillich's theology of culture is explored by Raymond F. Bulman. Bulman is particularly interested in how Tillich appraised technology and its influence on culture. Tillich's more optimistic (although still dialectical) view towards technology is clarified through a comparison to the dour French Protestant Jacques Ellul. Whereas Bulman is inclined to see a continuity in Tillich's approach to culture, John Stumme sees more discontinuity between the early and late Tillich. Essentially Stumme argues that Tillich in his later years was less critical of modern culture than he was in his earlier Socialist period. The contributions of Professors Thomas, Ross, Bulman, and Stumme were all initially presented to the North American Paul Tillich Society at its 1976 meeting in St. Louis.

There are other important dimensions of Tillich's understanding of culture that receive consideration in this volume. Tillich's interest in art and aesthetics is examined by Donald R. Weisbaker, who draws on some previously unpublished materials found in the Tillich Archive at Harvard. His work illumines Tillich's well-known interests in symbols. Robert Bryant sharply criticizes Tillich for his tendency to deal with abstract or overly generalized concepts in his writings on the theology of culture; he finds Tillich long on theory and short on specific insight into practical problems. Bryant feels that this deficiency in Tillich's thought is rooted in Tillich's too-abstract approach to christology. (Bryant's essay adds some fuel to the long-standing criticism of Tillich's christology as the "Achilles Heel" of his theology.) Frederick Reisz, Jr., on the other hand, finds both Tillich's perspectives on religious socialism and his doctrine of God as Spirit richly suggestive (and largely untapped) sources for contemporary liberation theologians. His essay shows how Tillichian categories can be applied to a different historical, cultural and political context, and is one of the most suggestive essays in the entire volume for the implications of Tillich's thought for today. I regret that this volume does not contain a study of Tillich from a feminist perspective, but it is clear that such work is going on and that, on the whole, feminist theologians have a positive sense of Tillich's approach to personhood.[7]

---

[7]See, for example, Joan Arnold Romero's "The Protestant Principle: A Woman's Eye-View of Barth and Tillich," in Rosemary Reuther, *Religion and Sexism* (New York: Simon and Schuster, 1974) 319-40. A more detailed treatment of Tillich and female experience is found in Judith Plaskow's 1975 unpublished Yale Ph.D. dissertation, *Sex, Sin and Grace: Women's Experience and the Theologies of Reinhold Niebuhr and Paul Tillich.*

Overall, the essays contained in this volume enable us to see Tillich more clearly amid the philosophical and theological currents of his day, and sharpen our sense of Tillich as a "boundary thinker." It is obvious, I think, that the group of scholars who acknowledge Tillich's influence are not sycophantic in their approach to his analysis and method, but are rather indebted to his critical spirit and his search for what he once called "beliefful realism." Whether one agrees or disagrees with Tillich's starting points in philosophy, theology or concept of culture, one cannot but be impressed by the creative ways that he sought solutions to old problems, and for the fresh ways that he addressed the problems of his lifetime. One might, in fact, say about Tillich what he once said about Marx, namely, that the questions that he asked were so important that it does not matter if his answers need revising.

I hope that this volume might add to the critical reassessment of Tillich's thought that is already going on in North America, South America and Europe, and that it will clarify for readers the resources that Tillich provides for an ever-changing theological situation.

Part I
TILLICH
AND THE WESTERN
PHILOSOPHICAL TRADITION:
CRITICAL ASSESSMENTS
OF HIS ROOTS, DEBTS,
AND PERSPECTIVES

Tillich
and Schelling's
Later Philosophy

JEROME ARTHUR STONE

We have always heard that Schelling exerted a strong influence on Til-lich, but until recently our study of Schelling has been largely limited to *Of Human Freedom* and *The Ages of the World*, unless we tried an exhausting study of German texts. *The Philosophy of Mythology and Revelation* was available only in a German edition of about 2,000 pages. One of Tillich's two dissertations on Schelling was available in German in the first volume of his *Gesammelte Werke*, while the other was extant in only a very few cop-ies in this country, not having been reissued since its appearance in 1910.

Recently this situation has changed. Some of Schelling's texts have ap-peared in translation and a number of studies have appeared. Both of Til-lich's Schelling dissertations are now available in English. With the appearance of this material and the continued interest in Tillich's early work, the interrelationship between these two thinkers will undoubtedly continue to be studied.

The Historical Significance
of Schelling in His Time

BEYOND RATIONALISM AND IDEALISM. Within his own time Schelling represents the "end" of German idealism in the sense that in his own development he had started with Fichte's use of Kant's moral categories as the basis for philosophy, moved on to a full-blown and vigorous idealism running side-by-side with Hegel, and then, in the transition to the second great period of his philosophy, the idealist elements in his thought had run up against their limits and this called for a re-orientation of philosophical procedures.[1] This re-orientation of philosophy, instead of involving a critical limitation on the part of philosophy in the vein of Kant, involved the philosophical investigation of the prior reality which is presented for philosophy's comprehension.

> Outside of that which pure thought discovers as being in the state of possibility, there exists *a reality external to thought.*[2]

Unlike idealism, this later philosophy of Schelling's does not start with thought but with reality. Unlike the critical philosophy, it calls not for a survey of the foundations and limits of reason but for a survey of that which is presented to reason. In this sense it is "empirical," but what is presented to reason for its comprehension is not sense impressions or the data of the sciences, but the activity of the divine in the world. It is this activity that philosophy is called upon to re-trace.

This activity of the divine in history, while presented to reason, involves breaks in the picture of the orderly and rational universe conceived by the Enlightenment. Hence Schelling's later philosophy represents a

---

[1] By Schelling's "second period," I refer to the period inclusive of *Of Human Freedom, The Ages of the World,* and *The Philosophy of Mythology and Revelation.*

[2] F. W. J. Schelling, *Philosophy of Mythology and Revelation, Münchner Jubiläumsdruck* of *Schellings Werke,* ed. by Manfred Schröter (1959): V:603. All references to this work are in the translation of V. C. Hayes, *Myth, Reason and Revelation* (Ph.D. dissertation, Columbia University, 1970); available from University Microfilms, Ann Arbor. See also Robert F. Brown, *The Later Philosophy of Schelling: The Influence of Boehme on the Writings of 1809 to 1815* (Lewisburg PA: Bucknell University Press, 1977). Recent studies also include James L. Esposito, *Schelling's Idealism and Philosophy of Nature* (Lewisburg PA: Bucknell University Press, 1977).

break in and a challenge to, not only the Idealist philosophy, but also to its approach to religion.

1. *The ultimate as the aporia of thought.* The first major break in the rationalist's coherent picture of the world is that the ontological ultimate has a surd character to it. It is unthinkable.

> In the phrase "that which is What is," we may distinguish the "that which is" feature from the "What is" feature. The "What is" feature contains "everything general."
> . . . The "that which is" feature, however, contains nothing general; it is not a *What*; in fact, "it is a reality which transcends all thought" to such an extent that the "What is" feature seems like "something super-added, something which came along later."[3]

2. *The Fall.* Another break with the coherence of rationalism is the notion of the Fall, the pre-temporal Fall. Schelling has conceived the Self,

> the "ungrounded act of egoity," the active rational will—as excluding itself, by its own act, from the world of Ideas and setting itself over against God. . . . As *will willing itself*, the self is . . . anti-divine (Gegengottlichkeit).[4]
>
> If sin is potentiated contradiction, it is also the potentiated irrational, the irrational that posits itself as such. . . . The irrational in its spirituality is the lie; it is absolute hostility to the rational, it is that which eludes the rational process and identity.
>
> All attempts to deduce sin can finally be reduced to two. One descends from man to nature and finitude, in order to discover there the principle of sin. The other aims beyond man, to God, seeking to discern in the divine decree the justification of sin as a means that is naturalistic, aetiological; the second is historical, teleological. Both, however, prevent the possibility of an unqualified No to sin. Hence it is necessary to remain on the human place, and thereby to renounce any deduction of sin.[5]

The original Fall, the pre-temporal Fall, was not that of Adam or an individual man, but an *Ur-mensch*, a primeval man. This Fall of the Spirit or Soul makes possible the origin and consequently the fall of individual souls.

> This Soul in which the Will has arisen is now no longer equal to the Soul in the Idea. It becomes, because of that Will, the individual soul, for it is precisely this will that

---

[3]Hayes, 210.

[4]Ibid., 253.

[5]Paul Tillich, *Mysticism and Guilt-Consciousness in Schelling's Philosophical Development*, trans. by Victor Nuovo (Lewisburg PA: Bucknell University Press, 1974) 104f.

constitutes its individual element. But with this first accidentally actual soul, there
is posited an infinite possibility of other souls.[6]

That this Fall represents a break in coherence for Schelling is quite
clear.

As "the beginning of a totally other world posited outside the Idea," one cannot say
it is necessary but just that is *is*. It is the original accident (*Urzufall*), since "it has
no cause outside itself" and since it is that "from which everything else that is accidental derives."[7]

3. *The transition from Negative Philosophy to Positive Philosophy.* The
Fall is an event, a pre-temporal event to be sure, which is external to reason and with which reason must come to terms. Another major break with
a philosophy of pure concepts is the activity of the Divine in history, overcoming the consequences of the Fall. This activity is also external to reason and with which reason must come to terms. This gives rise to the
transition from Negative Philosophy to Positive Philosophy.

Schelling uses the term "Positive Philosophy" in three senses. In the
most restricted sense it is the Philosophy of Christianity. In a wider sense
it is the completion of Negative Philosophy. In the widest sense it is the
Philosophy of Religion, embracing the Philosophy of Mythology and the
Philosophy of Revelation.[8] It is to the second sense that most references
to Schelling's Positive Philosophy refer and it is this sense that we shall
examine here.

Negative Philosophy deals with concepts and essences, in contrast
with Positive Philosophy, which deals with facts and existence. The former
is a necessary and useful preliminary to the latter. Concepts are needed
in understanding existence.

Negative Philosophy is, then,

speculative metaphysics in which an autonomous reason seeks to . . . find the
structure of (noetic) reality and its first or ultimate principle.

This whole discussion, of course, is in the realm of the hypothetical. From the
supreme essence one can deduce nothing but other essences: from the Absolute

---

[6]Schelling, *W.*, V:646.

[7]Hayes, 249.

[8]Kuno Fischer, *Schelling's Leben, Werke und Lehre* (Heidelberg, 1923) 795.

Idea nothing but other ideas. . . . From a *What* one cannot deduce a *That*. The negative philosophy cannot explain the existent world. Its deduction of the world is not a deduction of existents but only of what things must be *if* they exist. . . . But we must *also* recognize the *necessity* for rational or negative philosophy as part of that "whole," which for Schelling is Philosophical Religion.[9]

The self henceforth longs for God himself. It wants to possess Him—Him, the God who acts, the God who is Providence, the God who, as *himself* a positive, factual Being, *can oppose the fact of the Fall*, the God who is Lord of Being. . . . The God who is above and beyond Reason can do what reason cannot do: He can make the self equal to the Law, i.e., free the self from the Law.[10]

The self cannot itself lay claim to the power to win this God. God must *come to meet* the self with his aid. . . . All we can do (and no philosophical pride can or should keep us from doing this) is gratefully to accept that which comes to us undeservedly and (as a gift of) grace, and which we cannot attain otherwise.[11]

This takes us beyond the religion of reason, beyond the Enlightenment.

At the end of the Negative Philosophy, I have only a possible religion, not a real religion. I have only "religion within the limits of pure reason." Those who perceive a rational *religion* at the end of rational science deceive themselves. Reason does not lead to religion, just as Kant's theoretical result shows that there can be not rational religion.[12]

But this is not the end of philosophy, because a true Philosophical Religion is Positive Philosophy, a philosophy which gives an account of what lies beyond philosophy but which comes to philosophy for its comprehension.

Without Philosophical Religion it is impossible to comprehend the real religions—Mythological and Revealed—or to interpret and give an account of them. By interpreting these two religions in the light of Philosophical Religion, one can best perceive that what we call Philosophical Religion has nothing in common with rational religion.[13]

---

[9]Hayes, 185.

[10]Schelling, *W.*, V:749.

[11]Ibid.

[12]Ibid., 750.

[13]Ibid.

Negative Philosophy starts with the idea of God as the Prius, the pure That, and asks how it is possible that the world derives from him. Positive Philosophy has the task of showing that:

> He reveals Himself as Lord of actual empirical existence. . . . If he is truly Lord of all Being, it follows that the full demonstration of God's existence will be the whole history of the human race.[11]
>
> Just as I am not satisfied, in the case of individuals who are important to me, to know that they exist, but demand continuing proof of their existence, so here: we demand that the divinity draw ever closer to the consciousness of mankind: we require that it be an object of consciousness not merely in its effects but in itself. But this too is to be attained only by stages, especially since it is demanded that the divinity penetrate not only into the consciousness of individuals but into the consciousness of mankind.[15]

Tillich has expressed this transition in Schelling from a philosophy of rationally deduced concepts to a philosophy of attention to the activity of the divine as follows.

> Reason concerns itself with knowledge of . . . the concept, of the essence of things. It deduces a priori the concept . . . and in this connection it is entirely incidental to the concept whether something actually exists.
>
> Whereas rational philosophy is aprioristic and deductive, positive philosophy is aposterioristic and empirical. Experience is the only means of proof in positive philosophy. . . . Its concrete tasks are to consider the creation as the freely posited beginning of the world process; the Fall as the beginning of the evolution of the history of religion; and the evolution of the history of religion, which culminates in revelation.[16]
>
> Because the free, personal God is the God who reveals himself, therefore revelation is will and act, and is opposed to reason. For reason lives in the necessary. . . . It can only be said of a God who acts that he reveals himself. Only a will can be revealed.[17]

4. *The theogonic interpretation of mythology.* A fourth area where Schelling's later philosophy moves beyond Rationalism and, to some ex-

---

[11]Hayes, 269.

[15]Schelling, *W.*, V:753.

[16]Paul Tillich, *The Construction of the History of Religion in Schelling's Positive Philosophy: its Presuppositions and Principles*, trans. by Victor Nuovo (Lewisburg PA: Bucknell University Press, 1974) 64f.

[17]Ibid, 137f.

tent, beyond Idealism, is his interpretation of mythology. After a long treatment of various interpretations of mythology, which he finds lacking, he sets forth a view that gives mythology a real, if subordinate and partially distorted, place in the human understanding of the divine.[18]

To begin, the overarching thrust of Schelling's treatment is that mythology went through four ascending stages: an original, blind, natural theism; a relative monotheism; polytheism; and true monotheism.[19] This is not the place to attempt an evaluation of this history of myths. While it has elements of forced theorizing in it, it is informed by much study, particularly in Hebraic and Greek areas, and contains provocative insights which remain to be sifted.

The mythological process is a product of the dynamics of the human mind itself.

> Both peoples and individuals are mere instruments in this process. . . . The representations do not *come* to them from outside; they are *in* them without them knowing how or why, for they come out of the depths of consciousness itself, and present themselves to consciousness with a necessity which leaves no doubt as to their truth.
>
> Mythology in general arises by means of a theogonic process . . . in which the human consciousness is seized and held fast by its own nature.
>
> The human *consciousness* itself (is) the true seat, the real generative principle of mythological ideas.[20]

Yet there is an objective content to these myths.

> As a result of the necessity with which the content of the representations is produced, mythology possesses from the very beginning a *real* and therefore a doctrinal meaning.[21]

As Hayes has it, "mythology deals with *real gods* from the very beginning of mankind's self-awareness, and the succession of gods—who had

---

[18]Hayes, 82-125; Schelling, *W.*, VI:1-95; Tillich, *Construction*, 127-35.

[19]Schelling, *W.*, VI:1-95; Robert F. Brown, *Schelling's Treatise on "The Deities of Samothrace," AAR Studies in Religion* (Missoula MT: Scholar's Press, 1976).

[20]Schelling, *W.*, VI:196, 206, 201.

[21]Ibid., 198.

God as their final ground and content—is a movement which *truly takes place* in consciousness."[22]

> In the mythological process, man is . . . dealing with . . . *powers that rise up in the depths of consciousness*—powers by which consciousness is moved. The theogonic process which gives birth to mythology is a *subjective* process for as much as it unfolds in *consciousness* and manifests itself in the formation of representations. But the causes and, therefore, also the objects of these representations, are the real theogonic powers *as such*, the very powers under whose influence consciousness is originally that-which-posits-God. It is not the mere *representations* of the potencies but the *potencies themselves* which form the content of the process.
>
> In this process the powers appear as a succession only in order to produce and re-establish the (lost) unity. Thus the *meaning of the process* lies not in a divergence but in a convergence. . . . The process itself is not one of separation but of re-unification. What gives rise to this process is . . . a power which takes exclusive possession of consciousness without the latter being aware of it.[23]

But the generation of the gods is also the becoming of God, the gods being moments of the whole, at least in relation to consciousness.

> Since only those gods are real who have God as their ground, it follows that the final content of the history of the gods is that of the generation . . . of *God*, a real becoming of *God*, in consciousness.
>
> The truth is certainly not in the individual moments; if it were there would be no process. . . . It is the end of the process and is therefore contained completely only in the process *as a whole*.
>
> The multiplicity of the gods as such is merely an *accidental* fact which is cancelled out in the whole; it is not the intention, not the final purpose of the process.
>
> One could compare the moments of which mythology is composed with individual propositions in philosophy. Each proposition of a true system is true . . . when it is conceived as belonging to an onward movement.[24]

Furthermore, mythology recapitulates the process of the unfolding of nature, being controlled by the movement of the same powers.

> The powers which rise up again in consciousness . . . and reveal themselves as theogonic powers, can be none other than those which produced the world.
>
> The potencies must pass through all the states and relationships to one another that they had in the natural process. . . . The mythological process unfolds *according to*

---

[22]Hayes, 157.

[23]Schelling, *W.*, VI:209, 211.

[24]Ibid., 200, 211-14.

the same laws and passes through the same stages as those through which Nature originally passed. [25]

THE MUNICH CATHOLIC INTERPRETATION AND CRITIQUE OF SCHEL-LING. During his own time Schelling received considerable attention and enthusiastic, if critical, appreciation from the Catholic theological community, particularly at Munich. He was often viewed as the "Catholic hope" against the Protestant Hegel.

Already in his earlier philosophy there was appreciation from the Catholic intellectuals, some of whom were instrumental in his coming to Munich in 1807. Thomas O'Meara has studied this appreciation intensively.

The Catholic intellectuals were busy "Christianizing," if not "Catholicizing," this Schelling, and to an extent they were anticipating or at least paralleling the philosopher himself, who was coming slowly to a new interest: life and history amid religion. The Catholics saw in the early movements of romantic idealism a counterbalance to Kant, to rationalism, and in some ways to Lutheran Protestantism. The ideas of movement and unity, of totality and diversity in nature, of philosophy through life and activity . . . would appeal to Roman Catholicism. [26]

Schelling's positive philosophy made an even greater impact.

It did not absorb Christianity into a larger, a-revelatory system, but placed Christianity, even the church, at the end of a historical process. . . . It included insight and experience, vision and emotion, the natural and supernatural and praeternatural.

Schelling influenced Roman Catholic theology in three stages: (1) Before . . . the initial move to Munich, Schelling's thought was in contact with a first group of Catholics—mainly churchmen such as Bishop Sailer or professors in Bavarian schools. . . . (2) Then came Schelling's presence in Munich after 1806. (3) Schelling's occupancy of a chair in 1827 influences a group of young Catholics who will be dominant theological voices during the middle third of the century (Staudenmaier, Deutinger).

The Catholic theologians had a number of pertinent criticisms.

---

[25]Ibid., 217f. Cp. *Ages of the World* for a discussion of the process of nature.

[26]Thomas O'Meara, O.P., "Schelling at the University of Munich (1827-1841): Romantic Idealism and Roman Catholic Theologians," (1974) (unpublished) 3. I am indebted in this section to O'Meara.

> The first issue is what well may be Schelling's "primal model," a linear process reaching from God to the end of history. . . . A Trinity is active in Schelling's philosophy, but that activity does not insure that the Incarnation . . . is truly historical. There is a difference between ontological realization and moral freedom; only the latter is the sphere of revelation and religious history. . . . When our theologians raise issues about the content of revelation or about the sovereignty of God's action in history they are . . . raising the issue of grace.
>
> A second focus of the critiques is freedom. . . . Freedom is the *sine qua non* for an encounter between a conscious being and history/grace. [27]

A full discussion of the influence of Schelling on Catholic theology would, of course, have to include a discussion of Walter Kasper, just as a full treatment of the theological impact of Schelling should include Berdyaev and even perhaps Charles Hartshorne.

Tillich as an Interpreter of Schelling

1. *The positive appreciation of the "later Schelling."* As an interpreter of Schelling, Tillich is best known to American readers as one who has attempted to restore an appreciation of the second major period of Schelling's work.

Schelling's *Philosophy of Mythology and Revelation* did not appear in an official edition until 1856-1861. In the meantime, the Berlin lectures of 1841-1842 were published in an authorized version by Frauenstadt and Paulus. This edition was a poor piece of work, put out by his enemies, and helped foster the pejorative estimate of his work.

> Fackenheim notes that the early critics were totally dissatisfied. If they were theologians, they looked to Schelling for an apologetic which they did not get, nor were meant to get. If they were positivists, they had even less sympathy with Schelling than with Hegel. And if they were Hegelians (as most of them were), they saw the most important criterion of judgment in systematic completeness, the very point in which Schelling was weakest; further, they were bound to regard his development after 1804 as an aberration or an outright betrayal. [28]

F. C. Bauer characterized the lectures as "Galimathias," while Eduard Zeller dismissed the whole business as:

---

[27]O'Meara, 7f, 14.

[28]Emil Fackenheim, "Schelling's Conception of Positive Philosophy," *Review of Metaphysics* 7:4 (June 1954): 564; quoted by Hayes, 21f.

a verbose, muddled, abstruse Scholasticism; a disagreeable mixture of speculation
. . . cloudy theosophy, arbitrary Biblical exegesis and ecclesiastical dogma.[29]

As a matter of irony, the most readily available of Schelling's later works in English have been two of the major works of the "later Schelling," *Of Human Freedom* and *The Ages of the World*. It was partly due to the encouragement of Paul Tillich that these works, especially the latter, were translated and certainly due to his influence that these works have received the reading that they have.

2. *The priority of will over intellect.* One of the major thrusts of Tillich's interpretation of Schelling is that Schelling belongs to the great voluntarist tradition, running from Augustine, through the Spiritual Franciscans and Bonaventura, Scotus, the German mystics, Luther and Boehme, that has emphasized the primacy of will over intellect.

Will is primordial Being, and all predicates apply to it alone—groundlessness, eternity, independence of time, self-affirmation!
The old proposition is here once again in place: the original being is will, and will is not merely the beginning but also the *content* of the first emergent being.[30]

Tillich sees this voluntarist line as continuing through Schopenhauer, Nietzsche, Bergson, Heidegger, and so on.[31]

3. *Existentialist elements within an essentialist framework.* The relation between essentialist and existentialist elements in Schelling is a crucial question, as Gabriel Marcel has insisted.[32] A good treatment of this problem has been given by Victor Hayes.[33]

A number of interpreters see Schelling as an existentialist or at least as a forerunner of existentialism. These include Karl Löwith, Walter Kauf-

---

[29]Eduard Zeller, *Geschichte der deutschen Philosophie* 2d ed. (Munich, 1975) 560-62; quoted in Fischer, 715f.

[30]Schelling, *Of Human Freedom*, trans. by James Gutmann (Chicago: The Open Court Publishing Company, 1936) 24; Schelling, *W.*, V:570; VI:1-11, 201-25.

[31]Paul Tillich, *Perspectives on 19th and 20th Century Protestant Theology*, ed. by Carl E. Braaten (New York: Harper & Row, 1967) 146, 192-95, *inter alia.*

[32]Gabriel Marcel, "Schelling fut-il un precurseur de la philosophie de l'existence?" *Revue de Metaphysique et de Morale* no. 1 (January-March 1957).

[33]Hayes, 35-44. I am in general agreement with Hayes in his treatment of Tillich as an interpreter of Schelling. Hayes does not elaborate, within the scope of his dissertation, Tillich's use of and transmutation of Schelling in Tillich's own system.

mann, William Barrett, and Emil Fackenheim.[34] Löwith's comments on
the Berlin lectures of 1841 are typical:

> with this last event in the history of classic German philosophy begins the "philos-
> ophy of existence" which Marx and Kierkegaard developed in opposition to Hegel,
> the one externally, the other internally.[35]

This break with Hegel occurred before the Berlin lectures, going back
to the essay *Of Human Freedom* (1809). Fackenheim suggests that:

> He pointed to freedom and existence as facts which no possible dialectical system
> could absorb; the step from rational system to existence was a *metabasis eis allo
> genos.*[36]

On the other hand, Copleston, Kenneth Hamilton, Schulz, and Gabriel
Marcel are not so ready to see Schelling as an existentialist. Marcel sees
Schelling as preparing the way, not for a philosophy of existence, but for "a
renewal of ontology on nontraditional foundations."[37]

Tillich's approach to this question is that in Schelling there is an existentialist outlook within an essentialist framework.

> Therefore there is an essentialist framework in his mind. Existentialism is possible
> only as an element in a larger whole, as an element in a vision of the structure of
> being in its created goodness, and then as a description of man's existence within
> that framework.[38]

Tillich is probably right here, for the breaks in the essentialist outlook
in Schelling, specifically the Fall and Revelation, do not destroy the place

---

[34]Karl Löwith, *From Hegel to Nietzche* (Doubleday Anchor Books, 1967) 113; Fackenheim, 566; William Barrett, *Irrational Man* (Anchor Books, 1962) 275; Walter Kaufmann,
Nietzsche (New York: Meridian, 1956) 11.

[35]Löwith, 113.

[36]Fackenheim, 567.

[37]Marcel, 81.

[38]Tillich, *Perspectives*, 245. See also Paul Tillich, "Schelling und die Anfange des Ex-
istentialistischen Protestes," *Philosophie und Schicksal: Schriften zur Erkenntnislehre und
Existenzphilosophie* (*Gesammelte Werke*, Band IV, Stuttgart: Evangelisches Verlagswerk,
1961) 133-44. Also relevant is Paul Tillich, "Existential Philosophy: Its Historical Meaning," *Theology of Culture*, ed. by Robert C. Kimball (New York: Oxford University Press,
1959) 76-111.

of reason. Negative Philosophy is still necessary, can still give an account of the essential structure of the divine, even though it cannot show its reality. In the Munich lectures *On the History of Modern Philosophy*, Schelling wrote:

> Any philosophy which does not remain grounded in the negative but tries instead to reach what is positive, the divine, immediately and *without* that negative foundation, will inevitably end up dying of spiritual impoverishment.

And from the Berlin lectures:

> How should I give up that philosophy which I myself founded earlier, the discovery of my youth? (My) task and purpose is not to put another philosophy in the place (of negative philosophy), but to add it to a new science until now considered impossible. This will restore (negative philosophy) to its true foundation and give it once again the orientation it lost when it went beyond its natural limits—i.e., when it was regarded as the whole, instead of simply a fragment of a higher whole.[39]

Furthermore, the Fall and Revelation are to be understood by philosophy, even though not deducted from philosophical principles. This task of philosophy has not yet been accomplished, and when it is this true philosophy will be also a true religion. But the task is possible and Schelling felt that he was making an advance in this direction.

> The *same* principles which operate implicitly and without being understood in both revealed and natural religion, are *consciously grasped and understood* in philosophical religion. Hence, philosophical religion . . . has the task . . . to *comprehend* those religions which are independent of reason and to understand the whole truth and characteristic significance of each.[40]

We must "expand the smallness and narrowness of our thoughts to the greatness of the divine thought."[41]

> The *content* of Revelation is nothing but a higher history which goes back to the beginning of things and on to the end. The *Philosophy* of Revelation will simply explain

---

[39]Schelling, *W.*, V:246; VI:758.

[40]Schelling, *W.*, VI:252.

[41]Schelling, *W.*, VI:403f, 419F, 422.

this higher history and trace it back to the principles which are known and given to it from elsewhere. [12]

4. *The Dialectical Principle within Schelling's Development.* Tillich's contention is that the development of Schelling's thought can be followed by tracing out the dialectical movement of a single problem. This is an important issue in Schelling scholarship.

> Is this "philosophy" merely a loose series of very different philosophies? Or are there systematic connections, threads hidden perhaps beneath the surface, which provide continuity and coherence? C. M. Schröder believes this question of the inner unity of Schelling's philosophy might be regarded as the central question in Schelling-studies. [13]

The dynamo generating the movements of Schelling's thought Tillich finds in the problem of the relation of the principle of identity to the moral categories. Thus the stages in Schelling's thought are neither disconnected nor adventitious reactions to various philosophical influences, from Spinoza to Boehme, but represent the stages in the development of the inner dialectic of Schelling's thought.

> Mysticism and guilt-consciousness, the feeling of unity with the absolute and consciousness of opposition to God, the principle of the identity of absolute and individual spirit and the experience of contradiction between Holy Lord and sinful creature: this is the antinomy for whose solution religious thought in the Church in every age has struggled and must continually struggle. [14]

In *Mysticism and Guilt-Consciousness* Tillich starts with a brief but insightful tracing of these two principles of truth and morality from the Greeks onward, including a masterful ten-page treatment of Kant from this perspective. He then traces the development of the principle of identity in Schelling's first major period, from Fichtean ethical mysticism through nature mysticism and the religion of aesthetic idealism to the philosophy of absolute identity (lampooned by Hegel as the "dark night in which all cows are black").

---

[12]Ibid., 422.

[13]Hayes, 29; C. M. Schröder, *Das Verhaltnis von Heidentum und Christentum in Schellings Philosophie der Mythologie und Offenbarung* (München, 1936) 11-15.

[14]Tillich, *Mysticism*, 27.

> The very reduction of the seven periods to two is the presupposition of every inner understanding of Schelling's development. The great turning point of Schelling's thought . . . occurred before the publication of *On the Nature of Human Freedom*. . . . However, the transition is not external but dialectical. It is not the interruption, but the completion in a grand style of what was begun. [15]

For a discussion of the light thrown upon the continuity of Schelling's thought by the 1913 discovery of a text by Franz Rosenzweig, the reader can refer to Hayes's brief discussion. [46] Entitled "Das alteste Systemprogramm des deutschen Idealismus," it called for a philosophical treatment of mythology. The text dates from 1796 when Schelling was twenty-one, but since it is unsigned and actually in the handwriting of Hegel, its evidential value seems low.

Tillich's Appropriation
of Schelling's Later Philosophy

While it is not my contention that Tillich is merely repeating Schelling's ideas, it is clear that Schelling was of great influence, probably the greatest single influence on Tillich.

SCHELLINGIAN THEMES AND THEIR APPEARANCES IN TILLICH. 1. *God is Not a Being.* The notion that God is not a being, not even the highest Being, finds strong confirmation in Schelling.

> If one holds that God is the Existent, one gives up the notion of God as a *mere* particular entity (*Einzelwesen*) with which the demonstration of earlier metaphysics were content. God *cannot* be a mere individual existent, and the God who is not *the* Existent could not be God. . . . God is related to things only because he is the *general* essence (*allgemeine Wesen*). This does not mean, of course, that he is the Existent in an abstract, non-determined way, but in the most fully determinate sense. He is the Existent which lacks nothing of what belongs to Being (*Sein*), the perfect and complete Existent, τὸ τιαντελῶς ὄν, as Plato called it. [17]

There is in Schelling some real anticipations of Tillich's notion of God as the Power of Being. In the first place, Schelling's voluntarism, charac-

---

[15] Ibid., 24.

[16] Hayes, 33.

[17] Schelling, *W.*, V:455. Cf. Plato, *De Rep*, V:477A.

terizing primal Being as Will, leans in this direction. Also the notion of a "potency" points in the direction of an ontology of power. Tillich's reference to Luther's notion that God is the power in the arm of the murderer finds echo in Schelling.

> The power (*Kraft*) with which even the sinner operates and by which evil is perpetrated is still a divine power (Cf. Ps. 18:26f). . . . Man has perverted the position of the potencies, and so God operates perversely in the perverse, i.e., he no longer acts as fatherly Will, but as Unwill. [18]

2. *The Triadic Structure of Life.* Characteristic of Schelling's thought is his view that life has a triadic structure. This is above all true of the divine life and, in a derivative sense, of human life. The essay *Of Human Freedom* is the easiest place to grasp the three divine potencies. Here the schematism is not as complex as in *The Ages of the World*, and Tillich, in *Mysticism and Guilt-Consciousness* uses this far more than the *Ages* for this reason.

For Schelling there are two aspects to the divine. First there is an *urgrund* or undifferentiated principle preceding all antitheses. But out of this indifference move three potencies. The undifferentiated Schelling will sometimes speak of it as Will, but at other times as the Absolutely-Absolute or Indifference. (*W*, V:548). To complicate matters, this Indifference, which in the discussion of human freedom was the Indifference underlying the three potencies, becomes in the *Philosophy of Mythology and Revelation* the Indifference underlying the split between the Unity and the Multiplicity of the divine. But my purpose here is not to trace the development of Schelling's Gnostic-like positing of layer upon layer of grounds.

Out of the ground move the three principles or potencies in a nontemporal but yet ontological order. [49] The first potency is that of darkness, irrationality, ego-centricity and contraction. The second potency is that of reason, light, the Other, and expansion. The first is contractive, and yet it is also searching or yearning for the second. The first potency is contractive as ego-centric and yet its poverty makes it go out of itself, al-

---

[18]Schelling, *W.*, VI:444.

[49]In *The Ages of the World* and *Philosophy of Mythology and Revelation*, he distinguishes between the three Potencies in the divine and the three Principles in nature and history.

though still in an ego-centric and possessive fashion, toward the other. This is brought out rather well in *Ueber die Gottheiten von Samothrake*:

> For it was the teaching of all peoples who counted time by nights that the *night* is the most primordial of things. . . . But what is the essence of night, if not lack, need, and longing. For this night . . . is the nature looking forward to the light, the night longing for it, eager to receive it. Another image of that first nature, whose whole essence is desire and passion, appears in the consuming fire which so to speak is itself nothing, is in essence only a hunger drawing everything into itself.[50]

The third potency is Spirit as love, as the union of the first two principles.

Tillich's discussion of the divine life owes much to Schelling, but perhaps we should be even more cautious than Victor Nuovo in seeing the similarities.[51] For one thing, in Tillich's view of the divine life, there is no Indifference before the differentiation of the triad. Also in Tillich the first principle is not so characterized as ego-centric or irrational. It is power. Also for Schelling there is a sense, clear in *Of Human Freedom*, that the first potency is the ground, whereas Tillich usually refers to God as such as the ground. When Tillich does refer to the first principle, he is more likely to refer to it as the Abyss or the Abgrund. Also for Schelling the first potency can be called the ground of God's existence, what makes God to be God, a very unTillichean notion.

The similarities are there, however, including the Spirit as love or the unity of the other two, and Tillich's logos has clear affinities to the second potency as the principle of reason and of revelation. Also similar are the notions, made quite clear in *Of Human Freedom*, that every nature requires its opposite in order to be revealed.

For Schelling the three potencies constitute, as principles, the structure of cosmic evolution. As Schelling puts it, employing trinitarian terms:

> The time before Creation is in a special sense the time of the Father, since being is still exclusively in *his* hand. The present time is in a particular sense the time of the Son. . . . The third time, which during the whole creation is *future* and to which everything is supposed to arrive, is the time of the Spirit.

---

[50]Schelling, *W.*, IV:352; *Deities of Samothrace* (W IV:352, 354).

[51]Tillich, *Construction*, 23-26.

> Thus it is permissible to think of the three persons as the successive rulers of the three . . . great world-ages.[52]

Thus for Schelling the three principles in the divine life are to be distinguished from these principles in nature or in man. In the divine life the dark principle is elevated to light. But in the temporal process of the world there is only a yearning, a *Sehnsucht* of the dark, irrational, and ego-centric toward the light, the rational, the Other. The pre-temporal unity of the principles, which is indissoluble in God, becomes dissolved in man because of evil. Yet, of all the creatures, man is highest because in him the elevation of the dark to the light, while not complete, occurs more fully than in any of the rest of the creatures. Finally, the separation of the first two principles within the temporal process leads to a final reunion in the divine life, in the Third Age.

For Schelling, as for Tillich, human life involves a separation from the divine ground, a resulting polarization within human life between the First and the Second, and a movement toward reconciliation of the polar elements with each other and with the divine, resulting in an enrichment of the divine life.

For Schelling the first potency or principle within both the divine and the created life is that of individuality and contraction; the second is that of meaning and expansiveness. Spirit, in both the divine and human life, is, as the third potency or principle, the unity of the other two. For Schelling, again paralleling Tillich, the first two principles have a prior unity within the divine life, are disunited in man, and are moving toward a reunion with each other within the divine life.

For Schelling, as also in a sense for Tillich, the divine life is enriched by the return of the separated. God yields the Ideas, that were in him without independence, to selfhood so that they may be in him again as independent entities. This separation for the sake of enriched reunion starts with the *ungrund* itself, which divides in order that there may be life, love, and personal existence. Every nature requires its opposite in order to be revealed. God's opposite is already within him, yet he requires man outside of him to actualize love.

---

[52]Schelling, *W.*, VI:463.

Primordial time and end time correspond. . . . The identity, which is realized in the eternal becoming of the divine life, is, from the standpoint of time, as much before as after the world process. It is the *status a quo* of existence and the *status ad quem* of cosmic events. "In the end, this final period is the perfect realization of the whole—hence it is the period of the complete incarnation of God when the infinite has become wholly finite without loss of its infinity. Then is God really all in all, the true pantheism" (7:484). "But if all things will have become subject to him, then the Son himself will also be subject to him who subjected all things to him, so that God may be all in all. For the spirit is not yet the highest; he is only spirit or the breath of love. But love is the highest. It is that which was there before the foundation of the world and before that which exists (as separate), but it was not yet there as love, rather—how shall we designate it?" (7:405f). Then Schelling called it indifference. *The eternal meaning of the world process is that indifference becomes love.* (Final italics mine.)[53]

Love unites, therefore requires separation. In reunion something new occurs. (Guy Hammond, *Man in Estrangement*, 160-70, has a good treatment of this theme of separation and reunion in Tillich.)

The 17th Century Angelo Silesius has this among his epigrams:

Der Vater *war* zuvor, der Sohn *ist* noch zur Zeit, Der Geist *wird* endlich *sein* am Tag det Herrlichkeit

This epigram is to be understood . . . as a number of thoughtful men of the Middle Ages understood it when they concluded from the fact that the Old Testament was the time of the Father and the time of the New Testament the time of the Son . . . that a third economy, a third time, was at hand: the time of the Spirit which was to bring the eternal gospel . . . as Abbot Joachim of Flores held.

For us, that succession has the further and general meaning that everything, i.e., the whole creation, i.e., the whole great development of things, proceeds from the Father—through the Son—into the Spirit.[54]

This Trinitarian economy combines the Augustinian-Boehme tradition of the Spirit as love or the bond of the other two with the ancient Alexandrine notion of the *anakephalaiosis*.

For Schelling, again as for Tillich, the divine is not a static absolute, as in neo-Platonism, but is a life of tension and resolution. This life is transcendent to the temporal flux of nature and history, but it is related to this world in two important senses. It can enter history at crucial points in

---

[53]Tillich, *Mysticism*, 113.
[54]Schelling, *W.*, VI:463ff.

man's history, even perhaps as the principle of evil (like Tillich's demonic), and also the final restoration is not merely a return to the static ground as in Plotinus, but is a reunion which enriches the ground. Historically, what has occurred is a sense of history, coming from Augustine, Joachim de Flores, and the fructifying imagery of Jacob Boehme.

A brief word concerning Schelling and Hegel on the triadic structure of the world process is in order here. In his mature thought Hegel has a concept of Absolute Spirit as a process of separation and reunion. The world of nature and of history is the working out of the divine process of self-differentiation and resumption of unity enriched through this particularization. The Absolute goes out from itself into the particularity of existence and returns in a way that overcomes alienation and results in a concrete fullness to the Absolute.

One difference between Hegel on the one hand and Schelling and Tillich on the other is that for Hegel the actualization of reunion is now occurring temporally. For Schelling and Tillich there is a break between the divine and the human so that there is a transtemporal unity of the potencies within the divine life while the reunion of the principles is not realized within present time, except by anticipation of the Age of the Spirit for Schelling and fragmentarily in the Spiritual Presence for Tillich.

For all three of these men there is a triadic structure to the course of the universe, with time as we know it constituting the middle between a beginning and an end; and for all three men the beginning involves a type of estrangement or isolation while the third stage is one of reunion and enrichment. (The parallels with C. S. Pierce are intriguing.) The question is, when is this third stage of reunion and enrichment to be found? For the mature Hegel it is right now in the process of completion. For the mature Schelling and Tillich the third stage is an endpoint, with all the paradox of speaking of the end of the process. However, for Schelling the stage of human history is one of growth and progress in a way that is not the case for Tillich.

This third stage is actually present though fragmentarily for Tillich in what he calls the Spiritual Presence. For Schelling the third stage will become present in Spiritual Christianity or the Church of John. [55]

---

[55]Schelling found confirmation of his view of the three ages of the Church in Neander's *General History of the Christian Religion and Church*, Bd. V. Abth. 1, pp. 438ff; Schelling, *W.*, VI:690n.

Having no external authority, this Church will exist because everyone will come to it through his own conviction, for in it each spirit will have found a home.

It will be a truly public religion . . . as the religion of all mankind.

Actually, this Church is still a Church of the future. John is to be the ruling potency of the Church only in the last time. His function cannot begin before . . . the Church shall have attained its final unity . . . at the time when the Lord comes, the final time of the Church.[56]

This triadic structure of the divine life and the human drama is mirrored in the theogonic process of mythology.

Between consciousness in its simple essentiality and consciousness in its realization, between the unity which is posited in it in a purely essential way and the unity which is effectively realized in it—this unity being the goal of the theogonic movement—there, between the two, is the world. The moments of the theogonic movement, therefore, do not have meaning exclusively for the theogonic process; they are of general significance.[57]

A full study of the relation between Schelling and Tillich's Christology would take us outside of the limits of this paper. However, a brief note of certain similarities, while not intending to gloss over crucial differences, is appropriate here. In the first place, for both men Christ is the true center of history where the redemptive process, ontologically grounded and cosmic in scope, reaches its turning point. In the second place for both men the word must take on personality in order for there to be redemption of the personal.

God affirms the will to selfhood by himself becoming an individual. "Only the personal can heal the personal, and God must become man in order that man may return to God." (7:380). The individual, selfish personality as such is subject to wrath. . . . Communion with God is possible only if God himself becomes an individual personality.[58]

In the third place, for both men an important aspect of the work of Christ is that here a finite man was not estranged from the divine. Tillich's

---

[56]Schelling, *W.*, VI:720, 719, 723.

[57]Ibid., 218.

[58]Tillich, *Mysticism*, 112.

image is that of transparency, of complete openness to the divine ground, of the sacrifice of his particularity. Schelling's imagery is similar.

> The incarnate Logos has made this being [of the Logos] completely submissive and obedient to the Father, thus sanctifying it (John 10:36, 17:19) and making it "the vessel, the attracting potency of the Holy Spirit."[59]

Tillich's summary of Schelling's position gives further clarification.

> Contradiction in potency leads God to assert his absoluteness and become an individual. Thereby, however, he becomes subject to wrath and the immanent self-negation of all self-hood. Once more, Yes and No stand in extreme contrast. The Cross of Christ is the solution of this supreme contradiction, that is, the self-sacrifice and self-annulment of the will to selfhood, raised to the absolute, divine will to power. "The true infinite entered the finite, not to deify it, but to sacrifice it to God in his own person, and thereby to reconcile it" (5:292).[60]

   A full study of the relation between Schelling and Tillich's view of the human drama should also include a deeper study of their views of fulfillment beyond death than we can give here. Let us note in passing that Schelling, like Tillich, has a notion of "essentification."

> The common view which sees death as a *separation* of soul and body, considers the body as a specimen of ore in which the soul is enclosed and hidden like some noble metal. Death is the separation process which frees the soul from this matter. . . . The other view would be inclined rather to compare the effect of death to that process in which the spirit (*Geist*) or essence (*Essenz*) of a plant is extracted. It is thought that all power and all life which the plant had in itself passes over into the sap which is drawn from a plant.

> So the death of man might be not so much a separation as an essentification, in which only the accidental comes to an end, but the *essence*, what man really *is*, is preserved. For no man appears in his life as he really *is*, but after death he does. Therein lies the joyfulness of death for some, and its appalling terror for others.[61]

   The distinction between Schelling and Tillich at this point would have to take account of Tillich's sense of symbolic language, of reunion with the ground, and whether the note of possible terror is included.

---

[59]Schelling, *W.*, VI:573f.

[60]Tillich, *Mysticism*, 111f.

[61]Schelling, *W.*, VI:599; cf. Hayes, 375, n. 82.

3. *Potencies and Polarities*. We have already indicated that for both men the first and second potencies, or polar elements, are in eternal tension yet union within the divine ground, are separated in the world process, reach both their this-worldly fulfillment and yet separation in man, and will find ultimate reunion in the final fulfillment.

The similarities in their notions of polarities are obvious and impressive, but a word of caution should be made. The excellent work of Victor Nuovo in translating and commenting upon Tillich's two dissertations puts us into his debt, but he could have been perhaps a bit more cautious in pointing out the differences between the two men at this point.[62] There is a complexity to Schelling's notion of the potencies in the divine life, evident even in *Of Human Freedom*, compared with Tillich's more restrained treatment. Tillich also distinguishes between three pairs of ontological polarities. Tillich's treatment of the polarities is also enriched by the distinction between the polarities in tension in essential being, in disruption under the conditions of existential estrangement, and in ambiguous relationship in the concrete actuality of life and history. Tillich's treatment is also extended by using the polar concepts as a powerful tool of cultural and historical analysis.

There are some important anticipations of Tillich's treatment of form and dynamics in Schelling. Indeed, this polarity may come closer than the polarity of individualization and participation to Schelling's polar view.

> In man, too, there is this same contradiction: a blind productive power, limitless in its nature, standing—in the self-same subject—over against a sober power which limits and forms it and therefore literally negates it. Every spirit's work shows to the judicious observer whether it proceeds from a harmonious balance of that activity or whether one of the two preponderates. A preponderance of productive activity is present when the form seems too weak as compared with the content, so that the content partly overpowers the form. The opposite is the case wherever the form forces back the content so that the work lacks fullness.

> The secret of true poetry is to be drunk and sober at the same time, not at different moments but at one and the same moment. This is what distinguishes the Apollonian enthusiasm from the merely Dionysiac. To present an infinite content—that is, a content which literally struggles against form and seems to destroy every form—to present such an infinite content in the most perfect, i.e., the most infinite form: this is the highest task of art.[63]

---

[62]Tillich, *Construction*, translator's introduction.

[63]Schelling, *W.*, VI:417.

It is interesting to note that we have here in Schelling the connection of dynamics with the infinite, form with the finite. This is part of the background of two points in Tillich which might prove puzzling. First, it is the abyss that makes God be God. Second, the substance of the work of art, what Tillich in his earlier writings, such as *The Idea of a Theology of Culture*, calls "import," is what is open to the ground, rather than the form.

Schelling's view of tragedy also has the germ of Tillich's notion of destiny, although without the polar element of freedom and with a gloom to it.

> In his sufferings, Prometheus is "the sublime prototype of the human self." Prometheus Bound contemplates without hope the irreparable and irreversible rupture caused by his act and its consequences. . . . Prometheus, however, was in the right. He *could not do* what he did. He was under a moral necessity. And herein lies "his tragic dignity." For "the truly tragic misfortune is not that which results from a voluntary act, but that to which we are driven by a moral necessity." Prometheus was therefore "in his right," although this did not prevent Zeus from inflicting continuing torture upon him.[64]

4. *The Incursion of the Depths*. There are a number of topics dealing with the inbreaking of the potencies or principles into the course of human life. It is not clear that Schelling thought of them as belonging together in any sense, although the phrase, "incursion of the depths," which the present writer uses, does indicate a commonality, especially when seen from Tillich's viewpoint.

a. *The demonic*. Schelling does not have as fully developed a notion of the demonic as does Tillich, but he does give weight to demon possession and the role of evil spirits in the New Testament.

> Demons are to the Jews pagan potencies, for everything pagan is to them demonic. . . . So the stories of the demoniacs at the time of Christ and in his presence, prove to be nothing but Jewish representations to which Christ has accommodated himself. These disease phenomena have real significance. It was natural that the battle Christ was destined to wage with Satan, i.e., with the real principle of Paganism, should be ushered in by external and physical phenomena.[65]

---

[64]Schelling, *W.*, V:665, 667.

[65]Schelling, *W.*, VI:669.

Here we have another example of the combining of subjective and objective elements in Schelling's hermeneutics.

> Still more mythological are the statements in II Peter 2:4 . . . "God did not spare the angels which had sinned," i.e., those who *departed* from the place which was supposed to be their center . . . by virtue of their tendency to rise out of potency and seduce the human will—God did not spare them but (what is natural and necessary consequence shall be looked upon as a punishment) he has bound them with shackles of darkness in Tartaros in order to keep them till the last judgment. . . . In this passage it would be foolish to deny the mythological character of the statements. . . . The Apostle Peter had not read Hesiod's Theogony and yet he speaks in very similar terms.[66]

In one section Schelling does have the beginnings of a concept of evil spirits as powers of destruction, formerly good powers turned evil. This is clearly anticipatory of Tillich.

> When man is relieved of his sovereignty (and the Fall of man is nothing but the loss of his sovereignty), then all those subordinated possibilities, potencies and spirits are able to rise up, and man now falls into their power whereas previously they had been in his. Indeed, insofar as those potencies were posited by the creation only as possibilities—to this extent they were all right, they were *good* (and in this sense one can speak of an original pure and good state of the angels). But when, by virtue of the guilt of man, the divinely posited unity, in which everything was to be comprehended under one head (man), is broken up and lost, the potencies come forth with a power and force which they were not destined to have, one which they should not have, and they appear as *evil* spirits.[67]

The major root of Tillich's concept of the demonic lies in Schelling's notion of the First Potency (A-) becoming, in the extra-divine world, the principle of ego-centricity (B). For it is clearly the abyss, not the *logos*, that underlies the creative-demonic.

> The unruly [*das Regellose*] lies ever in the depths as though it might again break through, and order and form nowhere appear to have been original, but it seems as though what had initially been unruly had been brought to order. This is the incomprehensible basis [*grund*] of reality in things, the irreducible remainder which cannot be resolved into reason by the greatest exertion but always remains in the depths.[68]

---

[66]Ibid., 681f, 680.

[67]Ibid., 674.

[68]Schelling, *Of Human Freedom*, 34.

This helps to explain an apparent ambiguity of Tillich's notion of the demonic. On the one hand the demonic seems to be a breakthrough of the divine creativity gone awry. On the other hand it seems to be the elevation of the finite to the infinite, so that it is hard to distinguish the demonic from idolatry. The apparent ambiguity is caused by the fact that it is the unruly element of the demonic, kept in bounds within the divine life by Schelling's Second Potency or Tillich's logos, which is the principle of ego-centricity or self-elevation. The connection between the demonic and the First Potency is clearer in Schelling than the connection between the demonic and the divine abyss for Tillich, but the connection, however muted, is there for Tillich also.

b. *Kairos.* Schelling does not have anything like Tillich's fully developed notion of *kairos*, but the germ of it is there. In the first place the transitions in the history of mythology represent real turning points in the relation of the divine to the human. And Christ is, above all, the great point of the entrance of the divine into the human.

> Facts like the resurrection of Christ are like lightning flashes in which the higher, i.e., the true, the inner history breaks into (and enters) the merely external history. To remove these facts is to change history into a mere externality. That which provides history's support, its value and its only meaning, is removed the moment these facts are taken away.
>
> Such facts, by which the inner history emerges externally, are but *few* in number, but no thoughtful person will regard this as sufficient reason to doubt them, for that would mean he was unable to recognize the inner and higher connection of things in general.[69]

c. *The Age of the Spirit.* More clearly significant for Tillich's development is Schelling's notion of the coming Age of the Spirit. On the one hand this supplies what Tillich would call the *telos* of history. On the other hand, transposing this from the future in fulfillment to the present in fragments, we have Tillich's notion of the Spiritual Presence, particularly when we remember that Spirit is the reunion of the first two principles.

> "He himself returns to the invisible realm and promises . . . the Spirit, the ideal principle who leads the finite back to the infinite (5:292). " . . . This inner dialectical movement, from the incarnate to the crucified to the exalted—from Jesus through

---

[69]Schelling, *W.,* VI:611f.

the Christ to the Spirit—constitutes the essence of Christianity. In this living sys-
tole and diastole the contradiction is conquered through grace and that identity is
fashioned which included guilt-consciousness overcome within itself. The principle
of mysticism triumphs, but not in the form of mysticism, not as immediate identity,
but rather as personal communion that overcomes contradiction: it is "the religion
of the Spirit and of freedom" (14:237).[70]

5. *Reason and the Irrational.* Is an autonomous philosophy possible in
the face of the Fall and Revelation? Yes. It is when philosophy truly faces
these that it becomes, in Tillich's phrase, truly theonomous. In *On the
Boundary* he claims that Schelling's later philosophy is the most truly
theonomous aspect of German idealism.[71]

We have already treated Schelling's notion of philosophy as having to
face non-rational factors. The first of these is the irrational event of the
Fall. Note parallels with Tillich on self-loss and concupiscence.

The spirit can choose to give itself freely to God or draw the world to itself. If the
latter, it is absorbed by the world.[72]

The second is the extra-rational activity of the divine in myth and
revelation.

Because the free, personal God is the God who reveals himself, therefore revelation is will and act, and is opposed to reason. For reason lives in the necessary,
and therefore in the natural.[73]

Tillich has recognized both of these non-rational factors in his own
thinking.

As we noted above, Schelling's positive philosophy is an attempt to
think philosophically about the divine activity in myth and revelation. It is
not stretching too far to see in Tillich's notion of a theonomous philosophy
a parallel to Schelling's positive philosophy, a philosophy which unites the
autonomy of reason with an ultimate concern for the divine ground and activity. The response of reason to the divine saving activity is, for Schelling,

---

[70]Tillich, *Mysticism*, 125.

[71]Paul Tillich, *On the Boundary: An Autobiographical Sketch* (New York: Charles Scribner's Sons, 1966) 51f.

[72]Schelling, *W.*, V:650-57.

[73]Tillich, *Construction*, 137.

to recognize it as wonderful. This note of unexpected joy, which Tillich touches in his treatment of the paradoxical nature of revelation, comes out at the end of *Ultimate Concern*, when Tillich exclaims, "'The saving power' is wonderful."[74]

6. *The Dynamics of Culture and Religion.*

a. *Autonomy, heteronomy, and theonomy.* Together with Hegel's early writings, Schelling's treatment of the history of the emancipation of reason and of the Church of the Spirit forms part of the background of Tillich's philosophy of culture, particularly the turning towards and from its depths.

The beginning of the Philosophical Introduction to the *Philosophy of Mythology* (Schelling, *W.*, V:437-76) is a history of the emancipation of reason. A recapitulating passage, referring to the time of Descartes, has been summarized by Hayes:

> Now Reason is free! or rather, it is emerging into freedom. Its age-long struggles—first against the blind authority of mythological religion, then against the external authority of the Church and Revealed Word, and now against the uncomprehended assumptions of natural knowledge—all this is past.[75]

Tillich summarizes part of Schelling's discussion:

> The Reformation . . . was marked by a turning away from tradition and a return to the original documents of revelation. But as a result consciousness fell into a new servitude, inasmuch as the authority of those "[written] monuments which originated under casual conditions without the force of necessity" could not blind consciousness internally (11:260). Moreover, this authority held sway for only a short time. Reason is the source of the final and definitive liberation. . . . "But consciousness that has fled from revelation has recourse only to natural knowledge which does not increase freedom, and to natural reason which, as the Apostle says, learns nothing from the Spirit of God . . ." (11:260). Rationalists have no justification to call themselves, among other things, free thinkers (11:260n). "For as before, consciousness was destined to be free from revelation, so it was destined once again to be free from natural reason" (11:263). It was Kant's deed to have accomplished this liberation. . . . At this point, Schelling expresses in a classic way the significance of the religious self-consciousness of German Idealism for the history of philosophy: It is the consciousness that guides the liberating power of Christianity to its perfect outcome. It is fundamental to the dialectical method . . . that nothing external or unintelligible, and, therefore, servile, be tolerated, not even re-

---

[74]D. Mackenzie Brown, *Ultimate Concern: Tillich in Dialogue* (New York: Harper & Row, 1965) 220.

[75]Hayes, 192f.

ligion. . . Everything conditioned enslaves, only the unconditioned, the act, makes free. Mythology is a process, therefore it enslaves. Revelation is a free act, therefore it sets free. "But by overcoming unspiritual religion intrinsically, revelation sets consciousness in opposition to it in freedom, and in this way mediates free religion, the religion of the Spirit, which, because its nature is to be sought and found only with freedom, can be realized completely only as philosophical religion" (11:255).

The escape from heteronomy is clearly indicated, as well the necessity of turning autonomy from bondage to itself and rooting it in the unconditioned. Tillich would differ from Schelling in that philosophical religion is not superior to revelation, although like Schelling he recognizes that revelation, while liberating, can also be the beginning of a process of heteronomy when the attempt is made to domesticate it. Actually Schelling's philosophical religion is not so far from Tillich's theonomy.

The emptiness of autonomy when turned from the unconditioned is recognized clearly by Schelling.

Man sought a completely free, critical knowledge, imagining that he would be content with this contentless . . . freedom. But there was a final disillusionment, for after freeing itself from the authorities represented by Church, Scripture, and Revelation, Reason now found itself to be in bondage to its own presuppositions.[76]

Schelling also has a clear notion of heteronomy, without this explicit term, as the above and the following passages make clear.

The Church itself, in order to overcome Paganism, became for a time a blind, external power.

No sooner had the Reformation cast off the external authority of the Church than it succumbed to the external authority of the written Word.[77]

Schelling's vision of the Church of the Spirit also contains the seeds of Tillich's concept of theonomy.

He sees the true catholicity and unity of the Church . . . in a simultaneous synthesis of Church and World, of Christianity and Culture. . . . Schelling conceives the "Church" of the future as . . . a synthesis of . . . Church and world, Christianity and civilization.

---

[76]Ibid., 189.

[77]Ibid., 188f.

> It will be a truly public religion—not as a State church or as a High Church, but as the religion of all mankind in which mankind will at the same time find the supreme knowledge.[78]

Yet there are periods in the past when there was an approach to what Schelling calls philosophical religion, and like Tillich, he finds special attraction to neo-Platonism for this reason.[79]

b. *Christianity as the fulfillment of Paganism.* While Tillich would want to turn attention from Christianity to Christ, the notion that the religious longings of mankind find fulfillment in the central revelation is a common notion to both men. Yet Schelling's appreciation of paganism must be assessed carefully in the light of his entire *Philosophy of Mythology* to indicate the differences from Tillich. The following passage hints at both the similarities and the differences.

> The content of all true religion is an eternal content. . . . A religion which is not from (the foundation of) the world and through *all* times, cannot be the true religion. Hence Christianity must have been in Paganism, and the latter must have had the same *substantial* content. (This agrees with our earlier statement that Christ was in Paganism—but not *as* Christ, which means *substantially*, not in his truth). . . . It is inconceivable that mankind could have survived through millennia without *any* reference to those principles in which alone salvation lies.
>
> Paganism—precisely because Christianity is not its absolute negation but its truth—also possesses in itself a relative truth. When we view the whole great pagan movement as the background for Christianity, then Christianity has a far greater and more powerful basis for its reality than the usual sophistical proofs of its truth are capable of giving it.[80]

c. *The dynamics of Christianity.* Catholicism, Protestantism, and the Church of the Spirit are typified by Old Testament and New Testament figures.

> In the Old Testament, *Moses* is the principle of permanence and stability, of what is real and substantial. *Elijah* is the fiery spirit who develops, quickens, moves, and urges on toward a future which is not yet known. *John the Baptist* concludes the Old Testament and with it the times before Christ. . . . Of the three apostles, *Peter* is the parallel to Moses. He is the law-giver, the principle of *stability*, the foundation. Paul . . . is the Elijah of the New Testament, the principle of movement, development

---

[78]Ibid., 416, 431; Schelling, *W.*, VI:720.

[79]Hayes, 187.

[80]Schelling, *W.*, VI:469f.

and freedom in the Church. Finally, the apostle *John* is the parallel to John the Baptist. Like him, he is the apostle of the future; he points to the future.[81]

Just as little as God has his being in one person alone, so little does the Church exist in only one of its Apostles. Peter is more the Apostle of the Father; he gazes most deeply into the past. *Paul* is the true Apostle of the Son, *John* the Apostle of the Spirit.[82]

Apart from the fact that for Tillich Paul is one who primarily speaks of the life in the Spirit, these characterizations of Catholicism and Protestantism in terms of stability and development and as both necessary do find echoes in Tillich's notion of sacramental substance and Protestant criticism. In Schelling, as in Tillich, these are polarities.

Each, however, presupposes the other. Peter remains the foundation, but it must be built upon if it is not to turn out unfruitful. Peter, therefore, requires Paul. But Paul also would be nothing without Peter. For what Peter has founded, Paul must develop—must free it, step by step, from its limitations and thus affect the whole future.

As with Tillich, the Catholic-Protestant polarity in Schelling is a driving force behind the history of Christianity.

If the Church were to persist, to consolidate, and to acquire a historical foundation and make progress, Peter *had* to rule supreme; for he is the body, the center, that which holds everything together. . . . Paul has always held a certain eccentric position in the Church. For whenever he was allowed to speak, whenever his words were heard and understood in all their stirring power, a commotion within the church was the result. Even in recent times, for instance, Jansenism only originated in the Catholic Church because certain pious and very sensitive men were struck to the heart by the fiery words of the Apostle Paul about the grace of God which is given freely and cannot be earned by (good) works. Just so, the writings of Paul are the main source of the spirited convictions of the most eccentric religious sect in England, the Methodists.

During the Middle Ages, to be sure, the Pauline principle always made itself strongly felt, though without success. . . . Those who recognized the true situation could have predicted early that a time would come when this principle would break through, emerge in free opposition to Peter's Church, and become a properly historical principle, the principle of a second and new era.[83]

---

[81]Ibid., 695.

[82]Ibid., 718f.

[83]Ibid., 701, 706.

While both Schelling and Tillich have positive appreciation for both Protestantism and Catholicism, there is a sense in which the true church is the Church of the Spirit or, for Tillich, the Spiritual Community. Once again Tillich takes the fulfillment of the Spirit in the future and makes it present fragmentarily and future eschatologically. Schelling's notion is borne out in passages like the following:

> The true Church exists in none of these forms alone. It is the Church which proceeds from the foundation laid by Peter and progresses through Paul to that end which will be the Church of St. John.[84]

d. *The dynamic typology of religion.* Although Tillich does not follow Schelling's treatment of mythology in detail, their treatment of the history of religion has generic characteristics. Most important is that the movement in the history of religion occurs through inner principles of development which are both objective and subjective at the same time, movements in the development of human consciousness and in the real spiritual forces that this consciousness is grappling with. Also they share a vision of a movement from a primitive *Urreligion* through polytheism to anticipations of the revelation in Christ. And paralleling the movement of religion there are also philosophical reactions which have a similar dynamic.[85]

THE TRANSMUTATION OF SCHELLINGIAN THEMES IN TILLICH.   It is clear that Tillich shares many themes with Schelling which he has either derived from his predecessor or which he has in common with him. It is also clear that Tillich has transmuted all of these themes in the process of assimilating them. There are three aspects to the direction that this transmutation takes.

In the first place there has been a purging of the fantastic elements in Schelling's thought. For example, there is a restraining of the ontological imagination. There is a complexity to Schelling's vision of the divine life, from the Absolutely-Absolute and the Indifference underlying the split between the Unity and the Multiplicity in the divine, on through the three potencies and the three principles. This whole business is much more re-

---

[84]Ibid., 702.
[85]Tillich, *Construction*, 93-101.

strained in Tillich. Schelling has an *Urmensch*, a suprahistorical beginning, an absolute and a relative prehistory, and so forth. All of this has been tempered in Tillich, partly through a sense for the empirical, partly through the influence of Christian tradition, partly through an awareness of the fantastic excesses of speculation.

In the second place there is, as we have suggested, a greater respect in Tillich's writings for the regulating influence of the Christian tradition. Tillich is a theologian, while Schelling never claimed to be one. This is especially clear in the development of the Christology. For Tillich the Christian tradition, while not binding, at least must be treated with respect. While Schelling is aware of the Christian tradition, he does not feel rooted in it. It is the divine activity, not the historical understanding of it in a particular religion, which is decisive.

In the third place there has been a shift between Schelling and Tillich from the language of speculation to the language of symbol. The description of the divine life or of the beginning and end of history has a self-assured, almost theosophical cast in Schelling, while Tillich speaks with a clear knowledge that he is speaking metaphorically of that which transcends all symbols. We have not only a greater respect for empirical inquiry, a greater awareness of the estrangement of human reason from the divine, informed by existential and historical considerations as well as the events of the twentieth century, but also there is in Tillich a greater sense of the Divine mystery.

On Revising Tillich:
An Essay on
The Principles of Theology

VICTOR L. NUOVO

I

It is said of Petrarch, that most representative of Italian humanists, that he refused to publish his works until the end of his life. In growing anxiety, aware of the passing of time, but unaware of the difficulties that he would cause his biographers, he spent his days revising his poetical works and treatises, and his letters to his many friends, so that in him art and life might become one—a spiritual creation.

Paul Tillich was also a reviser. Being a philosopher rather than a poet, he was concerned not with his individual works, but with his system and its presentation. Like an artist he viewed his system as a unique spiritual creation that was expressive of life, and not of his life only, but of his community and of his era.[1] He showed little interest in republishing his early works, preferring to leave them in obscurity unless they fit as parts of his

---

[1] *Das System der Wissenschaften*, in Paul Tillich, *Gesammelte Werke* (hereafter referred to as GW), ed. by Renate Albrecht, 14 vols. (Stuttgart: Evangelisches Verlagswerk, 1959-1975) I:223-24.

overall systematic program; and those that he allowed to be reissued were
often first revised. Consequently, Tillich's *Gesammelte Werke* is not a critical and comprehensive collection, recording earlier and later versions of
his works, but an authorized version of works selected by him, some of
them doubly translated and revised, a record to posterity of his
achievement.

In spite of this effort, Tillich's work remains unfinished. His presentation of his system has left us with not a few unsolved problems and with
many obscurities. There are reliable reports that Tillich was dissatisfied
with his *Systematic Theology*; that, had it not been for the practical demands of publishers, a much longer and a more complete work would have
appeared at a later time. In his last public address, he discusses the in-
adequacies of his *Systematic Theology*. [2] This work, which we may presume
was to complete the systematic efforts of Tillich's long career as a philosophical theologian, was, he says, too narrowly apologetic. His concern in
Systematic Theology was limited to the confrontation of Christianity and
European secular culture. Now his concern has broadened to include the
entire history of religions. Tillich states that the theologian must take a
more affirmative attitude toward other religious traditions than his own.
Although he need not and in fact cannot depart from his particular religious
situation and its symbols, the theologian must learn to recognize the concrete forms of religious realization that have appeared elsewhere in the
world. There are other *kairoi* besides those moments of creative synthesis
upon which his own tradition was founded.

By studying the history of religions, the theologian will discover, perhaps, that all of these creative moments are united by a single inner aim:
"The Religion of the Concrete Spirit," the triumph of theonomy, that is
both present and future. From this standpoint we may envision a new theology that is, on the one hand, pluralistic, so far as it acknowledges a manifold of moments of spiritual realization, moments that are not united by the
continuities of tradition and historical community, and, on the other hand,
monistic, so far as it looks to the theonomous power that unites them all.
This new theological structure will not require the theologian to abandon
his particular past in order to be open to some future spiritual realization.
There is already some indication that his own symbols will be renewed by

---

[2]"The Significance of the History of Religions for the Systematic Theologian," in Paul
Tillich, *The Future of Religions* (New York: Harper and Row, 1966) 91.

this openness with even greater intensity. The new theology will oppose the secular attitude but not reject it. The claims of the advocates of autonomous secular culture and the Enlightenment to knowledge, moral goodness, and artistic expression, are just. So is their criticism of religion so far as it tends toward irrationalism and the demonic. The creative moments in the history of religion include this criticism. The opposition of theonomy and autonomy is dialectical. They include each other. But cut off from theonomous expression, secular culture becomes empty. The secular theologian, in spite of his Christocentrism, reduces Jesus to an ethical teacher. How is this theologian to be distinguished from a mere moralist?

If we are to take seriously Tillich's last public word, then it is necessary that we not merely represent his theology, but revise and reconstruct it. Tillich has provided us with guidelines for this effort in his last lecture, and in his earlier Bampton lectures he has left us an example to follow.[3] In the present essay I shall attempt to revise Tillich's theology, but from a different standpoint than the one presented in these works. There is, I believe, a fundamental error in Tillich's conception of the constitution of theology, of the relation between theology's form and substance, and consequently of his understanding of the principles of theology. The origin of this error can be traced to Tillich's notion of theonomy and its relation to autonomy. I shall argue that autonomous reason does not inevitably or necessarily empty itself of meaning and that autonomous forms are adequate to express the unconditioned; that the concept of theonomy, therefore, serves only an apologetic and not a constructive purpose; that it is possible to construct a theology founded upon rational principles alone without depriving theology of its depth; and that the validity of the symbols of historical religions and the future that they promise can be fairly judged by these principles.

In the course of this essay, I shall look in the direction of Kant. Kant shall be my touchstone, although I do not believe that he would have approved of everything that I say here nor of the way that I say it. Whether this approach is justified must depend finally upon the validity of my arguments and the truth of the revised theological principles which it is my purpose to present. However, there are historical reasons that justify this turning to Kant at the outset. The question of theonomy, whether there is

---

[3]Paul Tillich, *Christianity and the Encounter of the World Religions* (New York: Columbia University Press, 1963).

a higher law that may surpass but does not destroy the law of reason, pre-supposes Kant. The term, "theonomy," although etymologically Greek, originated during the early nineteenth century, according to the Oxford English Dictionary in Germany. Its use represents the effort of theologians to find a solution favorable to their discipline to the difficulties raised by the rational criticism of religion, whereby autonomous reason was set against heteronomous dogma and law.

The opposition of autonomy and heteronomy comes most sharply into focus in Kant's theory of morality, but it appears also in his critique of theoretical reason, in the regulative function of reason whereby reason has the capacity to set limits for itself, to be a law to itself. Autonomy is simply that quality of the will by which it governs itself by universal moral laws independent of any other object of volition, be it pleasure, reputation, or divine favor. Heteronomy is the subjection of the will to any other principle. [4] The concept of theonomy is supposed to mediate the opposition that Kant so sharply defined. But there can be no mediation if Kant is strictly adhered to. Theonomy would be a form of heteronomy. There is no higher law. We must not assume that it is our duty to obey a command, even if it is said to be from God, unless we have judged it worthy of adoption through the moral faculty of reason. [5]

But Kant does allow that there is one situation where the moral law can properly be represented as the law of God. In the conflict of good against evil, the victory of moral goodness can be assured only by founding an ethical commonwealth, a union of wills under moral laws alone. The constitution of such a society, which is not a public commonwealth subject to public laws and legality, requires the concept of a supreme lawgiver, whose will is identical with the sum of all moral duties and who, because moral worth is revealed, not in external acts but in the inner disposition, knows the heart. [6] As supreme lawgiver, God represents the universality and consistency of moral laws and the just power that is able to establish ends that are conformable to this law. This is the origin of our concept of God. [7] We

---

[4]Immanuel Kant, *Foundations of the Metaphysics of Morals*, English translation by Lewis White Beck (New York: Bobbs-Merrill, 1959) 59.

[5]Immanuel Kant, *Religion within the Limits of Reason Alone*, English translation by Theodore M. Greene and Hoyt H. Hudson (New York: Harper and Row, 1960) 174ff.

[6]Ibid., 90.

[7]Ibid., 95.

may call this "theonomy," but it is a theonomy wholly subordinated to the rationally determined laws of morality. This does not mean that somehow God is subordinate to reason, but that God is supremely rational, just as God's will can be said to be perfectly good without meaning that God is subordinate to goodness. The rational laws of morality do not constrain the will of God or any other "holy will," for such a will is by nature "necessarily in unison with the law."[8]

In Tillich's use of it, theonomy takes on a different and perhaps more profound significance. He makes theonomy into a speculative metaphysical principle that is supposed to overcome the opposition of autonomy and heteronomy in the sphere of morality or in any other—art, politics, science, etc.—because it is the transcendental unity of both. By means of this principle, Tillich attempts to reverse the relation of morality and religion. One important consequence, however, of this dissolution of the opposition of autonomy and heteronomy, and of this overturning of Kant, is the legitimization of historical religion, of what from the Kantian standpoint and that of the Enlightenment can only be heteronomous doctrines, institutions, and laws. In other words, Tillich's use of the principle of theonomy, although apparently metaphysical, serves an apologetic purpose.

The speculative metaphysical standpoint that is characteristic of Tillich's theology has its foundation in German Idealism, as Tillich readily admitted. The union of the idea of autonomy of freedom with Spinoza's idea of substance gave rise to the Idealistic system of the post-Enlightenment.[9] But it was only by way of Kant that the idea of freedom was raised to a metaphysical principle and that the soil was prepared for the growth of German Idealism and beyond it to Existentialism; Tillich is the heir of these developments. Therefore, to view him in the light of Kant is not arbitrary or unjustified.

II

Whatever evolution Tillich's conception of the aim and method of theology may have undergone, there is one unchanging element in it, namely, his belief that mere reason is insufficient to carry out the tasks of theology,

---

[8]Kant, *Foundations of the Metaphysics of Morals*, 31.

[9]F. W. J. Schelling, *Of Human Freedom*, English translation by James Gutmann (Chicago: Open Court, 1936) 17, 25.

that the substance of theology, which renders it positive and concrete and affirmative, is disclosed in revelation. Revelation is "the breakthrough of the unconditioned into the world of the conditioned."[10] It is the manifestation of mystery, and yet does not destroy reason, but reveals its depth.[11] Revelation is always concrete. It may be borne by a community or by an individual, but most often by an individual, a spirit-bearing Gestalt, who stands for the community.[12] The paradigm of revelation is the incarnation.[13] Revelation is the synthetic unity of the particular and the universal, of existence and thought, of flesh and the logos. The method of theology is theonomous so far as it is governed by this principle. Its achievement, its realization as a genuinely theonomous science, depends upon the historical situation, the openness of symbolic or cultural forms and structures of spiritual life to the transcendent source of being and meaning. Thus, the incarnation is not only the paradigm of revelation, but of every spiritual-creative act. The possibility of theology as a theonomous science is conditioned upon the possibility of the theonomous culture. Not only revelation, but all spiritual creation, in science, morality, politics, and art, is a "breakthrough" through conditioned or finite forms.[14]

This conception of theology is profoundly apologetic. There are, however, at least two kinds of apologetic theology. One, natural theology, consists of the rational justification of theological beliefs. Most natural theology of this kind is concerned with the rationality of belief in the existence of God, who is just, omnipotent, and so forth. But other themes are also investigated, for example, the possibility of the immortality of the soul or of an original creation, or the rationality of belief in the resurrection of the body or in revelation. Natural theology, which not long ago was out

---

[10]Paul Tillich, *Religionsphilosophie*, GW, I:298, English translation in *What is Religion?*, ed. by James Luther Adams (New York: Harper and Row, 1969) 29. The translation given here and all others of Tillich are mine unless otherwise noted.

[11]*Religionsphilosophie*, GW, I:297-99, English translation, *What is Religion?*, 27-30; "Philosophy and Theology," in *The Protestant Era*, trans. by James Luther Adams (Chicago: University of Chicago Press, 1948) 90-92; *Systematic Theology* 3 vols. (Chicago: University of Chicago Press, 1951-1963) I:79-81, 108-109, 112 (hereafter referred to as ST plus volume and page).

[12]ST, I:111. Cf. also, *Das System der Wissenschaften*, GW, I:214f.

[13]ST, I:151.

[14]*Das System der Wissenschaften*, GW, I:274; ST, I:148-50.

of fashion, now seems to be enjoying a modest renaissance. However, its achievements have little to do with our present concern with Tillich. On the whole, this kind of apologetics is non-speculative. Theological doctrine and philosophical inquiry remain external to each other. [15]

There is another kind of apologetics whose method is founded upon the presupposition of the identity of a particular theological doctrine of expression, perhaps the central theological doctrine, with the principle of truth. This principle is viewed as the norm not only of constructive theology and religious expression, but also of every intellectual endeavor. This norm does not remain unchanged in its use. An exchange takes place. The religious expression gives its authority to thought, just as it receives, through the act of interpretation, the attributes of pure thought. It becomes a principle.

Whether this process is justified, whether, for example, the wisdom or logos of God is the structure of creation and the pattern of truth, is a very ancient question. This is the question of the philosophical significance of myths and miracle stories and prophetic visions. Were the ancient poets and prophets and apostles ecstatic metaphysicians who presented their doctrines figuratively? Is an allegorical interpretation of their productions justified? It would be tempting to examine this question and its history here, for such a review would bring to light Tillich's place in the history of philosophical theology and the abiding questions that he addressed in his theology. But to do so would require too long a digression and resources that I do not possess. Suffice it to say that implicit in the present revisioning of Tillich's theology in the direction of Kant is a rejection of this kind of apologetics. At least for the sake of argument, I shall accept the judgments of Spinoza, who attributed to the prophets and apostles moral insight only[16]; of Hume, who considered the union of historical faith and philosophical doctrine as a coincidence only and of no real philosophical value[17]; and of Kant, who denied that there is any speculative value in revelation, so that it and the doctrines that represent it can never be made

---

[15]Cf. Alvin Plantings, "Introduction," *God, Freedom, and Evil* (New York: Harper and Row, 1974).

[16]Benedict de Spinoza, *A Theologico-Political Treatise*, English translation by R. H. M. Elwes (New York: Dover, 1951) 9, 33, 40.

[17]David Hume, *The Natural History of Religion*, ed. by H. E. Root (Stanford: Stanford University Press, 1956) 43.

into a principle of truth; who, on the other hand, attributed to Scripture and its story of salvation, a practical, that is to say, a moral validity; who, therefore, located the principle of theological affirmation ("What may I hope for?") in pure, practical reason. [18]

By using the term "profound" to characterize Tillich's manner of apologetic theology, I am not suggesting that in comparison with it natural theology is superficial. It most certainly is not. "Profound" in this instance signifies that Tillich's apologetic motive is not explicit; it lies beneath the surface. The same use of the word occurs in the sentence, "Peterson is profoundly mistaken," meaning that Peterson's entire point of view of a particular issue is wrong; that his error lies not in any single judgment, but in the standpoint from which all of his judgments are made. Therefore, the error is not apparent in any one of Peterson's judgments. It is primordial. It may even be called radical. Thus, we may call Tillich's theology radically, or primordially, or profoundly apologetic, meaning thereby that the apologetic motive lies at the root of his theology, that his theology as a whole is built upon it. I shall give some examples to illustrate this point.

Tillich's concept of a theonomous norm is an adaptation of the Incarnation to the theory of meaning. A theonomous norm, which has validity not only in theology, but also in every *Geisteswissenschaft*. For example, ethics, political philosophy, intellectual history, metaphysics, aesthetics, is "born in a definite historical place, and therefore has the concreteness and particularity of an individual spiritual creation. It is not intentionally universal [i.e., it does not call attention to itself, but sacrifices its form to unconditioned form], but it is universally valid."[19] His concept of "the creative," which is the fundamental category of spiritual realization, is a variation on the same theme. "Because thought and existence are united in every creation, therefore, every creation is at once individual and universal. The more an actual entity is at the same time individual and universal, the clearer is its creative character. The highest form of the creative is therefore the spirit-bearing Gestalt."[20] "The universal, spirit-

---

[18]Immanuel Kant, *Critique of Pure Reason*, B832-47, English translation by Norman Kemp Smith (London: Macmillan, 1933) 635-44; cf. also, *Religion within the Limits of Reason Alone*, English translation, 11.

[19]Tillich, *Das System der Wissenschaften*, GW, I:241; ST, I:136.

[20]Ibid., GW, I:212.

bearing, individual Gestalt is the highest metaphysical symbol," which is
to say, it reveals or expresses the absolutely unconditioned.[21]

In his *Systematic Theology*, Tillich defines the norm of theology as "the
New Being in Jesus as the Christ." He tells us that this formulation is
based upon St. Paul's saying: "If anyone is in Christ, he is a new creation"
(II Cor. 5:17).[22] New Being is the theonomous or unambiguous re-creation
of all that "participates" in Jesus as the Christ, who is the spirit-bearing
Gestalt in whom the ambiguities of reason, life, and history are overcome.[23] Form and participation are, of course, not St. Paul's but Plato's
terms. Christianity is true, because its principle is the principle of truth
everywhere.

The assertion that Jesus is the Christ is a paradox.[24] In an early essay,
Tillich explains the necessity of paradox in all discourse about the unconditioned, that is, in all metaphysical discourse. Paradox is unavoidable, because the unconditioned is not an object but rather transcends the
separation of subject and object. This, according to Tillich, is the primal
paradox (*die Urparadoxie*). It occurs at the point "in which the unconditioned becomes an object." The paradox is located in the object that bears
the unconditioned and not in our discourse about it.[25] Here again we perceive the symbol of the incarnation. The norm of theology is represented
as the norm of first philosophy. Of course, Tillich believed that all metaphysical concepts were necessarily symbolic. A symbol is a concept "that
expresses something else than its proper immediate meaning." Metaphysical concepts must express or point to the unconditioned.

The profound paradox of having to comprehend the unconditioned in
terms of the conditioned is inherent in metaphysics.[26] The symbols of
metaphysics may be drawn from myth, which is "the most immediate form
of theonomous metaphysics," or from science. Dogma, which is "the attempt to use scientific concepts as theonomous symbols," is the synthesis

[21]Ibid., GW, I:198.

[22]ST, I:49.

[23]ST, II:119.

[24]ST, I:50, 56-57, 123, 151.

[25]*Die Überwindung des Religionsbegriffs in der Religionsphilosophie*, GW, I:367, English
translation in *What is Religion?*, 122-23.

[26]*Das System der Wissenschaften*, GW, I:254.

of both.[27] Valid metaphysical symbols are ones that express "the unity of the real itself." This unity is a "coincidence of opposites," of thought and being, of existence and logos. Metaphysical symbols comprehend the paradox of the ultimate identity of the conditioned and the unconditioned.[28]

"Justification through faith" is another theological norm that prevailed in a previous age, but which continues to have validity for Tillich not only in theology but in his theory of meaning.[29] Thus, his representation of the conflict of autonomy and heteronomy echoes the opposition of law and gospel. When in the history of culture religious expressions lose their theonomous power they become rigid and empty. Paradox, then, becomes mere logical contradiction. Then autonomous reason rightfully opposes religion, and in the ensuing conflict the victory of autonomy is assured:

> But the victory is a costly one. The right of autonomy to oppose heteronomy becomes wrong [*Unrecht*] *because autonomous form is law.* Rationality and technology operate according to laws, *but it is impossible to live under the law.* Whenever the unconditioned is comprehended only as the unconditional validity of logical or ethical or aesthetic form, the living dies. *For there the unconditioned is a judge who condemns every individual form because it has not fulfilled the law. . . .*[30]

The law kills; the spirit gives life. The breakthrough of unconditioned meaning into autonomous form is called "grace."[31] Cultural creativity is grace. The theonomous breakthrough of autonomous forms does not negate them, but "fulfills" them.

More could be said about Tillich's concept of spirit (*Geist*).[32] Spirit is creation in all cultural spheres, the unity of form and actuality.[33] Spirit is

---

[27]Ibid., GW, I:279.

[28]Ibid., GW, I:256.

[29]ST, I:47.

[30]*Die Überwindung des Religionsbegriffs in der Religionsphilosophie*, GW, I:387, English translation, *What is Religion?*, 152.

[31]Ibid., GW, I:379, English translation, *What is Religion?*, 140; also, *Das System der Wissenschaften*, GW, I:214: "The unity of *intention of the universal* and *realization in an individual*, this and nothing else is creation and spirit. Here too religious discourse has fashioned a symbol when, in opposition to legalism on the one hand and to lawlessness on the other, it preaches that genius [*das Begnadetsein*] is a state of being filled with God. Spiritual creation is 'grace'."

[32]ST, III:21-25; *Das System der Wissenschaften*, GW, I:210-18.

[33]*Das System der Wissenschaften*, GW, I:191, 210, 284.

the spirit of love that creates community.[34] Spirit is truth, the unity of autonomy and theonomy.[35] These three symbols of Christian theology—the Incarnation, law and grace, and the Holy Spirit—are constitutive of Tillich's thought, of his theory of culture as well as of his theology. They form one principle: the incarnate logos is the spirit-bearing Gestalt, who through his creative deeds fulfills the law and reunites thought and existence in the original ground from which they both arose. The whole of Tillich's thought can be summed up in this formula. In some measure, perhaps in a large measure, theological conviction depends upon the ability of an author to echo the past convincingly to demonstrate that in dealing with a current problem honored formulae are applicable. The more widely applicable these formulae are, the stronger the conviction. In Tillich's system, which comprehends the whole of reality, they receive the widest possible application.

To some, this working together of Christian religious expression and philosophical concepts is precisely what gives value to Tillich's theology. The circularity of the method exemplifies the symbiosis of faith and understanding which is characteristic of the best of Christian theology. One need only consider Augustine, Anselm, Bonaventure, and the anonymous author of the prologue to the Fourth Gospel to see that this is so. I confess that I find it attractive. The rich symbolic expression of the church joined to the profoundest searching of the intellect in a life that is both spontaneous, because deeply learned, and reflective, is surely a great cultural achievement. Two forms of life have become one, and yet they remain also separate. A *communicatio idiomatum* occurs between them. This life seems far more profound than Kant's unilateral interpretation of Christian theological symbols. Kant justifies the interpretation of religious symbols and beliefs in terms of moral concepts, regardless of whether the interpretations given agree with those based upon history of tradition, by appealing to the autonomy and primacy of reason.[36] By doing so, he seems to deprive the symbols of life by uprooting them from the soil of tradition. But Kant may yet be justified, for when I examine Tillich's theological formulations, and those of his predecessors in this form of theological life, in

---

[34]Ibid., GW, I:264-65; *Morality and Beyond* (New York: Harper and Row, 1963) 88-95.

[35]*Das System der Wissenschaften*, GW, I:293.

[36]Kant, *Religion within the Limits of Reason Alone*, English translation, 9, 11.

search of the connection between reflection and religious expression, I
find none. The natural growth of symbols and thought, when examined,
proves to be something factitious. Theology, as Tillich conceives it, is a
cultural activity, a creative achievement, a form of life. But it may not be
the form of life best suited for the pursuit of truth and justice, for it is based
on a social norm that is not of guaranteed universality, which indeed seems
heteronomous, howsoever it be called. The only universal social norm is,
as Kant has shown, the moral law of freedom.

III

In Tillich's *Systematic Theology*, theological construction is based upon
two principles: a formal criterion and a concrete norm. Tillich defines the
critical principle or formal criterion of theology as follows: "Only those
statements are theological which deal with their object in so far as it can
become a matter of being or not-being for us."[37] By formal, Tillich means
that the principle is abstract, that it is without content, that it applies to
theology in general, or what means the same thing, it applies to no theology in particular. It is a critical principle, which is to say, it is a rule by
which we distinguish genuinely theological assertions from those that are
not, or the criterion for determining valid theological concepts. In fact,
there is only one concept, "being-itself," that satisfies this criterion; the
remaining theological expressions are "symbols."[38] By the same token,
there is only one theological assertion that "means what it says directly
and properly," namely, "God is being-itself."[39]

A theological system founded upon this critical-rational principle would
be autonomous, but it would be empty of content.[40] The norm provides the
substance that is necessary for a truly theonomous theology. In his *Systematic Theology*, Tillich distinguishes between a formal and a material
norm.[41] The formal norm is the institutional authority that sanctions the

---

[37]ST, I:14. This is, of course, the second version of the formal criterion. One might call
it the objective as opposed to the subjective version of the criterion. The first is, "Only
those propositions are theological which deal with their object in so far as it can become a
matter of ultimate concern for us." ST, I:12.

[38]ST, I:239.

[39]ST, I:238.

[40]ST, I:49; *Das System der Wissenschaften*, GW, I:275, 277.

[41]ST, I:47.

construction of material norms. Material norms are doctrines, dogmas, etc. They make up the content of theology. Formal criterion and material norm constitute the poles of theological activity. They are instances of the two *Urelemente* of cognition, thought and existence, which, in *Das System der Wissenschaften*, are identified by Tillich as the basic constituents of every spiritual action.[42] The criterion represents the thought pole of systematic theology; the norm represents its existence pole. The division corresponds in general to the themes of Volume I and Volume II, respectively, of *Systematic Theology*. A spiritual act is the creative union of thought and existence (or, what is the same, one that unites "power and meaning").[43] Thus, to complete the parallel, Volume III of the same work, whose theme is "Life and the Spirit" (and "History and the Kingdom," which is but an extension of the former theme), combines the considerations of the two previous volumes.[44] Norm and criterion differ with respect to their origin. The criterion is a philosophical concept, formulated and clarified through reflection and argument. It is scholastic, universal, autonomous. There can be only one criterion of theology. The historical provenance of the criterion is incidental to its meaning. The norm is the product of spontaneous life. It must never be cut off from its root. Norms grow. Their emergence is through "a historical process which, in spite of many conscious decisions, is on the whole unconscious."[45] "The norm grows, it is not produced intentionally."[46] Norms are symbols. They reveal the depths of reality that can be reached in no other way, least of all by rational inquiry.[47] In contrast to the single concept of theology, norms are manifold. They not only grow, they also die.[48] Norms have actual existence. We encounter the criterion only through the norm. Norms are symbols that have the quality of immediacy. They are particulars.

Why does theology need the norm as well as the criterion in order to carry out its systematic task? We have noted Tillich's answer to this ques-

[42]*Das System der Wissenschaften*, GW, I:118.

[43]ST, III:22.

[44]ST, III:12.

[45]ST, I:48.

[46]ST, I:48, 52.

[47]*Dynamics of Faith* (New York: Harper and Row, 1957) 42ff.

[48]Ibid., 43.

tion: being-itself is an abstract concept and lacks the concrete presence that theology demands. It lacks content. But to be consistent with Tillich's realism, in contrast with nominalism, being-itself cannot be said to be an empty concept, but rather the richest of all concepts. Being-itself "is not the highest abstraction, although it demands the ability of radical abstraction. It is the expression of the experience of being over against non-being. For this reason, the medieval philosophers called being the basic transcendentale, beyond the universal and the particular."[49] Being is not *ens commune*, but the cause of existence, the infinite power of being. Why then does this richest of concepts become empty, an abstract concept that requires something more to be thought concretely? An answer consistent with Tillich's point of view might be as follows: The experience of being over non-being, what, theologically expressed, is the power of God to create something out of nothing, has now been made into a concept, a rule. It is no longer immediate, intuitively present. It is the form of the concept, the fact that it is now thought abstractly, that makes it empty. In this form it can exercise only a negative, regulative function. A rule as such has no immediacy. It is not "positive and productive."

However, although norms do differ from the criterion in that they are particular, belonging to a historical faith, whereas the latter are universal, they are both rules. They have the same logical function. Norms differ from the criterion by being subordinate to them. Their right to be norms depends upon their capacity to express, for a time, the ground or power of being. If norms are rules, deriving their right to be such from the criterion, then they are also formal, for formality is just the characteristic of being a rule. And as such they too must be thought abstractly. Norms are rules. They govern the interpretation of the sources of theology, scripture, and tradition. A normative exegesis of scripture is one that applies the rule, of justification by grace, or eternal life, or the New Being, to the text. Thus, since they apply to a multitude of texts or elements of tradition, norms have generality.[50] Yet Tillich would not want to say that norms are

---

[49] ST, II:10.

[50] Norms are general rules, but they are not universals. They must, to be valid, express the universal, namely, being-itself. In this respect they are rational, for universality is the essential characteristic of rationality. When, however, they claim this universality for themselves, then they become heteronomous. Their claim of universality, as well as their rational dogmatic form is then a lie. Cf. *Das System der Wissenschaften*, GW, I:279.

empty for this reason. But if he would not, then on the same principle he cannot say that the criterion and a theology founded solely upon it must be empty. The formality of a rule does not deprive it of its content. If it did, it would lose its validity as a rule. It would govern nothing.

There is a parallel between Tillich's conception of the criterion of theology and the categorical imperative. The categorical imperative expresses the formality of the moral law, its universality and unconditionality. Tillich rejects the categorical imperative as the sole principle of morality. He argues that because it is formal and lacks specific content, it has no concrete use.[51] It must be supplemented by ethos, the immediate felt-values of a community, and it must be filled with love.[52] But this is a mistaken view of the categorical imperative.[53] To be sure, the categorical imperative does not generate or produce specific duties, to that extent it is formal and without content, but neither does a norm generate scripture and tradition to which it is related as a hermeneutical rule.

What the categorical imperative states is that moral duty cannot be based upon the particular interest of a rational being or of a community of rational beings, and that duty's incentive is always itself. By means of this rule we can determine in whatever situation what is or what is not rightfully our duty. Rather than driving out content, the rules of moral duty acting through the imagination are likely to bring to mind a manifold of possible uses. This is just the power of a formal principle when it is properly understood. Examples of duties may serve to give force to the formal rule, may bring it intuitively close, for example, "Always keep your promises," "Never lie," "Never exploit another creature." But without the formal rule, these would soon lose their force when once their validity was questioned. Likewise, parables and simple tales may make a moral point sooner and more effectively than an abstract argument, for example, the story that the prophet Nathan tells to King David (II Samuel 12:1-7). But unless David had an a priori sense of right, Nathan's story would have had no force. Just as Tillich misinterprets the categorical imperative, regarding it as empty because it is a rule or law, so does he misinterpret the criterion of theology.

---

[51]ST, III:45-50.

[52]*Das System der Wissenschaften*, GW, I:269-71.

[53]I am aware that what follows is not adequate to stand as a conclusive refutation of Tillich's criticism of Kantian ethics and plan to follow this essay with another dealing with this issue at length.

It is regulative, yet at the same time it calls to mind the appropriate content that conforms to it. Indeed, just as it can be said that the categorical imperative is the a priori condition of King David's moral experience, so the criterion of theology can be said to be the condition of religious experience, of the holy.

The concept of being, therefore, must be thought abstractly, but is not thereby the emptiest of concepts, not an abstraction or mere concept or logical construction. It is, if Tillich's realism is to be believed, the richest of concepts and this richness is not lost to rational thought, rather by it this concept is brought to light. Because it is the richest of concepts, being-itself is most properly predicated of God. There is no reason why a rational theology cannot be constructed upon this principle, and in the following section I shall attempt to prove this by developing, in outline to be sure, just such a theology.

Before proceeding to this task, I shall make one further observation concerning the differences between a norm and the criterion of theology. Norms, such as eternal life, justification, and New Being, differ from the criterion not only because of the manner in which they are present to consciousness, the one concretely, the other abstractly, but because of their content. The criterion is an ontological principle. Norms, on the other hand, at least those that I have mentioned, are directly or indirectly moral. Now there is one sense in which the criterion of theology can be called negative or unproductive. The assertion that God is being-itself does not entail that God is just, or good, or merciful. These are the attributes that inspire in us a love of God or a respect for him. In this respect, being-itself is a nihilating principle. By itself, it cannot become the principle of hope. But it is nonetheless capable of producing positive theological content. We should, then, distinguish at least two senses of "positive." Positive may mean simply having a content. That is to say, a principle is positive if by means of it something can be posited or asserted. If we can assert on the basis of the formal criterion that God is one only, that he is the cause of all existence, that he is radically different from everything else that exists, so that he is not a being besides others, then we have a positive theology. There is a second sense of positive, namely, having a content that can be affirmed, that is worthy of respect. On the basis of an ontological principle only, we can assert the power of God, but not the goodness and justice of God, and without the confidence that God is just and good there can be no respect for God, although there may be fear, or deep anxiety, or perhaps even a grudging admiration of his power and ingenuity. Without this confidence there can be no hope, no good beyond the transitory power of human achievement. The power to assert these attributes of God must come from a source other than ontology. In the final section of this essay I shall propose, as did Kant, that *this* positive content can be established on the basis of another rational principle, namely, the highest good.

IV

The criterion of theology, that God is the infinite power of being, being itself, the cause of existence, exercises, for the most part, a negative role in theology. This is not because it is without content, as though it were the supreme abstraction, but because of the peculiar nature of its content. As a theological principle it is radically monotheistic and deistic. This is its content.

As a philosophical concept, being-itself, or the being of that which is, has dominion over all the realms of consciousness. It is the *prius* of all thought. Explanation of any kind, especially philosophical explanation, begins and ends with it. It transcends all the categories of being, including substance. Being-itself (*das Sein selbst*) is not an entity (*ein Seiendes*), nor the most universal class of entities; it is rather the unconditioned condition of all entities and their attributes.

God is not an entity, but the being of every entity. That being-itself is one only (but not an individual) seems analytically true. If, then, being itself can be predicated of God, then there can be one God only. Being-itself is infinite. Because nothing finite can be God, there cannot be many gods, nor can a tribal god be made absolute. To be sure, although there can be one God only, the infinite power of divinity can be represented in manifold ways. Our interest in the powers of life and death, our perception of power in nature and human life, may finally lead us to consider that infinite power upon which they all depend. By making many of these powers central, for example, the productive and destructive powers of nature, the beneficial power of the hero to provide order and human skills, the religious emotions of dread, fear, joy, admiration, and even hope, arise. But among these, the affirmative emotions cannot abide, so long as they are founded upon finite powers. They have no lasting foundation.

The radical principle of monotheism is the doom or fate of all the gods of this world and of every concrete hope that they inspire. It is a nihilating

principle that sweeps away every historical faith. In this light, I must disagree with H. Richard Niebuhr's theory of radical monotheism. He claims
that being-itself is a principle of value as well as an ontological principle,
that the concept of being gives rise to the assurance that "because I am,
I am valued, and because you are, you are beloved . . . that whatever is,
is good, because it exists as the one thing among the many which all have
their origin and their being, in the One."[54] The proposition, "Whatever is,
is good, because it exists," is true in one quite trivial sense. A thing may
be called good when it is more or less a perfect instance of its kind. I understand this to be the meaning of the scholastic transcendental "good."
But to be good in this sense does not mean the same as to be valued or to
be beloved. That something is more or less a perfect instance of its kind
implies neither that it is in itself worthy to be valued or beloved, nor that
its ultimate cause is benevolently disposed toward it. Of course, it does
not imply the contrary of this either. If it did, no theological hope would be
possible. Nevertheless, "cause of existence" must not be confused with
"creator of the world."[55] If God is the cause of existence and exercises the
ultimate power of being and not-being, then indeed with him all things are
possible, or so it seems from our limited standpoint. But we have no way
of knowing what, out of an apparent infinity of possibilities, God would
choose, if indeed he has the power of choice, to bring into existence. Likewise, things are true because they are what they are. But this does not
imply that they are truthful nor that the ultimate power that produced them
is truthful in any but the weakest sense. Truth and goodness are not powers of this world as are nature and life. But if they are unconditioned, as it
seems they must be, it is not within the capacity of onto-theology to bring
this fact to light.

The critical principle of theology may also be called the principle of
Deism. By Deism I mean the theological doctrine that God and the world
are radically different. The infinite power of God cannot be said to be
bound necessarily to this world. Deism does not exclude the possibility of
Pantheism. God may be the substance of everything; whatever exists may
be only an actualization of divine potency. Yet from another perspective the

---

[54]H. Richard Niebuhr, *Radical Monotheism and Western Culture* (New York: Charles
Scribner's Sons, 1960) 54.

[55]Kant, *Critique of Pure Reason*, B659, English translation, 525.

world has its own being. The necessities by which we describe its organizations and operations are finite. They cannot be extended to God. In other words, God cannot be said to be bound by the laws of nature, even if nature be his nature. The infinite power of God must be bound by no necessity except that of its own nature, which is unknown to us. Infinite potency and freedom may be attributed to such a God, but neither truth, nor goodness, nor justice, nor mercy.

Tillich defines our attitude towards the infinite power of being as "ultimate concern." This is his well-known and widely adopted definition of religion. Ultimate concern, however, is much too vague a concept to represent the variety of possible attitudes that we have towards the infinite power of being. No doubt we have a concern for the ultimate power that produced us. This concern may take the form of fear, or deep anxiety, or even that pathological love that we sometimes find arising within ourselves for the agents of power who exercise a capricious dominion over us, but the same power may also produce scorn in us. Our concern for the infinite power of being may also take the form of interest. Whenever, in the manifestations of this power, in nature or in history, we perceive an apparent design, that is, so far as reason and the understanding enable us to gain a degree of detachment from the display of divine power, we may wonder or admire or even enjoy what we perceive, even though the object of our admiration cannot be said to be there for our benefit. Such an attitude may mark the beginning of science or cognitive concern. The effect of this attitude is detachment from every power external to us and the discovery of an absolute greatness that resides within ourselves, which is not ourselves, but is truth and goodness to which we can aspire. Kant believed that it is only when a degree of detachment is attained, only when our rational powers come into play, that religion emerges from superstition.[56] No doubt he meant moral religion. But it may be that with the awakening of rationality, which is autonomous, a natural religion is possible whose point of departure is the interest that the productive power of nature cannot fail to evoke from perceptive and intelligent creatures. This, however, is an un-Kantian thought as much as it is an un-Tillichian one, for Tillich followed Kant in rejecting all natural theology pursued by the theoretical faculty of

---

[56]Kant, *Critique of Judgment.* English translation by J. C. Meredith, 2 vols. in one (Oxford: Clarendon Press, 1952) I: 114.

reason alone. It was, nonetheless, a consideration for which Kant was not unsympathetic.[57]

So far, then, as our theological reflections are based only upon the ontological criterion of theology, we cannot attribute goodness to the infinite power of being. The principles of Deism and radical monotheism can at best allow us to develop a negative theodicy. The awareness of our nothingness in this immense theater of God's power silences our complaints. We may indeed wonder at the vastness of the world, its intricate structure, at a power of infinite creativity, and our insignificant place in all of its displays. We may acknowledge that this power is the ultimate cause of our existence, but the affirmative attitude that such reflections may inspire within us cannot exceed a mood of melancholy and resignation. Hope, however, must have another source. It originates in the possibility or the right to attribute goodwill to God. To attribute such qualities as goodness, justice, and mercy to God is to demand it of God. The justification of this demand arises not from metaphysical reflection, but from morality. Theology, then, must have two principles: the unconditioned power of God and the unconditional demand of the morally good will. Only upon these two principles, which are not the same, is it possible to construct a theology that is both positive and affirmative.

V

The categorical imperative is the law of freedom; it is the absolute form of truth and goodness. Freedom is not the power to contradict the moral law, but the power to resist every heteronomous claim upon our will. Submission to alien laws, to the irrational as such, is not freedom but the greatest bondage. This freedom may be called autonomy, which Tillich correctly defines as "the obedience of the individual to the law of reason, which he finds in himself."[58] This rational concept of freedom, which, when it is practically employed, is the basis of morality and must be distinguished from Tillich's speculative concept of freedom, which is the power of the creature to exist, to "stand outside" of its essence, to dissolve its unity with the divine life.[59] These two concepts of freedom must be kept

---

[57]Kant, *Critique of Pure Reason*, B652, English translation, 520.

[58]ST, I:84.

[59]ST, I:255; II:31. Compare with ST, II:20.

distinct. In this essay, my primary concern is with the former. About the latter, I say only that I am not sure that it can be called freedom at all. If it is freedom, it is a power that can be used only once and then is lost. We can recognize it only after having lost it. It is not so with the rational freedom that morality brings to light. This freedom is always renewable. In the theoretical realm, it is the power of reason to renew its inquiry into received knowledge and to apprehend unnoticed facts; it is the spontaneous play of abstract concepts that generate new hypotheses and new syntheses. If being is infinite, so is the capacity and ingenuity of reason to comprehend it. Their relationship is not one of conflict, [60] but of mutuality. This spontaneity or play of abstraction is the origin of artistic creation as well. But it is only in the moral realm that the validity of these gentle powers is secured.

Autonomy is freedom from God's infinite power. Our moral nature entitles us to question God, to call him to account. In the light of this freedom, the infinite power of being is "might that has no dominion over us."[61] But to challenge God, to insist that God hear the just complaints of his creation presupposes that God is just, or that he ought to be. The right to postulate that God be just arises out of the freedom that morality discloses. This demand is that the world be a moral world, one of perfect freedom, one in which not only moral perfection but also happiness, the harmonious realization of all creaturely desires that are consistent with a mutual good will, is attained. That this demand is not a mere wish, but an a priori judgment of pure practical reason, is the point of Kant's so-called moral argument.

The initial premise of this argument,[62] which amounts to a moral or ethico-theology, is the inseparable connection of morality and hope. Every rational being has reason to hope for happiness, so far as he has made himself worthy of it by his virtuous life. There is an "inner practical necessity" that relates morality and happiness. This is not a very strong argument, but a plausible one. Virtue may be its own reward, as it is with Kant. But

---

[60]*Das System der Wissenschaften*, GW, I: 119.

[61]Kant, *Critique of Judgment*, English translation, 109.

[62]For the following I rely mostly upon Kant's *Critique of Pure Reason*, English translation, 635-44. But I have also taken into account his *Critique of Practical Reason*, English translation by Lewis White Beck (New York: Liberal Arts Press, 1956) 114-53, and *Religion within the Limits of Reason Alone*, English translation, 5n.

virtuous actions have consequences in the phenomenal world, and it seems reasonable to hope that these consequences be happy rather than unhappy, not only for the individual who produced them but for everyone affected by them. It would seem reasonable to hope anything contrary to this. Therefore, we can make it a duty for every rational being, that he will the happiness of himself and others so far as it is consistent with morality.

From this point on, Kant's argument becomes rather complex. There are at least three parts of it. First of all, there is the relation between morality and happiness. According to Kant's ethics, happiness is never the ground or motive of morality, but the reasonable consequence of it. Although we have the power to make ourselves worthy of happiness, we do not have the power to secure it. This power resides in God. It is reasonable to suppose, if there be an omnipotent and benevolent creator, that he should will that those worthy of happiness attain it. But since the happiness to be attained must be exactly commensurate with an individual's moral worth, God's capability of securing it for every rational creature must consist not only of power but of knowledge. The idea of the highest good is the perfect correlation of happiness and virtue. This idea can be comprehended completely only by a rational being who knows the moral worth of every individual, who is omniscient, but also perfectly just and wise.

The second part of the argument has to do with morality as a social system. For Kant, morality is a system of free wills. Every moral action is accompanied by the idea of a system of morality, of an "ethical commonwealth." This idea is also not the ground but the ideal consequent of moral action. What seems to govern this part of the argument is a variation of the principle that the whole is greater than the sum of its parts. An ethical commonwealth is a union of free wills. But the principle that coordinates or harmonizes these wills does not reside in any individual. It is an ideal that includes all. There must, then, be a "supreme reason," "a supreme will that comprehends in itself, or under itself, all private wills."[63] God, then, is the perfect harmony and consistency of all rational wills and moral deeds, the transcendental principle of society.

The third part of the argument raises the question of immortality. Although the ideas of a perfect harmony of wills and of the highest good are

---

[63]Kant, *Critique of Pure Reason*, English translation, 638.

ideas only and unlikely to be realized in the phenomenal world, for rational creatures seem inept at social organization, and not everyone is virtuous, and happiness is not in fact commensurate with virtue, nevertheless, it remains the duty of every rational being consistent with the ideals of pure practical reason, to seek the highest good possible in the world. It seems self-evident that we ought to endeavor to achieve the best that we can conceive. This, then, must be the command of reason. But it would be unreasonable to suppose that reason would command the impossible. If, therefore, the best cannot be achieved in this world, then there must be another, noumenal world, where this goal can be reached. In this world, then, we postulate a "moral world," and the sum of all actions in this world belong to that world, together, one would expect, with the ideal consequences of those actions, like "treasure in heaven." The sum of all virtuous wills in this world constitutes a mystical body "so far as the free will of each being is, under moral laws, in complete systematic unity with itself and with the freedom of every other."[64]

If this argument is valid, then the aim of this essay, of constructing a theology on the basis of autonomous rational principles, has been reached. A rational theology is conceivable quite apart from theonomy or revelation. One final consideration remains: to determine the relationship between rational theology and historical religion.

In his *Religion within the Limits of Reason Alone*, Kant presents his theory of religion not as a system of postulates of pure practical reason, but as a hermeneutics of religious tradition and a theory of history. He begins with a historical religion, Christianity, and attempts to show that the principles of Christianity are consistent with pure rational religion. There can, he states, be only one religion (because there is only one morality). He argues that whatever claims to be a religion and cannot be reduced to these rational principles is not religion but a cult.[65] This may seem to some to be an unsubtle attempt by Kant to replace religion with morality. However, I believe that he is justified, and for the following reasons. Both religion and morality make absolute demands upon the rational will. In anticipation of any objection to this assertion, I refer to Tillich's definition of "ultimate concern": "Ultimate concern is the abstract translation of the

---

[64]Ibid., English translation, 637-38.

[65]Kant, *Religion within the Limits of Reason Alone*, English translation, 11.

great commandment: 'The Lord, our God, the Lord is one; and you shall love the Lord your God with all your heart, and with all your soul, and with all your mind, and with all your strength.'"[66] But a rational conscience cannot entertain two absolutely unconditional demands. Either one must exclude the other, or they must be reconciled by interpreting one in terms of the other. Tillich chose to subordinate morality to religion, claiming that the rational form of morality had to be filled with religious substance. But Tillich's argument is based upon a misunderstanding of Kant's ethical formalism. If, as I have argued, autonomous reason does not empty itself of content and substance by following its own laws, then to impose a theonomous norm upon it is heteronomous. Kant chose the opposite course, the one that is favored here: to interpret religion in terms of morality.[67] And this is justified, for there is an ethical content in more religion, and religion is, after all, something that rational beings do. But if Kant's hermeneutical method is justified, then it should be applicable to other historical religions besides Christianity, for example, to Buddhism. That it can be applied in a profound and not a superficial way has been demonstrated by Kant in his *Religion*, for example, in his analysis of the concept of radical evil. I began this essay referring to Tillich's hope for a theology that would take seriously the history of religions, and now return to it, but from a different and, I believe, more promising standpoint.

But for Kant, historical religion is not only something to be interpreted. He believes that it plays a decisive role in the conflict of good against evil. The mystical body of virtuous wills must be more than an idea. It must have a place (or places) within history, and this means a social reality that is established neither upon natural bonds nor upon public laws and force. It must be a social reality whose principle is freedom, a voluntary moral association. The Church is such a society, although imperfectly conceived and realized. The Buddhist Samgha is another candidate for this designation, and there may indeed be others. When this practical aim of Kant's theory of religion is taken into account, then it appears as a theory of his-

---

[66]ST, I:11.

[67]The opposition can be stated quite nicely as follows: in his *Religion* (English translation, 9), Kant wrote, "A religion which rashly declares war on reason will not be able to hold out in the long run against it." Tillich would doubtless reply, "Reason which rashly declares war on religion will not be able to hold out in the long run against it."

tory whose goal is freedom in society. History is the development of the idea and the reality of voluntary associations whose principle is mutual good will and whose transcendental ideal is God.[68]

---

[68]I have taken the liberty of borrowing the expression "voluntary association" from Professor James Luther Adams, without whose inspiration I would not have thought these thoughts. But I cannot claim his approval of the way that I have used it. If, however, in the course of my reflections I find myself in his vicinity, then I shall regard myself as richly rewarded for my efforts.

Critical and Religious Consciousness: Some Reflections on the Question of Truth in the Philosophy of Religion[1]

ROBERT P. SCHARLEMANN

The point of departure for Tillich's reflections on the philosophy of religion as we find them in his early essays, "Die Überwindung des Religionsbegriffes in der Religionsphilosophie" (1922)[2] and "Religionsphilosophie" (1925),[3] is a question which is otherwise seldom discussed in the philosophy of religion. It is a question about the possibility of a philosophy of religion at all, though not in the sense of the transcendental question of the condition of the possibility of something that is al-

---

[1] Translation, with a few minor alterations, of an address presented at the annual meeting of the Paul Tillich Gesellschaft at Hofgeismar, Germany, on April 30, 1976. The footnotes have been added.

[2] *Gesammelte Werke*, I: *Frühe Hauptwerke* (Stuttgart, 1959) 367-88. English translation in *What Is Religion?*, translated by James Luther Adams (New York, 1969) 122-54 (abbreviated hereinafter as WR).

[3] Ibid., 297-364. English translation in WR, 27-100.

ready actual. What is involved in the question meant here is not the effort
to provide a basis for an actual philosophy of religion through reducing it to
the condition of its possibility. Instead, it is the endeavor to solve the difficult problem that the very question about the essence of religion serves
to make a true answer impossible. By asking, "What is religion? What is
the essence of religion?," we erect a barrier which from the outset prevents our reaching the truth about religion. Religion is in the peculiar situation that it can lay claim to truth only so long as the question of the
essence and truth of religion is not posed. Once the question is raised,
truth has already vanished. Religion, as it presents itself, can then no
longer be true, and a judgment which intends to state what religion is cannot possibly be a true one.

We must be clear about what is being asserted here, for Tillich's somewhat curt statements do not make evident what is really at issue. Obviously the source of the problem is not simply the fact that theoretical
thinking is always abstract in comparison with the life process which it
seeks to understand and that such thinking accordingly can cast a false
light on living religion. On the contrary, the problem lies in the fact that the
otherwise innocent question, "What is that?," assumes outright destructive power when it is directed toward religion. In view of a religious phenomenon one cannot even ask, "What is that?," without thereby making
the phenomenon disappear. Hence philosophy of religion appears to face an
insoluble dilemma. If it keeps its philosophical character, it loses its object,
it is no longer philosophical because it is not permitted to raise the question
of the essence of the phenomenon. Tillich expresses this state of affairs in
his "Religionsphilosophie" thus: On the one hand, "the stronger, more
original, and purer that it is," the "more explicitly" does religion make the
claim that it excludes conceptual generalization; for that reason religion
feels itself under an "attack on its innermost essence" when it is called
"religion" (GW, I:297; R, 27). On the other hand, however, philosophy
cannot allow itself to be forbidden to ask the question of essence. Hence,
in view of religion, philosophy is in the peculiar circumstance "that it either
must dissolve the object which it seeks to grasp or must cancel itself in
the presence of [its object]" (ibid.; R, 28). Three years earlier Tillich had
expressed himself similarly in his essay "Die Überwindung des Religionsbegriffes in der Religionsphilosophie." At that time he wrote, "'Religion' is

the concept of something that is destroyed precisely through this concept" (GW, I:368; R, 124).

These observations make it clear that what is involved is a problem which we might entitle "critique and religion." At stake in the controversy between critique and religion is not only the content of certain religious objects but the truth of religion itself. Critical consciousness, which has become more and more at home in the thinking of Western peoples since the time of the Enlightenment, is characterized by the fact that it feels as untrue as any immediate relationship to actuality. What is true is only that relation to reality which has been mediated by an answer to the question whether the phenomenon really is what it presents itself to be. With critique, consciousness takes final leave of the condition in which it can simply accept things as they actually present themselves. By contrast, a religious consciousness retains, at least at one point, an immediate relation to reality, namely, at that point where it stands under the immediate impression of the phenomenal God. About everything else such a consciousness can be questioning and critical; about the reality of the phenomenal God it cannot be so. Instinctively religious consciousness knows the very thing that critique, in its own way, discovers; it knows that the actual God disappears as soon as one places the truth of the appearance in question. The difference between critique and religion is that the former is prepared to let the God disappear and to retain at most the status of a condition necessary for morality, whereas religion will forgo its questioning before it will let the God disappear. At one point critical and religious consciousness must accordingly find themselves at irreconcilable odds because what critique aims at is what religion must unconditionally exclude.

For arbitrating this conflict, Tillich demanded a "conquest" (*Überwindung*) of the concept of religion. He himself sought in two different ways to fulfill this demand. In the first place, he endeavored to develop a normative philosophy of religion in which religion and philosophy meet in the unconditional as that which is intended in religion and which at the same time is presupposed by the philosophical questioning that conditions everything. In the second place, he set up the method of correlation in which questions arising from existentialist analysis and symbols coming from religious traditions are so interpreted that they refer to each other and complement each other. What remained undeveloped in Tillich's own work were certain suggestions inherent in the concept of "absolute para-

dox" as Tillich sketched that concept in an unpublished essay, "Rechtfertigung und Zweifel" from the year 1919.[4]

What I should like to do in the present essay is, first, to sketch the dilemma to which Tillich makes reference in his philosophy of religion and to
do so on the basis of the inner logic of the dilemma. This will be followed
by an attempt to conceive of the essence of religion precisely as paradoxical. Finally, the last section offers an outline of the kind of consciousness
corresponding to this conception of religion, a consciousness we might
well call a "second naiveté."

I

In demanding a transcendence (*Überwindung*) of the concept of religion, Tillich intends to reject a procedure of thought according to which
we understand a concrete religious phenomenon through a general concept
of essence. Such a concept consists of a synthesis of a singular with a universal, which can be expressed in a judgment. If, for example, we have a
certain occurrence in view and make the judgment about it: "That is a religious rite," we comprehend the singular occurrence by the general
thought "rite." The concept can then be further analyzed if we go on to say
such things as this: "A rite is a religious rite when it re-presents a constitutive event, say, the creation of the world." Religion, as it understands
itself, resists such a conceptualization of itself. Why?

The reason can be given by reference to the position of the subject and
object terms in a judgment. In a judgment, which distinguishes the elements synthesized in the concept, the subject is necessarily the relatively
singular whereas the predicate is the relatively general. "That is an oak,"
"an oak is a tree," "a tree is an entity (something that is something)"—in
such a series the predicate is always general in comparison with the subject. If religion, then, wishes to lay claim to universal validity, as it does
when it looks at itself, it cannot occupy the position of the subject in a judgment; it must take the position of a predicate and, more exactly, of the universal predicate. That very necessity is the source of both the conflict
with philosophy, for which the universal predicate is not religion but being,

---

[4]"Rechtfertigung und Zweifel" (1919). A typescript is on hand in the Tillich archives at
Harvard and in Göttingen. Despite bearing the same title, this essay is not the same as the
one published in 1924.

and also the uneasiness that religion feels over against conceptual thought, since conceptual thought in this case seems to be on the side of philosophy. Religion prohibits judgments such as these: "Religion is the feeling of absolute dependence, or the feeling of the numinous, or faith in the transsensible, or a state of being grasped by the absolute." For in such judgments religion loses its place as the universal predicate by being subordinated to another predicate. If, however, it retains the place of the universal, it gets into conflict with philosophy. The place which philosophically is occupied by being is taken religiously by religion. This gives rise to the question: "What then is the universal predicate itself—religion or being? What is the last predication we can make about a phenomenon—that it is an entity, or that it is a religion?"

Yet religion cannot even permit that question to emerge; for the very formulation concedes victory at the outset to being and to philosophy. When we ask, "What *is* that?," we already presuppose, as the basic concept, being and not religion. Language and conceptual thought do not even permit us to pose the question neutrally, even if we tried to do so, for they reflect the fact that the original experience connected with questioning is not the universality of religion but the universality of being. That we can ask questions at all is in itself a clear proof that the self-understanding of religion, according to which religion is the highest predicate, is false. Hence this self-understanding can only be true if the question of its truth is never raised. Conceptual thought, which equates the universal with the predicate, must endanger religion because it impels religion to understand itself as highest predicate—something which religion can be only so long as no one asks whether that is what religion is.

Religion's instinctive mistrust of questions and an analysis of predicate thinking agree on this. If the question of the essence of religion is raised—indeed, if the question *can* be raised—then the self-understanding of religion appears to be false. But since critical consciousness does not allow anything to remain unquestioned, it must also direct the question of truth toward religion. In doing so, however, it loses the possibility of ever arriving at an affirmative answer because its very questioning has in the meantime destroyed religion as religion.

A way out of this dilemma is offered by another consideration, one which still moves in the realm of conceptual thought. It is essential to conceptual thinking that it synthesize the singular with the universal. Everyday thought and scientific thought fulfill this requirement by subordinating the singular, as the subject of a judgment, to the universal, as the predicate. If thought could be carried out in some other manner as a concept, then the difficulties connected with the concept of religion might be soluble. Might the universality of religion perhaps consist in its being not the highest predicate but the final subject of all judgments? Normally, to think is to judge that the singular belongs to a universal. Consequently, in our daily and scientific thinking about religion we believe we can understand Christianity, Buddhism, Hinduism, and so on, by conceiving them as religions and by conceiving religion in turn as, say, a movement toward the unconditional. Might it not be possible to carry out thinking in an inverted way by ordering the universal to the singular and thus forming the judgment "Religion (= the universal) is this (= the singular there)"? In such a case we would form the thought "Religion is Christianity, Buddhism, Hinduism, etc.," rather than the thought "Christianity etc. are religion."

The sense of this inversion must be carefully noted. The universal is here defined by its concrete workings. In such an inverted concept, which still remains a synthesis of universal and singular, religion is indeed universal even though it is no longer the predicate of some singular subject. Instead, it is the subject of a judgment in which the predicate is not a universal concept but a concrete formation. From that point nothing would prevent us from arriving at the conclusion that religion is being. That is to say, the basic concept of religion as being would give expression to the fact that the deed or activity in which religion is most purely concretized is nothing other than the concrete activity that we also designate as "being." In such a case there can be no conflict between religion, which always has to do with the one final subject, and philosophy which always has to do with the universal predicate. "Religion as being" is the basic concept, and "Religion is being" is the basic judgment in which philosophy and religion converge and on which a philosophy of religion can be built. The content of what Tillich called the unconditional is, under this aspect, religion as being. The unconditional judgment is the judgment that religion is being.

How this convergence of the one subject with the universal predicate works out can be briefly sketched with reference to Tillich's notion of correlation. The predicate "being" eventuates in a question; for when we assert that something is a being, we are only asserting that it is something and not nothing. In turn, if we put the further question of what "being" is, we cannot provide an answer on the basis of a still more universal predicate because there is none. With the concept of something as a being, conceptual and discriminative thought, which moves in an ordering of the singular to the universal, reaches its limit, where the only thing it can do is to use a tautology as an answer: "Being is being; being is that which every being qua being is." Thus the question of being so opens up the universal predicate that no judgment and no concept can close it any more. A tautology cannot close it because tautology does not provide any defining predicate, it only repeats the subject. The question which is thus opened can be closed only by a judgment on the part of an inverted thinking, in which we say, "Religion is being." The subject and predicate are here intentionally inverted. The question, "What is being?," expects an answer that will begin with being as the subject term: "Being is. . . ." What happens instead is that the answer has the form: ". . . is being." The question is formulated: "What is being?" in the sense of: "What is it that being is?" The answer is given: "Religion is being." Hence one no longer asks what *religion* is. In that sense the concept of religion is transcended. One *asks*, rather, what *being* is and receives the *answer* that *religion* is being. Being is itself nothing, but religion is being. This is to say that being is never the subject and religion is never the predicate of an ultimate judgment. But in the concept, "religion is being," and in the judgment, "Religion is being," religion as a predicate concept is transcended; it is taken up into the concept of the unconditional. With this double suggestion, then, that religion is never the predicate for the concrete effects and that the most appropriate predicate for religion is being, one can indeed grasp religion.

Such a solution does not, however, provide an answer to the question of what the essence of religion is. The striking thing about Tillich's correlation is the fact that the assertion "Religion is being" is *not* an answer to the question of the essence of religion, despite the fact that it appears to be so; rather, it is an answer to the question of what *being* is. For that reason this solution, which is characteristic for how Tillich construes the philosophy of religion, seems to me not to have taken hold of the problem with the same degree of radicalness as did the unpublished essay of 1919 bearing the title "Rechtfertigung und Zweifel." For the concept of absolute paradox, which Tillich there tries to develop, reaches deeper than does that of the correlation of religion and being in a normative philosophy of religion or in a correlation of religion and philosophy. The absolute paradox points to a kind of thinking in which conceptuality itself is made to disappear. In a rough fashion one might designate what is meant here as the possibility of thinking in "disappearing concepts." What that is, how it is possible, and what significance it has for the question of the truth of religion are the questions to be discussed in the next sections.

II

There are two forms of judgment whose content is, as it were, disappearing concepts—tautology and paradox.[5] In a tautology the disappearance derives from the nonfulfillment of an expectation. A tautological assertion has the form of pure identity, $A = A$. Normally when we begin to make an assertion, "A is . . . ," what is expected in order to complete the judgment is a predicate concept that further determines the subject. In a tautology, however, the expectation is disappointed because what is provided is only an iteration of the subject—for example, "Religion is religion." What does such a judgment assert? Actually nothing. But precisely that *is* asserted, for tautology is a judgment-form through which we give expression to nothing. In other words, it is not the case that a tautology makes no assertion. We do in fact make an assertion with it, but *what* we assert is precisely nothing. There is a difference between not asserting at all—keeping quiet—and asserting but asserting precisely nothing. By "nothing" we mean that to which the particle "not" in negative judgments points. What this particle means we cannot grasp directly as such, even though we do readily understand it in context; for as soon as we think it, it is not nothing but something, an object of thought.

What "not" signifies cannot be an object, and yet thinking, in order to be thinking, must have an object. How then is it possible to think and yet to think nothing? It is possible through tautological judgments. What we are thinking when the expectation of a defining predicate is first awakened and then disappointed is the very same as what is meant when we use the particle "not" and understand it in its connection without any further ado. If we wish to isolate the "not" as such from its context and make pure negativity the object of thinking, that can take place in that, through the dou-

---

[5]Identity $(A = A)$ and contradiction $(A = \text{non-}A)$ are two principles of thinking. When they are turned into judgments (instead of being expressions of principles) of thought, they are tautological and paradoxical, respectively. They then form the "disappearing" concepts of which this paper speaks. The fact that principles are disappearing concepts when they become judgments is the logical counterpart to Tillich's thought that the content of such assertions as "God is" contradicts the form in which the assertion must be made because the opposition between subject and object which is contained in the form of the assertion goes counter to what the assertion intends to say (thus *Ges. Werke*, I:378-79).

ble movement of expectation and disappointment which lies in a tautological judgment, we let nothing appear upon any randomly chosen object. The "not" is itself neither subject nor predicate of the judgment. Rather, it makes an appearance, and it is grasped, through the procedure of erecting a subject of judgment, as though to be further shaped by a defining predicate, and then of immediately withdrawing the subject by merely reiterating it. A tautological concept empties itself and in so doing objectifies nothing.

In recent philosophy of religion it was Ian Ramsey who made most explicit use of tautology in order to clarify the distinctiveness of some basic religious utterances.[6] Ramsey makes a distinction between empty and significant tautologies. It is true, according to his analysis, that these religious utterances are, logically viewed, tautological; but the difference between a mere tautology and a religious utterance is that the former expresses nothing whereas the latter mediates a cosmic meaning. Religious assertions are "significant tautologies." One might adduce "God is God" as an example. In form such a judgment is tautological. Whether it is a religious assertion depends on whether it effects a cosmic "disclosure" or "discernment." If it does, then it is true; for it allows its intended object to appear. The truth of the assertion consists precisely in its actually bringing about insight into the intended content. If the assertion itself has no effect, it is empty and untrue; and no amount of further testing will help toward proving its truth.

The manner in which a tautology achieves its aim—if I might explicate this theme somewhat differently from Ramsey—can be elucidated under two aspects, each having to do with one reason for our lack of insight. In the first place, a tautology serves the purpose of directing our attention to the fact that we should not overlook the subject of a judgment in haste to occupy ourselves with the predicate. We are told, "God is God"—that is to say, he is not what we think him to be when we subsume him under a predicate, such as the predicate "first cause" or "being itself." He is other than that; he is what he is. Similarly, "religion is religion"—it is not what we like to think it to be when we try to grasp it as a "directedness toward the absolute" or something similar. In these examples what the tautology does is to deny the relative nothingness of the singular, which serves as

---

[6]Ian T. Ramsey, *Religious Language: An Empirical Placing of Theological Phrases* (New York, 1963, c1957).

subject of the judgment, and to deny it by emphasizing it through iteration. In this case, accordingly, a tautology denies the prior denial of the singular which had taken place through our hastening from the accidental singular to the universal implicit in a predicate.

Under a second aspect tautology emerges when we have to do with final explanatory reasons. Such reasons cannot be based on higher reasons since there are none; they can only be cited in the hope that they are self-evident. "Why is the state of the world as it is?" we might ask by way of example. At first we can adduce various historical, social, economic, political, and other reasons. They can in turn be based on cosmological and finally on ontological reasons. At the end, however, the last reason can no longer be based on anything else, it can only be cited—"God is God, that's why the state of the world is what it is." Obviously this second use of tautology is a variation on the Aristotelian theme that first principles cannot be proved but only intuitively known.

The result of an investigation of the use of tautology as one form of disappearing concept is twofold. First, a tautological assertion asserts nothing. Second, it asserts the highest or ultimate. Hegel already knew that; being is nothing. Pure being and pure nothing have the same logical form. A concept that can be discriminated as a tautology is a disappearing concept because it does not represent an identity in a difference; it is an identity that remains an identity and only gives the illusion of a difference. Hence, the thought of pure being—"A = A," "a tree is a tree," "God is God," "Religion is religion"—must really be the thought of nothing. The concept disappears in the process of its being formed and in so doing it conceives nothing. It does conceive, but what it conceives is nothing. "A = A" is thus the thought of pure being but also the thought of nothing. What differentiates between the two possibilities is, according to Ramsey, that in the one case the tautology is significant and in the other it is empty.

The questionable feature in Ramsey's analysis and consequently in every attempt to see the truth of religion in a tautological concept lies in the nondefinability of the content signified. A cosmic disclosure, a revelation, is to take place through the assertion, "God is God." To the question of *what* is revealed, one can only answer, "That God is God." But then we can no longer determine—to say nothing of critically testing—whether there is really something revealed or only putatively so; and we cannot in principle test whether the judgment which is to explain and to be the basis for all others should be formulated as "God is God," or as "Being is being" or as "Nothing is nothing," or even as "I, the singular that I am, am I."

This prompts us to look to a second form of disappearing concept—paradox. If "A = A" is the formula of a tautology, then "A is not A" is the formula for a paradox. In a tautology, the thought disappears because the expectation awakened is not fulfilled; the completion of the thought that is started wipes the thought out because in place of the predicate there is only, as it were, an open space brought about by the denial of the subject named. A normal concept has the form of "A is B"—"an oak is a tree," "religion is directedness toward the absolute." Paradox stands thus between pure identity, which a tautology expresses, and an identity in difference, which a normal judgment expresses.

What do we think of by means of such a paradox? In order to elucidate this, we might consider a second example. Let us assume that the paradoxical sentence that occupies us is this one: "Religion is not religion." With that sentence we wish to define the essence of religion. Let us further assume that we are using the word "religion" to designate an event taking place in the church or some other cultic community in contrast to one occurring in a house of parliament. First we attend a parliamentary debate for an hour, then a high mass. We ascertain that the former exhibits both similarities with and differences from the latter. If we then call the latter process "religion," we have a subject concept with concrete content. We know what the word "religion" is to designate in this particular case. But we are asking what the essence of religion as so meant is; we are looking for an appropriate predicate concept for the subject. We find the predicate concept initially in the concept of the genus which expresses what is common to the two events or processes in order then to distinguish religion by a specific characteristic. If we call the pertinent genus "rite," so that the two phenomena are both in some sense rites, what remains is only to ask what the specific element is which distinguishes religion from other rites. We must, however, bear in mind that religion cannot be subordinated to a generic concept without sacrificing its essence. According to this requirement the essential concept, which names the genus and specific difference, must be thought in such a way that we form the judgment: "The essence of religion (i.e., of this concrete process we have in mind) consists in this that it is a rite which is not a rite." A religious rite is distinguished from other rites specifically by the characteristic that it is not a rite. The essence of religion is to be not religion.

One can multiply examples of such paradoxical formulations indefi-
nitely: "Religion is not religion," "God is not God," "a religious myth is a
myth that is not a myth," "a religious faith is a faith that is not a faith," and
so on. An example which Tillich adduces in the 1919 essay mentioned earlier is the concept of law in Paul, a concept that the apostle used in order
to deny the applicability of just this concept to the God-man relation. The
situation of that time was one in which religious was concretely designated
through law. Of this law, which defined the God-man relation by giving
expression to the will of God, Paul asserted the paradox: "The law of God
is not the law of God," or, more generally: "Religion is not religion."

That the concept involved in such thoughts and judgments disappears
is clear. What starts out to be a connection of subject and predicate remains uncompleted because what is put in place of a defining predicate is
a positing followed by an abrupt removal of the predicate. What does such
a disappearing concept grasp? Can it grasp anything at all? Or is such a
concept not only a disappearing concept (*verschwindender Begriff*) but a
conceptual swindle (*begrifflicher Schwindel*) as well? The thought is "executed" in the double sense of the word; it is affirmed and denied at the
same time. It is affirmed because it does indeed posit something; it posits
religion as. . . . It is denied because what it posits is the denial of positing
the subject so. "Religion (that is, any concrete thing thought of as religion)
is not religion (that is, something other than how it is thought); but it is
that." In any definition of the religious, this is to be so. Can the paradox
that appears here grasp anything at all and arrive at truth?

In order to see how it is just the paradox that can grasp the essence
of religion and set forth its truth we must consider something that is self-
evident to the religious consciousness though it has long since been for-
gotten by critique; namely, that what marks an object as a religious one is
its immediacy. In religion, as the religious consciousness still understands
it, thought and object come together in such a way that one cannot even
make a difference between them. In the immediately religious state the
thought of God is simultaneously the being of God; that we think of God,
and that God exists, are one and the same. Critique destroys this relation
irrevocably; for as soon as we begin to question and are in a position to
discriminate, a difference between thought and reality has already been
made. In order to restore the lost relation a critical consciousness might
try initially to find an object corresponding to the notion of religion or of
God. But none can be found since none exists. Rather, the religious ele-

ment is precisely the unity between thought and object which critique has lost. The failure to find a religious object gives rise subsequently to the question whether the truth of religion might perhaps consist in a thought's sacrificing itself in its difference from its object and thereby presenting its truth. It is this possibility that a paradox seeks to realize. The activity of thought in which we designedly set up a concept in order forthwith to take it away—something, incidentally, that we could not do without a temporal distance between the two moments of the paradox, and something that consequently makes a paradox intolerable in formal logic—permits the concept to be taken up into the object that it is seeking to grasp. The religious object is not nothing; it is that concrete rite, the myth actually told, the history, the present person, the reigning idea that we have in view. But it is these things not as they exist there but insofar as our concept can be absorbed by them. An object becomes an expression of the essence of religion when our concept of it disappears into it. The paradoxical concept is formed, like all concepts, through connection of a subject with a predicate but since the predicate is, as it were, only an open space—a denial of the object cited as predicate—this concept connects thinking with the object by allowing the object to be what it is; the unity which comes about in that way is religion.

Perhaps this can be elucidated in the following way. As we think the thought "A is not A," our thought reverts to the object which was its point of departure. Something concrete provided the occasion for the thought. By asking what that thing *is*, we subordinate it to the concept of being. Thus we judge that religion, in the given case, is a rite. But by canceling the concept of being—that is to say, the concept through which we have objectified the rite as something—in the thought of a genus that is not the genus, we revert to the concrete object since it is the only thing still remaining in order to fill out the content of the negated genus, the open space. The singular thing is in this case something like an entity coming out of nothing, a creation *ex nihilo*. The singular, we should note, is not in itself nor in conjunction with a universal religious object; but in its reversion to the singular from the negativity of the open predicate, our thinking grasps the content which is meant by religion. We are readily tempted to fill out the content of the genus (about which we have said that is not that) with another genus. We might be inclined to say, for example, that religion is not religion because it is essentially illusion or implicit secularity, or as in Feuerbach, an anthropology that is not yet conscious of itself as such.

The noetic discipline that is required here, if we wish to grasp the essence of religion, is one which enables us to refrain from filling the open space with anything other than the subject with which we took our start. It is true that religion is essentially not religion; but it is not true that, on that account, religion must be something else, like secularity or anthropology. The essence of religion is the open region from which the concrete comes as out of nothing.

At this point we can see an important difference between tautological and paradoxical concepts. In a tautology, as Ramsey's example shows, we cannot say *what* is mediated through the cosmic insight or *what* the content of this insight is. Hence there is always a suspicion that someone who claims to have experienced such an insight and to have seen a content of cosmic significance greater than what the words normally mean is only deceiving himself. He intends to express the content through a tautology. But can he be certain that he has actually seen something if he cannot make a distinction in content between empty and significant tautologies? Does a religious tautology express anything more than nothing?

In a paradox, by contrast, it is possible to name the content. If we say, "The process going on there is essentially a rite that is not a rite," we define it as a religious rite. The content to which we refer is that singular rite of which we are speaking; it is the same content for anyone who thinks this thought. The specific difference in the predicate concept is, further, nothing other than the denial of the genus which is made in view of the same rite of which the general concept was initially predicated. What fills out the open space that is thus left by the denial of the genus is again nothing other than the singular thing, the concrete occurrence, to which our thought has reference. There is no disclosure of an indescribable content but only a return to the singular with which the thought started. Thinking converges again with the concrete content, and this recourse itself is the thinking of the religious content.

III

The preceding considerations have prepared a connection with critique. Critique is possessed of the power to make the concrete Gods, the phenomena of religion, disappear. It drives the Gods out by asking what they are. The answer to that question can only be negative in the sense that the phenomenal God is in any case not God because the questioning itself provides the questioner with a standpoint outside of the reality of that God. But outside a true God there could not be anything. If we are outside of the phenomenon, then it is not the true God that is appearing there. But—and now comes the turning point—just this negative answer confirms the deity of the appearing God. If the essence of religion is to be thought of as not religion, then the result of critique, which makes it impossible for religion to be religion, accords with the intended content of the religious phenomenon. The critical question, in being posed, denies the deity of the God it faces. By doing so, it forms in advance the very concept which grasps the essence of the God; and by grasping the essence in fact, it overcomes the purely critical standpoint.

Interestingly enough, the Heidelberg theologian Karl Daub, who in the early nineteenth century was the preeminent representative of speculative idealism in theology, hinted at this idea, though without carrying it out, and he did so in the framework of a Hegelian theory of identity.[7] He makes a double assertion, first, that the word "God" (in all of its variations as they appear in the several types and grades of religion) is identical with the concept and the concept in turn identical with the reality; and, secondly, that the identity between our thinking and God's being consists in the fact that the difference between thought and reality, which we make in critical thought, is already resident in the word and the idea of God itself. Thus, if we ask where religion, or God, appears, the answer in Daub's sense is this: "God is present in the word and the thought 'God'; he is identical with them, that is where he exists." But—we immediately object—the word "God" is surely not the reality that the word means. To this objection the Daubian answer would be given: "The difference that you have just asserted between the word and the thought and the reality is a difference in the word and idea itself. It is peculiar to the idea 'God' that it announces

---

[7]"Über den Logos. Ein Beitrag zur Logik der göttlichen Namen," *Theologische Studien und Kritiken* 6 (Heidelberg, 1833): 355-410. "Der Gedanke, sich der Gegenstand, unterscheidet das als Namen mit ihm identische Wort von sich und teilt mittelst seiner sich, den Gedanken, der Menschheit, für ihre Erkenntnis seines Gegenstandes mit" (400); "ohne Gott im Wort ist das Wort ein von der persönlichen Subjektivität gemachtes" (404). In his *Einleitung in das Studium der christlichen Dogmatik aus dem Standpunkte der Religion* (Heidelberg, 1810) 133, Daub remarks that God, out of eternal love, gave to truth a shape under which alone it could be manifest to human beings but that at the same time he gave human beings the power to distinguish the *Gestalt* or the *Sinnbild* from the truth or the cognition of truth.

the presence of its intended object, and shows its truth through expressing the difference between idea and reality. God is present in the idea, but he is present in such a way that he is identical with the difference that is resident in the idea." God is the difference between "God" and God.

A similar line of thought can be seen in Tillich's theory of symbols. In general a religious symbol is, for the religious consciousness, identical with its intended object; for religious consciousness, the symbol is the reality it means. In that sense Tillich could repeatedly warn against viewing a symbol as "only" a symbol as though it were a sign for a reality and not the reality itself. Nonetheless, viewed from the standpoint of a philosophy of religion, no actual symbol is the unconditional to which it finally points. Every symbol is transitory, its effective power comes to an end; and in that sense it is indeed "only" symbolic and not unconditionally real. But there is an exception to this transitoriness—the symbol of the cross. For what the cross symbolizes is the symbolic character of all symbols. Thus, if someone contends that the cross is a symbol of the unconditional but is not itself unconditional, this contention only confirms the unconditional content of this very symbol. The difference which Daub finds in the speculative idea of God Tillich finds in the symbol of the cross. In both cases, however, the distinctive feature is that the denial of the reality of the symbol or the idea is inherent in them. By expressing the denial one only gives utterance to something that, on their part, the symbol and the idea already express. This is to say that what the disappearing concept in a paradox grasps is precisely the difference in the identity which consitutes the essence of religion.

One cannot disguise the strangeness of this kind of thinking. But the reason for it lies in the fact that we have to do here with a consciousness other than the naively religious or the critical one. We might call it the "second naiveté," since its thinking is in a certain respect naive, in that it can take the concrete singular thing at face value, while it is at the same time critical because it has already passed through a questioning of the object. Such a thinking is no longer an unreflective oneness with the object of thought nor is it a critical distance which loses the object; it can put itself at a distance from its object because it is able to transcend itself and return to the object. In a second naiveté, consciousness is already beyond the alternative of religion and critique in their isolation from each other.

This has certain consequences for the question of truth. We can understand truth as the agreement or correspondence between thinking and the object thought, consciousness and intended being. The naively religious consciousness has truth because it still stands under the immediate impression of the appearance of the unconditional, without either being able to or wishing to question it. Critical consciousness, by contrast, remains without truth because it cannot bring about any mediation between thinking and the thing thought. If it tries to mediate the religious object, the unconditional, it only confirms the unreality, the negativity, of the alleged content. At best it can recover the religious objects as postulates necessary for the practical experience of freedom. Second naiveté, which moves noetically in paradoxes, is not initially a consciousness of an object but the consciousness of a consciousness of the object; it is reflexive. Yet it converges with the object by letting it emerge out of the negativity of the open predicate in the paradox and by letting its concept be taken over by the object.

A familiar example—one to which Kierkegaard devoted a treatise and Kant a footnote—can be used to make this relation clear. In the Old Testament story of God's command to Abraham to sacrifice his son, Isaac, the narrative has to do with a religious act that is dubious because it violates all morality. Kierkegaard observes in "Fear and Trembling" that the scandalous feature of the command under whose force Abraham stands is just the fact that it could not be justified before any court, not even that of the spirit who reigns over Greek tragedy. Ethically viewed, what Jahweh commands is senseless murder. Yet Abraham obeys. The unfathomable and puzzling aspect of the act of faith, which Kierkegaard can ascertain in Abraham but for his part not repeat, lies in the impossibility of mediating it. It is the religious consciousness as such that is at work there and that so tantalizes Kierkegaard because it is prepared simply to obey the phenomenal God without a reason. Kant, by contrast, states an opinion entirely in the spirit of critique. He thinks Abraham should have replied to the purportedly divine voice thus: "It is completely certain that I should not kill my good son; whether you, however, who appear to me, are God—of that I am not certain nor can I become certain"—not even if the voice thundered down from the visible heavens.[8] This Kantian reply would settle the whole problem in favor of critique. Hence, Kant on one side, and Abraham,

---

[8]*Der Streit der Fakultäten* (Hamburg, 1959) 62.

understood in Kierkegaardian fashion, on the other side represent the contradictory relation between critical and religious consciousness.

What, then, is the third consciousness, the one we are calling second naiveté? It is the consciousness which does not seek truth immediately in religion itself nor in critique but in the correspondence between the underlying content of religion and that of critique. Religion and critique both make direct reference to the phenomenon, in the case of Abraham to the voice of Jahweh which makes itself heard with unconditionally imperative power. The one (religion) heeds, the other (critique) rejects, the claim of the phenomenon. Second naiveté, in turn, makes no direct reference to the phenomenon but rather to the previous consciousness of the phenomenon, shaped now as religion and now as critique. What second naiveté objectifies is not the phenomenon but the consciousness of the phenomenon. The reality making its appearance is given to consciousness in a dual and self-contradictory form. The question of truth does not, therefore, consist in the possible agreement between consciousness and intended object but initially in the agreement between the religious and the critical consciousness. If those two are in agreement, in spite of the contradictory form, then consciousness and appearance also agree; for the phenomenon in itself is that which gives itself now in the one way and now in the other.

Do the two agree? The story of Abraham provides an answer to that question too, though beyond what Kierkegaard and Kant had to say about it. At the end of the narrative the angel of the Lord performs for Abraham the critical task by instructing him in what, from a critical point of view, he ought to have seen at once; namely, that in fact he ought not to kill his son. At that point religion and critique agree. But the truth does not lie with the one or the other alone; it lies in the two forms of consciousness together. The intended content of religion is something that makes its appearance in the double movement between naive reception and critical distance. In order to grasp it one must proceed with categories of thought that can follow this movement. In its paradoxical way of thinking, second naiveté already has the critical question of truth behind it. The question of truth can, to be sure, still be raised; but it is no longer a question of religious truth, for this naiveté no longer needs to ask whether currently ruling Gods are true since it knows that, critically viewed, they are false. At the same time it also knows that the untruth of the Gods is precisely the essence of the true God, the one who is truth itself. This naiveté knows that it does make a difference whether Abraham does not kill his son out of belief or out of unbelief in the apparent God—the one contradicts the other—yet it also knows that the truth of the matter lies in the fact that it is the essence of the one member of the opposition to be what it is not. And that is the truth which consists in the convergence of religious and critical consciousness.

Second naiveté is reflexive in that it has reference to its object not directly but through a first-order religious or critical consciousness. Truth, as it was there for religious consciousness, consisted in the fact that it neither could nor wished to withdraw itself from the impress of the apparent God; for critical consciousness, the untruth of religion consisted in the fact that it (critique) was not able to restore the divine object from which it had withdrawn itself by means of the question of the essence of the phenomenon. The truth, as second naiveté reaches it through religion and critique, consists in the fact that this consciousness can accept the religious objectivity as it presents itself because such a naiveté, by virtue of critique, does not fall prey to the temptation to understand the religious object as an empirical, ethical, or logical one. Truth lies in the agreement between what religion as such receives and what critique as such destroys.

So if we ask the question "Did Abraham in truth hear the voice of God?" the answer is this:

(1) To a religious consciousness—to Abraham himself—what was heard was the voice of God because the difference between the concept "voice of God" and the concept "what I now perceive as a voice overwhelming me" did not yet exist. Abraham did not ask whether he had really heard God.

(2) To the critical consciousness—a Kant as he reflects on the story of Abraham—the voice heard was not that of God, for the distinction between concept and reality, which critique draws, cannot be overcome by critique itself. If we *ask* whether a voice comes from God, the answer can only be No.

(3) To a metacritically naive consciousness—second naiveté—the voice audible to Abraham is the voice of God under the condition that one never actually hears it or thinks one has heard it, just as a command is a command of God only when it is not carried out in actuality. Such a nonactual actuality, as it is an object of second naiveté, cannot be perceived directly but only indirectly by means of the religious and critical consciousness on which second naiveté reflects.

If I am not mistaken, second naiveté, as just sketched, is the form of consciousness which corresponds to the symbol of the cross as Tillich interprets it. That symbol makes reference to other symbols—it is not a symbol standing alone—in a manner that corresponds exactly to the relation between second naiveté and the object-related religious or critical consciousness. Schematically the relation can be represented thus:

$$\text{2nd niaveté} \ldots \left\langle \begin{array}{l} \text{religion} \ldots \ldots \text{phenomenal God} \\ \text{critique} \ldots \ldots \ldots \ldots \ldots \text{nothing} \end{array} \right\rangle \text{symbol of cross}$$

Second naiveté perceives its object by going through the religious and critical consciousness. Its object (the cross) appears to it not directly but in the agreement between religion and critique. If this is so, then Tillich's symbol of the cross represents a Christian understanding of the concept of religion ("religion is not religion") in which the essence of religion is intuited in the cross of Christ—in the cross not as an isolated symbol but as a symbol that refers to the phenomenal God and effects the unity between religion and critique.

Conclusion. In this paper I have put forth a thesis that can be understood as a thesis about Tillich's philosophy of religion and also a thesis about the question of truth in the philosophy of religion. Under the first aspect the thesis can be formulated thus: Tillich was right in basing the understanding of the essence of religion on the paradox, even though he himself did not actually construct his philosophy of religion on such a basis. Under the second aspect the thesis reads: The truth which religion intends is present neither to the religious nor to the critical consciousness alone but to the second naiveté which knows how, by means of a paradoxical conception, to grasp the object that is reflected in both forms of object-related consciousness.

Tillich's Telescoping of Ontology and Naturalism

ROY D. MORRISON II

The relationship between Tillich's ontology and that perspective generally known as philosophical naturalism is a riddle which continues to evoke reexamination. The difficulty of interpreting his position arises partly from the preconceived notion that naturalism is fundamentally antithetical to idealism or to an idealistically oriented ontology. It cannot be denied that, in the past, "naturalism" has had formulations which were monolithic which seemed to make it an enemy of idealism and of theology. However, Tillich formulates a philosophical theology which is dialectical, and which employs the method of synthesis. He develops third alternatives to antitheses which have traditionally been regarded as mutually exclusive. The third alternative often involves a merging or coalescence of elements from both poles of the antithesis. This means that definitions, attitudes and value judgments which were appropriate prior to his synthesizing enterprise may have to be revised.

We intend to argue, first, that Tillich has a complex, dialectical relationship to naturalism and that he telescopes one "form" of naturalism into his ontology. To whatever extent his ontology is idealistic, this assertion means that Tillich's system tends to identify or to synthesize some aspects of idealism with some aspects of naturalism. Second, we believe that it is possible to identify a philosophical principle which will illuminate his problems and his procedures as he formulates the relationships of his ontology to the positions known as idealism, naturalism and supernaturalism. We shall call this concept the principle of continuity.

Third, we contend that the fundamental motivation in this particular application of Tillich's method of synthesis is the achievement of a non-reductive doctrine of reality and of man. That is, the reductive aspects of naturalism are eliminated when that position is assimilated into dialectical ontology. Tillich then has the good conscience to designate his own position as ecstatic or self-transcending naturalism. The argument is not that Tillich *is* a naturalist. Rather, it seems, Tillich's modification of definitions and categories makes such a charge obsolete or irrelevant—unless supported by careful and extensive semantic qualification. His intention, we believe, was to terminate the assumption that naturalism was monolithic and *ipso facto* reductive and unsuitable for the theological enterprise.

In developing this discussion, it is helpful to recall a distinction that Tillich makes between types or "lines" of philosophy. After presenting this distinction, we shall treat his conceptions of ontology and of naturalism. Finally, we shall set forth the technical issues and procedures in his enterprise of telescoping or dialectical synthesis.

Early in his career, he distinguishes between two streams of philosophy which flow from the Renaissance. There is the "methodical line" which includes Descartes and finds its mightiest expression in Kant's *Critiques*. This line also includes Spinoza's *Ethics*, English empiricism from Bacon to Hume, and the later nineteenth-century positivists. The methodical approach quantifies and objectifies reality. It seeks *experimental* verification based upon a correlation of rational, intelligible structures and sense data. Tillich has high praise for the methodical line. He regards it as unequivocal and as characterized by overwhelming success. "Every doubt of the correctness of this method can be dispersed by experiment," and technology is constantly proving that all criticism against it is untenable. [1]

The other main philosophical stream is designated as the "non-methodical line." For Tillich, this second line is symbolized by Jacob Boehme,

---

[1]Paul Tillich, *The Interpretation of History* (New York: Charles Scribner's Sons, 1936) 123f.

a sixteenth-century German mystic. The non-methodical line includes the mysticism and nature-philosophy of the middle ages, and the romantic elements in the thought of Schelling and of Hegel. During the nineteenth century, this tradition closely approached the empirical and naturalistic branch of the methodical line. However, at the turn of the nineteenth and twentieth centuries, it presented itself as a "philosophy of life" and protested against the methodical formalism of the Kantians. Tillich states that this second "line" of philosophy was not connected with rational, methodical science. Rather, its attitude included an intrinsic resistance to the methodical approach of the mainstream of Western philosophy.

According to Tillich, the non-methodical, mystical stream of philosophy was and is a minority point of view—with little power or influence. However, it constitutes a deliberate challenge to the reductive consequences of the worldview which results from the methodical approach to reality and to knowledge. It systematically de-emphasizes the notions of calculability, mechanism, and static structure in the interpretation of reality. It engages in a controlled modulation of technical reason's quest for precision in semantics, concepts, and in the delineation of metaphysical categories. This enterprise results in a pronounced *fluidity* in the character and relationships of all major categories, meanings and symbols. This point is important for our understanding of Tillich's telescoping of naturalism and ontology. Psychology is treated as ontology, and nature is identified with Being. Consequently, it may appear to Tillich's readers that some form of idealism is decisive for the non-methodical theory of reality. The mature culmination of the non-methodical line is to be found in Tillich's own later writings—formulated by incorporating ontological and "voluntaristic" elements from the thought of such diverse figures as Augustine, Boehme, Schelling, Hegel, Nietzsche, and Heidegger.

Tillich commits himself to the non-methodical line of philosophy partly because he feels that methodical philosophy is inherently *reductive*. That is, it objectifies reality and eliminates the dimension of transcendence. He attributes the rise of contemporary existentialism to the domination of technical reason and the consequent objectification of reality.[2] Hence, he seeks to *overcome* that form of naturalism which has objectification, or "objectivity," as its major philosophical goal. A second reason for Tillich's

---

[2]Paul Tillich, *Systematic Theology* (Chicago: University of Chicago Press, 1951) 1:100 (hereafter cited as *ST*).

devaluation of methodical thinking is his commitment to the mystical principle of *union*, or dialectical identity. This means that a form of dialectical
monism becomes decisive for his entire system.

It should be observed that, while committed to the non-methodical approach, Tillich simultaneously seeks to preserve and to defend the methodical, scientific view of the world. Throughout the entire system, his
intent is to avoid interference or mutually excluding confrontations between the two lines of philosophy. One outcome is that the non-methodical
ontology points to a dimension of reality which is metaphorically located
"inside" physical reality. This principle of non-interference explains why
Tillich can commit himself to mystical, dialectical ontology and yet defend
the indispensability of scientific inquiry[3] and the inviolability of the laws of
nature.[4] Tillich's non-methodical approach is not intended to annihilate methodical thinking and technical reason. Rather, the intent is to provide an
ontological hermeneutic for reality as man experiences it through the ontic
categories of finitude. Likewise, Tillich's ontology is not intended to reject
naturalism as such, but to *overcome* those forms of naturalism which he
considers reductive.

Ontology

Tillich defines philosophy as that cognitive approach to reality in which
reality as such is the object. Philosophy "is that cognitive endeavor in
which the question of being is asked."[5] This is the question of what it
means to *be*. In his opinion, all philosophy inescapably revolves around this
mystery. Another word for this inquiry is "ontology"; hence, it is the name
for the center of all philosophy. Ontology does not deal with "trans-empirical realities" or with a "world behind the world."[6] Dualism is emphatically
rejected. Ontology is considered to be an analysis of things as they are in
order to discover the principles embodied in them. Philosophy does not
deal with the "subject matter *as such.*" Instead, it deals with the *consti-*

---

[3]Paul Tillich, *Theology of Culture* (New York: Oxford University Press, Galaxy, 1959)
11f, 130.

[4]*ST*, II:6.

[5]Paul Tillich, *Biblical Religion and the Search for Ultimate Reality* (Chicago: University
of Chicago Press, Phoenix, 1955) 5. Cf. *ST*, I:18, 163, 62 n19.

[6]Ibid., 7.

tutive principles of reality, the *texture* of being itself—which is effective in every dimension of reality.

In dealing with the question of method, Tillich asks, "How is ontology distinguished from what has been called metaphysics?"[7] He answers that ontology is the foundation of metaphysics, but that it is not metaphysics itself. In *Systematic Theology*, Volume I, published in 1951, Tillich defined ontology as an "analysis of those structures of being which we encounter in every meeting with reality."[8] He regards this as the original meaning of metaphysics. However, he states that the preposition, *meta*, now has the irremediable connotation of dualism—the assertion that there is another world of transcendent beings. Therefore, he decides that the term ontology is perhaps less misleading than the term metaphysics.

Later, in *Love, Power and Justice*, published in 1954, he distinguishes even more sharply between ontology and metaphysics. There, he insists that ontology deals only with elements that are universally constitutive of everything that is. All events, persons, and all objective particulars are left to scientific analysis and to metaphysical constructions. Ontology "elaborates" scientific and metaphysical knowledge through its own critical analysis.[9] Tillich makes a similar distinction in the *Theology of Culture*. There, science is granted the exclusive right to the description of all objects and their interrelations in nature, in history, and in man's experience. Philosophy is granted exclusive claim to the description of the structures and categories of being itself—and of the *logos* through which being finds manifestation.[10]

Tillich is trying to accomplish several goals in making the kinds of distinctions cited above. First, he seeks a meaningful distinction between two major dimensions of reality—the ontic and the ontological. The ontic dimension deals with the traits of objects and of beings in the subject-object structures of spatio-temporal reality. Ontology deals with reality as it is "before" it has split or divided itself into subject and object—"before" there are objects in physically determined space and time. Therefore, in

---

[7]Paul Tillich, *Love, Power and Justice* (New York: Oxford University Press, Galaxy, 1954) 23.

[8]*ST*, I:20.

[9]Tillich, *Love, Power and Justice*, 19, 23.

[10]Tillich, *Theology of Culture*, 129.

some contexts, for Tillich, the term metaphysics is interchangeable with scientific inquiry and both terms are restricted to the dimension of ontic reality. Second, he wishes to maintain the distinction between the two dimensions in such a way that no technical dualism will emerge. Such an outcome would violate his principle of ontological identity and the dialectical monism upon which the entire system rests.

Third, while maintaining that the ontology is non-dualistic and immanental, he intends that it should have a certain metaphorical "distance" from ontic reality. Ontological reality *precedes* ontic reality logically, though not chronologically. This dialectical distance or priority evokes a sense of "transcendence" without resort to any classical form of supernaturalism. Fourth, Tillich seeks to restore Western man's sense of transcendence within a conceptual framework which will endure. That is, he seeks to make the ontology invulnerable to the devastating attacks of methodical, objective thinking and of the Kantian type of criticism. To accomplish this fourth goal, the ontology must be posited in a "place" which is "beyond" the province of objective reality and of objective thinking.

The last observation leads directly into a consideration of the precise epistemic and metaphysical *status* of Tillich's ontology. One fruitful approach to this question involves his development of "third alternatives"— as a general methodological principle—in his philosophy and in his theology. Again and again, Tillich attempts to transcend or to "overcome" an intellectual impasse in Western thought by formulating a third alternative—in a situation where two antithetic concepts appear to be mutually exclusive. As a relevant example, he informs us that he has fought supra-naturalism throughout his writing career, not in order to support naturalism, but because he has "tried to overcome the alternative between naturalism and supra-naturalism."[11]

Non-objective thinking is an integral part of the enterprise which seeks to overcome difficulties through the use of third alternatives. Early in his writing career, Tillich reached the conclusion that "objective" thinking was not satisfactory for the restoration of man's original religious words. Actually, this judgment is a major point of departure for his entire existential-phenomenological enterprise, which attempts to transcend or to supplement "technical" reason and the methodical line of philosophy.

---

[11]Paul Tillich, "Reply to Interpretation and Criticism," *The Theology of Paul Tillich*, ed. by Charles Kegley and Robert Bretall (New York: Macmillan, 1964) 341.

Original or archetypal words have been robbed of their original power by our objective thinking, and the scientific conception of the world, and thus, have become
subject to dissolution. In face of what the archetypal word "God" means, rational
criticism is powerless. In face of an objectively existing God, atheism is right. [12]

Believing that objective thinking and the pursuit of an objectively existing God lead to dehumanization and to the complete disenchantment of
reality, Tillich develops concepts which are "non-objectivating." Such concepts, from his point of view, are neither objective nor subjective. In order
to avoid both poles of the antithesis, he is led to the "choice of psychological notions with a non-psychological connotation." [13] Tillich cites Heidegger's work as the most radical example of this type of conceptuality. The
most dramatic case in point is his designation of *Sorge* (care) as the general
character of Existence. Also from Heidegger, Tillich accepts the notion
that Time, or temporality, is ontologically in a relation of identity with *personal* existence. This doctrine establishes a kind of continuity between a
crucial, universal category of human experience and the depths of reality.
Physical reality is somehow "life." This means that an inner dynamic or
ontological "life" is posited, rather than the static, objective, mechanical
picture of reality that is presented by those forms of naturalism which exclusively employ technical reason. It also means that Tillich's system seriously seeks to dynamicize Western man's conception of ultimate reality.

Tillich employs such psychologically oriented conceptuality for two purposes. One is the overcoming of antitheses; the other is the formulation or
constitution of his ontology. The second point here is crucial for an understanding of the nature of "ontology." In Tillich's philosophy, the term "ontology" means that all of reality is constituted by—and is understood in
terms of—categories which are psychological or anthropological in character, or in origin. It is equally important to note, however, that these concepts are not regarded as *mere* psychology in the ordinary or reductive
sense of that term. Rather, they are understood as being indicative of the
universal traits of all reality—of Being itself. Ontology thus establishes a
relationship of *continuity* between the character of human experience and
the character of ultimate reality. Man is not "alienated" from a mechanical

---

[12] Tillich, *The Interpretation of History*, 46f.

[13] Tillich, *Theology of Culture*, 94.

reality, or from a world that has no positive relationship to his kind of thinking and meaning. The inner *depth* of reality is somehow "psychological"—
but in an unconscious and impersonal manner.

Tillich assumes this ontological-psychological conception of reality
while employing his procedure of overcoming antitheses through dialectical third alternatives. Therefore, he can assert that it is a mistake to ac-
cuse ontology of introducing subjectivity into philosophy. The charge is
unfounded, he insists, because the *function* of the psychologically oriented
concepts is to describe the ontological character of reality in a manner that
transcends both the subjective and the objective sides of our ordinary experience.[14] Ontology does not speak of objects as such. In a non-objectivating manner, it speaks metaphorically of the structure of "life" which is
"above" the split between subjectivity and objectivity.

Tillich himself has employed a term which may point toward the precise status of his ontology. In dialogue with Nels Ferré, he states that his
idea of God is "transcendental" rather than "transcendent"—if the latter
term means a dualistically supranatural incarnation, a realistic eschatology, or a "world" behind the world.[15] Kant formulated a status for his metaphysics which is generally designated as "transcendental idealism."
Because his categories were supplied by the mind, the position has sometimes been considered to be "subjective." That is, the metaphysical categories were subjectively *located*, but they were epistemologically
constitutively objective in that they were universal and necessary in relation to all human experience. Tillich does not locate his ontology "inside"
the human mind, but neither does he make it dualistic or *objective*—in relation to spatio-temporal reality. At the same time, he indicates that it is
in the place that is no place, *pure reason.*[16]

In the light of these considerations, we suggest that the epistemic and
metaphysical *status* of Tillich's ontology is "transcendental." In order to do
justice to the unique, non-objectivating character of the system, it is perhaps more precise to employ the term *dialectical transcendentalism* because (1) Tillich formulates the status through the instrument of
dialectical third alternatives, (2) he never intends that the contents of the

---

[14]Paul Tillich, *The Courage to Be* (New Haven: Yale University Press, 1952) 25.

[15]Tillich, "Reply to Interpretation," 341.

[16]*ST*, I:26.

ontology should be reduced to either the objective or the subjective, and (3) some of the components of the ontology are employed in a manner which is—implicitly—both regulative and constitutive, i.e., both ideational and objective.

Consequently, the status of the ontology itself perhaps provides an outstanding example of Tillich's dialectical notion of "overcoming." His *intention* is that the ontology should deal with reality in an exhaustive manner. He apparently wants it to perform the same kinds of functions or to cover the same scope of thought as did the metaphysics of other philosophers. Despite the "placeless," dialectically transcendental status of the ontology, in his actual *practice*, Tillich closely approaches Aristotle's meaning of metaphysics: an analysis of the general principles of everything that *is*. Therefore, in overcoming the antithesis between objectivity and subjectivity, a strong element of some kind of objectivity is retained and incorporated in the dialectical third alternative. In other words, the discussions of ontology and of Being are intended as discussions of something that is *really* real.

Since psychology is treated as ontology, the *distinction* between objectivity and subjectivity tends to disappear. Or, more precisely, the category of subjectivity tends to fall into disuse. The ontology does not deal with objects of empirical experience; rather, it draws upon material from both the empirical and the non-empirical dimensions of reality and then deals with the "texture" of everything that *is*. The *texture* is the object of the analysis. On this dialectically transcendental level, the constitutive principles of all categories are given the same status; everything is placed on a single ontological "plane." Mythological, ontological non-events (for example the "transition" from essence to existence which occurs in the Fall) are granted the same degree of seriousness and the same degree of reality as physical, empirical events. We may call this Tillich's principle of *ontological equalization*. It operates throughout all of his philosophy and his enterprise of theological symbolization. The procedure is feasible and intelligible to him because his system is undergirded by the postulate of the primordial, dialectical unity of thinking and being. Through dialectics and the elimination of the category of subjectivity, Tillich seeks to overcome the threat posed by methodical philosophy when it declares transcendental concepts to be somehow unreal or intrinsically unverifiable.

When Tillich is primarily concerned with the ontic dimension of reality, he takes seriously the principle of identity which is associated with formal

logic and the law of non-contradiction: a thing cannot be itself and the opposite of itself at the same time. However, the conceptual apparatus of his
ontology assumes a *dialectical* "Principle of Identity"—which he accepts
from Schelling. Tillich explains that this identity is not a strict, undifferentiated unity. Rather, identity implies *difference*. That is, ultimate reality,
the Absolute, is a subject at the same time that it is an object. [17] Within the
realm of *essence*, "life," or a process can possess its own identity and simultaneously possess contradictory or antithetic identities. All opposi-
tions, antitheses, and polarities and categorical boundaries are mutually
dissolvable. Everything coincides: unity with plurality, particularity with
universality, finitude with infinity. Thinking and being are identical. Unconscious Being transmutes itself—through a "dialectical transition"—from
essence, to existence and back to essentiality.

Of crucial importance here are the metaphysical and theological consequences which Tillich draws from the identity of thinking and being.
Since they are one and the same, he can assert that a psychological *state*,
such as "ecstasy," is the exact correlate to self-transcendence as a state
of reality. Such a state is psychology and ontology at the same time. To be
in the state of ecstasy is to be in *union* with Being itself. Tillich believes
that this construct of ecstatic, ontological identity overcomes the alternative between naturalism and supernaturalism. It provides an idea of God
that is not reducible to either of those positions. This notion of God as an
ontological-psychological state of identity underlies his entire theological
system. [18] Thus, Schelling's dialectical Principle of Identity is the major instrument in Tillich's attempt to overcome the alternative between naturalistic and supernaturalistic conceptions of ultimate reality.

If ontology is the study of Being, and if Being is a non-physical, psychologically oriented kind of "stuff," or "power," or "substance," a meta-
physician might ask if Tillich's ontology is idealistic. Certainly, Being is a
notion which has a long history within the idealistic tradition and is inseparable from the notion that reality is somehow "mental" in its constitution
and/or its source. Tillich holds, however, that his ontology is not idealistic.
The ontology is beyond the subject-object split, and hence it is beyond the

---

[17]Paul Tillich, *Mystik und Schuldbewustsein in Schellings philosophicher Entwicklung*
(Gutersloh: Bertelsmann, 1912) 69.

[18]*ST*, II:8.

applicability of the categories of finitude—which include mind, matter, etc. The distinction between mental and non-mental reality cannot be employed. The use of the dialectical third alternative gives Being a status which is not reducible to the traditional metaphysical positions of materialism or idealism. In this sense, Tillich believes that he has overcome one (if not *the*) distinguishing characteristic of philosophical idealism. He is not disturbed by the residual idealistic connotations of the terms Being and essence.

For Tillich, then, ontology is the study of the all-pervading structures of reality—not as they are found in objects, but as they can be discerned in the texture of being which precedes the subject-object split of reality. His ontological analysis reveals Being to be dynamic, dialectical and yet ultimately mystical and monistic. This ultimate unity lies behind Tillich's striving for what he calls "ontological universalism."[19] The power and reality of Being are knowable by man partly through philosophy and partly through existential encounter and mystical reunion. The construct affirms the universal presence and availability of ultimate reality for all men—whatever term one might employ: spirit, Being, Courage, God, or the God above God.

The notion of continuity is most congenial to the notion of mystical monism in metaphysics. The notion of discontinuity is a correlate of the notion of dualism in metaphysics. If continuity and discontinuity are conceived as abstract, problematic principles in metaphysical thinking, they can be instrumental in grasping the dialectical complexities in Tillich's system. A philosophy which postulates discontinuity or dualism as an ultimate characteristic of reality must explain how there can be systematic, causal, and intelligible relationships. A philosophy which postulates continuity or monism as the character of ultimate reality must explain how there can be change, individuation and subject-object relationships. An absolutely unqualified monism or continuity principle tends to preclude genuinely distinct objects or states or subjects which need to be metaphysically or cognitively related to each other.

The subject-object structure of reality seems to reveal different *kinds* of reality which are somehow discontinuous. Also man's moral intuition

---

[19]Paul Tillich, *The Protestant Era* (Chicago: University of Chicago Press, Phoenix, 1948) xxiii.

and theological analyses seem to reveal two different spheres of reality or activity—one of which is privileged, or more real, or morally superior to the other. Some element of dualism or of discontinuity seems to be a metaphysical prerequisite if we are to account for the demand placed upon us by this intuition of radically differentiated kinds of reality and behavior. Since Tillich's system postulates an ultimate and enduring monism—a principle of continuity—his procedure entails a perennial problem: how to maintain the original postulate while introducing enough discontinuity and dualism to account for the epistemological correlations demanded by subject-object experience, and for the radical theological distinctions between the finitude of man and the infinity of ultimate reality. The principle of continuity is demanded by the monistic orientation of his methodology and his ontology. The principle of discontinuity, however, provides the conceptual foundation for his existentialism, for his sustained polemic against Hegel, and for his alternative to (reductive) naturalism and supernaturalism.

Naturalism

Like the word idealism, "naturalism" is a somewhat symbolic term referring to a cluster or constellation of concepts and their consequences. Tillich uses the word in several ways in different contexts, and there may not be a single meaning which links all of these various usages in an intelligible, consistent manner. However, there are two central meanings which can be gleaned from his various analyses and contextual implications.

Tillich's first central meaning can be called reductive naturalism. A system of naturalism is reductive if it is mechanistic or materialistic. It cannot then acknowledge the ontological "life" of reality. The Unconditioned is beyond the split or distinction between objectivity and subjectivity. Therefore, any form or naturalism that has objectification as its goal will necessarily be reductive. The positivistic and empiricistic forms of naturalism exclude the mystical or ontological reality of universals. They classify concepts like Being as extreme abstractions and, hence, as unreal. Insofar as it uses nominalistic, technical reason, reductive naturalism employs the principle of epistemological continuity—otherwise expressed as the *continuity of analysis*. It therefore denies reality to the ontological dimension of things. The crucial concept here is continuity. And, from Tillich's point of view, even an "idealistic" metaphysics can be a reductive form of naturalism if it fails to acknowledge a discontinuous depth within reality.

In its quest for precise conceptuality and for objectification, reductive naturalism interrupts and abstracts from the dynamic, indecisive process of life. It thereby falsifies reality and disenchants the world by reducing it to mechanical and rationalistic relations. The most serious charge against naturalism, he states, is its failure to maintain, or to acknowledge, the infinite *distance* between the whole of finite reality and its ultimate ground or depth.[20] In this context, the crucial, technically operative meaning of "distance" is discontinuity. However, it is a discontinuity within the framework of Tillich's dialectical monism.

Every aspect of this reductive naturalism is not objectionable to Tillich. He explicitly states that naturalism's criticism against supranaturalism must be accepted.[21] That is, he agrees with the limiting consequences of the principle of metaphysical and epistemological continuity on two points. First the categories and forms of nature cannot be extended beyond the realm of finitude to form a trans-empirical world. Space, time, causality and substance cannot be attributed to God or to the Unconditioned because such a procedure transforms infinity into finitude. Second, ultimate reality is not knowable through man's finite perceptual equipment or through the epistemological procedures which are necessary within subject-object structure. Consequently, there can be no natural theology for Tillich because natural theology, whether employed by Aquinas or by others, assumes the direct or analogical applicability of natural categories and symbols to that which is beyond nature.

Tillich's second meaning for the term naturalism is a positive one. As a contrast to the first meaning, one could call it non-reductive naturalism. Actually, his non-reductive "naturalism" is intended as a third alternative to the antithesis between supranaturalism and naturalism. Historically, these two choices have tended to be regarded as mutually exclusive and as exhaustive of the metaphysical possibilities. Believing that he has "overcome the alternative" between supranaturalism and (reductive) naturalism, he informs us that he still holds "emphatically to this position

---

[20]*ST*, II:6.

[21]Ibid. Tillich uses the terms "supranaturalism" and "supernaturalism." In many contexts, they are interchangeable.

which could be called self-transcending or ecstatic naturalism."[22] Some amplification is required here for two reasons. First, he still uses the term naturalism to name his new position, his third alternative. Second, supranaturalism seems to be completely eliminated.

Some clarification is provided when he distinguishes between two major types or forms of naturalism.

> When we use the word "naturalism" we should be clear about what type we have in mind. Today we call the mechanistic or materialistic type of naturalism a reductive naturalism....It denies that mind and life have any independent reality. They are supposed to be epiphenomenal; ...secondary and superficial, and not a part of any substantial reality. That is not a profound philosophy at all. But it is only one form of naturalism.[23]

The other form is "ecstatic naturalism." This form is "great" and is represented by Nietzsche—whom Tillich designates as a naturalistic prophet.

In *Courage to Be*, he defines naturalism as the "identification of being with nature and the consequent rejection of the supernatural."[24] It is worth observing that this identification tends to dissolve the previous philosophical antithesis between "idealism" and "naturalism." Two possible consequences can be designated. First, *everything* is now to be regarded as *being*—and hence as idealistic. Or, as a second possibility, the term idealism must be abandoned because it has been transcended or overcome. Then there would no longer be any basis for an antithesis. Reflection on Tillich's dialectical relation to idealism suggests that he would prefer the latter of these two possibilities. In this non-reductive definition of naturalism, the principle of continuity tends to become the sole instrument or criterion for distinguishing between metaphysical and epistemological positions. Certain difficulties in semantics and conceptuality accompany this methodological shift because Tillich continues to express himself in terms and categories drawn from classical idealism. Also, in *Courage To Be*, he speaks of "romantic" and "voluntaristic" types of naturalism. He defines

---

[22]Tillich, "Reply to Interpretation," 341.

[23]Paul Tillich, *Perspectives on Nineteenth and Twentieth Century Protestant Thought*, ed. by Carl E. Braaten (New York: Harper & Row, 1967) 205f.

[24]Tillich, *Courage*, 118.

voluntarism as a view in which nature is seen as the "creative expression of an unconscious will or as the objectification of the will to power."

Later, he describes voluntarism as a philosophical perspective in which "will" is the decisive element of reality. In an interesting, and rather personal, survey, Tillich states that voluntarism, as a movement, began in the nineteenth century with Schelling—before Schelling became a philosopher of life.[25] In the course of this survey, written in 1963, Tillich returns, in principle, to the distinction between the major "lines" of thought in philosophy which he had employed in 1926 in *The Interpretation of History*. The anti-voluntaristic, or non-voluntaristic line of thought includes Aquinas, the nominalists, the British empiricists, Kant, and—to some extent—Schelling and Hegel. It should be noted that this list deeply overlaps the roster of names and positions which was designated as constituting the "methodical line" of philosophy. The voluntaristic line, on the other hand, runs from Nietzsche to Schopenhauer; it includes Bergson, Heidegger, Sartre and Whitehead. It traces back through Schelling to Jacob Boehme—the ecstatic sixteenth-century mystic who, Tillich states, was dependent upon Luther's voluntarism. The first clear appearance of voluntarism, according to Tillich, is in Augustine—who makes an ontological identification of will, love, and original being. In this entire analysis, the operative notion of voluntarism is very closely affiliated with that which he elsewhere designates as the non-methodical line and as the ontological approach.

Also, the entire analysis gains its intelligibility from Tillich's own ontological, i.e., non-psychological, interpretation of will. The semantic spectrum of the term is expanded to encompass both conscious, purposive will and the unconscious process of reality.

> Will is the dynamics in all forms of life. Only in man does it become conscious will. In voluntaristic philosophy will is not restricted to a conscious psychological act. Nevertheless, the word must be used. If you understand will as the dynamic element in all reality, then it makes sense.[26]

The powerful element of theism in Augustine's thought might not enable him to subscribe, comfortably, to Tillich's interpretation. Nevertheless, for the latter theologian, the voluntaristic notion of will is identified ontologi-

---

[25]Tillich, *Perspectives*, 191.

[26]Ibid., 196. Cf. *Morality and Beyond* (New York: Harper, 1966) 19: "Only man. . . ."

cally, with being itself—and unconscious being is dialectically identified with nature.

Tillich makes a pointed assertion which indicates the level of transcendentalism or abstraction on which his enterprise is proceeding. For him, the nature of the natural (the nature of reality) is not specified by the decision to define naturalism as the identification of nature and being. The definition does not reduce reality to any classical metaphysical position—and, it does not interfere with the freedom of intellectual inquiry. Philosophy and science are still free to determine whether nature is organic, progressive, structured by laws, or interpretable through mathematical abstractions.

In one sense, Tillich's own philosophy is specifying that nature is Being—that it is ontological. In another sense, he is simply not concerned to specify what the ultimate nature of the natural is because it is beyond the categories that we use for making such specifications. The Unconditioned, or the ultimate "import" of reality, is neither idealistic nor materialistic for him. He does not wish to choose any particular *model* or metaphysical position for nature—just as he does not wish to choose between the four classical epistemological relations between what he calls subjective and objective reason.[27] He designates these four positions as realism, idealism, dualism and monism. He avoids reductive commitment to any one of the positions and argues, instead, that all interpretive efforts assume the principle of intelligibility. All philosophical and theological arguments assume that the mind (subjective reason) is able to "grasp" reality (objective reason). He is content, then, to make the identification of Being and nature—thereby taking up voluntaristic, non-reductive naturalism into his own position and yet preserving the infinite distance between finitude and infinity.

It is from this supposedly noncommittal perspective that Tillich employs the principle of discontinuity to attack Hegel's "idealism," and his alleged essentialism and metaphysical hubris. In charging Hegel with essentialism, Tillich means that the relationship between essence and existence, the *transition*, is seen as a continuum. There is no gap, no infinite qualitative difference. In charging Hegel with metaphysical and intellectual hubris, Tillich means that reality is depicted as rationally comprehensible

---

[27]*ST*, I:333, "Reply to Interpretation."

in all of its dimensions. There is no non-rational depth or dimension beyond the dominion of systematic and categorical thinking. An interesting observation must be made, however. Insofar as Hegel's idealism is condemned because it is determined by the principle of continuity, Tillich is rejecting a principle which is shared—in some decisive manner—by reductive forms of naturalism, by the non-reductive naturalism of John Dewey and John H. Randall, Jr., and by Tillich's own dialectical monism. Both Dewey and Randall insist that the principle of continuity (in its metaphysical and epistemological implications) is (a) naturalistic, (b) non-reductive, and (c) ultimately grounded in and guaranteed by the evolutionary monism of Hegel's metaphysical vision. [28]

Hence, Tillich's criticism appears to entail the suggestion that metaphysical *monism* is reductive—as well as the naturalistic principle of epistemological continuity—unless both are sharply qualified. The former must be qualified by introducing a limited, dialectical dualism. The latter must be qualified by postulating an epistemological method or an epistemological relationship which differs from that of empirical science. Tillich makes both qualifications and retains the principle of continuity as well as the principle of discontinuity.

In countering the principle of continuity, Tillich envisions a unique dialectical discontinuity between objective reason, subjective reason and the *depth* of reason. The term reason, as it is used here, tends to become synonymous with the whole of reality. Reason is *One*. And yet, it is three. And, that third, primordial element in reason is discontinuous in the sense of being completely non-rational and undifferentiated. Here, Tillich appropriates Schelling's notion of the *prius*—that pre-categoreal, dynamic reality which Hegel designated as the "night in which all cows are black." This is a crucial point which leads Tillich to regard Schelling as an existentialist with the corrective necessary to overcome Hegel's essentialism. It is also one major source for Tillich's concept of the Unconditioned. This *prius*,

---

[28]Tillich and John H. Randall, Jr. taught joint seminars and engaged in dialogue. In Randall, there is a parallel to Tillich; i.e., a blending of teutonic idealism, a principle of continuity, and traditional "naturalism" to achieve a new allegedly non-reductive form of naturalism. Randall explicitly cites Hegel and Dewey as the sources for his notion of metaphysical continuity. See his *Nature and Historical Experience: Essays in Naturalism and In the Theory of History* (New York: Columbia University Press, 1962) 237. Also, see Randall's "The Nature of Naturalism," *Naturalism and the Human Spirit*, ed. by Yervant Krikorian (New York: Columbia University Press, 1944) 372f.

this Unconditioned, is within all of the structured elements of reason; yet, it is free. It is not subject to the rationalistic determinism of Hegel's Absolute.

The Unconditioned thus constitutes and symbolizes Tillich's overcoming of the principle of continuity and the reductive forms of naturalism which rely upon it. In this sense, the Unconditioned is positive and creative—though it is placeless and "neutral." Tillich argues that the Augustinian type of philosophy leads to the "ontological awareness of the unconditional." In this context, awareness, he states, "is used as the most neutral term, avoiding the connotations of the terms intuition, experience, knowledge."[29] It connotes ecstasy as an ontological-psychological *state* of self-transcendence. Because of its neutrality, the Unconditioned does not destroy the rational coherence of the physical system or modify the inviolable structures of nature. It brings no supernatural intervention and it makes no theistic imposition of authority upon the individual centers of human personality. This same "neutrality" makes it technically invulnerable to methodical epistemology—since, ontologically speaking, it does not "exist."

The Unconditioned is not a matter of experimental observation or publicly empirical verification. That is, it cannot be approached or evaluated by the scientific method. Rather, the term points to an "element" in every religious experience which makes it religious.

> The term "unconditioned" or the adjective made into the substantive, "the unconditional," is an abstraction from . . . sayings which abound . . . in great religious literature. The unconditional is a quality, not a being. It characterizes that which is our ultimate and, consequently unconditional concern, whether we call it "God" or "Being as such" . . . or whether we give it any other name. It would be a complete mistake to understand the unconditional as a being the existence of which can be discussed. . . . Unconditional is a quality which we experience in encountering reality.[30]

The unconditioned can be assigned a variety of names; however, when considered as being-itself, it claims the category of the highest ontological rank. Here, Tillich is raising the question of the most fundamental concept which must be applied to reality or to nature, whether it is change or rest,

---

[29]Tillich, *Theology of Culture*, 22f.

[30]Tillich, *Protestant Era*, 32 n1.

dynamics or statics, becoming or being. He argues that becoming includes and overcomes *relative* non-being. But being-itself is the negation of absolute non-being: "it is the affirmation that there is anything at all."[31] This argument reaffirms Tillich's stance as an ontologist. He participates in the dynamicizing of Western man's metaphysics by incorporating the dialectical principle of life and the concept of the restless Unconditional. At the same time, he rejects the basic postulate of process philosophy: that change is the fundamental character of reality. However, the distinction is not without ambiguity. He exalts the concept of being but modifies it with the principle of becoming. The procession from essence to existence to essentialization depicts reality as "life," in the *activity* of self-realization.

Tillich's self-transcending naturalism and the Unconditioned are ultimately associated with his nature romanticism. In recalling his youth, he states that his life has been lived on the boundary between theology and philosophy, between reality and imagination. He contemplated the sea and was deeply impressed with its moods: aggression, tranquility, and the ecstatic quality of the gales and waves. Thus, the sea provided for him the imaginative element for the doctrine of the Unconditioned—considered as the eruption of the eternal into finite temporality. This means that the self-transcendence of nature is ultimately attributable to a "quality" which erupts without disrupting, which pervades without invading, which dynamicizes reality without violating the structures which provide objectivity for reason and for the physical system of reality. This concept of romantically inspired eruption is probably as helpful as anything in understanding the relation which he envisions between the Unconditioned and the dimensions of reality that are structured by categories. He also informs us that it is nature romanticism which occasions his predominantly aesthetic-meditative attitude toward nature, rather than a scientific, technical attitude. "It is the reason for the tremendous emotional impact that Schelling's philosophy of nature made upon me although I was well aware that this philosophy was scientifically impossible."[32]

Schelling is also a decisive influence in Tillich's doctrine of natural evolution and the telescoping of being into physical nature. Schelling states his

---

[31] *ST*, III:26.

[32] Paul Tillich, "Autobiographical Reflections," *The Theology of Paul Tillich*, 4.

romantic vision of the monistic philosophy of the future in the following manner:

> One had to acknowledge the great antiquity of the physical, and how the physical, far from being the last, is rather the first from which everything, even the development of the divine life, originates.
>
> In a short time the contempt with which, after all, only the ignorant still look down on everything physical will cease. Then there will no longer be any difference between the world of thought and the world of reality.[33]

This quotation contains the principle of the identity of being and physical reality—a vision of the identity of thought and nature. It also contains that monistic, synthesizing conceptuality which facilitates the evaporation of the antithesis between metaphysical idealism and that position which Tillich calls the "voluntaristic forms of naturalism." Lastly, but of equal importance, it assumes a certain evolutionary order and a certain hierarchy of levels of complexity and self-realizaton in reality. This aspect of Schelling's thought is clearly reflected in Tillich's doctrine of the multi-dimensional unity of being. The inorganic is given a certain priority, for it is the first condition for the actualization of all subsequent dimensions. Hence, Tillich states that,

> This is why all realms of being would dissolve were the basic condition provided by the constellation of inorganic structures to disappear.[34]

However, the immanental power or quality of the Unconditional pervades this inorganic, physical system and ontologically "precedes" it. Consequently, there can be no reduction to materialistic forms of naturalism.

In sum, Tillich's philosophy attempts to overcome all forms of reductive naturalism by providing decisive roles for discontinuity and for the Unconditioned. At the same time, Tillich's self-transcending naturalism is profoundly indebted to the prince of idealists, F. W. J. Schelling. The ontological source, the *voluntaristic* power of reality, is inclosed within the empirical universe. Nature and being are dialectically "identified." The Unconditioned erupts into the categories of finitude, but it *qualifies* finite real-

---

[33]Friedrich Schelling, *The Ages of the World*, trans. by F. W. Bolman, Jr. (New York: AMS Press, 1967) 90.

[34]*ST*, III:19 (1963).

ity; it does not evoke spatio-temporal events through an act of intervention. Nature, as a physical system, is derivative in relation to the primordial unity of thinking and being. However, this is an ontological—rather than a chronological—assertion. On the other hand, spirit and consciousness, *as they appear in man*, are chronologically derivative in relation to the physical system. Man has the capacity for self-transcendence because nature itself is self-transcending.

The Resultant Synthesis

In bringing ontology and non-reductive naturalism into a synthesis, Tillich intends to formulate an alternative to naturalism and supranaturalism. At times, he states that his position is neither natural nor supranatural. The reader thus tends to expect a construct which is equally removed from both poles of the antithesis. Our analysis, however, indicates that this is not the case. Tillich flatly *rejects* supranaturalism. He intends to "overcome" naturalism (as well as idealism). It must be noted that the operative meaning of overcoming for Tillich is akin to Hegel's dialectical notion of *Aufheben*. That is, the perspective to be overcome is partially rejected and partially preserved and incorporated. In this procedure, the supposedly passive system may have a dramatic effect upon the system which conducts the overcoming.

As we have seen, Tillich's positive naturalism is deeply interwoven with classical German idealism. In fact, in his conceptual apparatus, the antithesis between "idealism" and non-reductive naturalism tends to evaporate—and the value of his struggle to avoid metaphysical idealism becomes debatable. Tillich is inextricably involved with the idealist tradition—partly because of his relationship with Schelling and Hegel, and partly because of his absolute reliance upon the concepts of Being and the unity of thinking and being.

An assessment of his relation to naturalism in general leads us to consider a *cluster of crucial elements and characteristics* of his mature position. First, Tillich's worldview reflects the total absence of theism and supranaturalism. Second, transcendence becomes a function of immanence—as is usual in an immanental system. Third, the non-centered Unconditional replaces the notion of subject-to-subject relations between man and ultimate reality. God is beyond subject-object structure and, hence, he is not a centered self. Fourth, the non-centered character of the divine emancipates man from heteronomy—the imposition of external authority and the implication of pre-ordained unworthiness. Man's autonomy is dialectically identified with—and dialectically distinguished from—theonomy—the power of being which is primordially united with man's inner essence. Thus, "essential man," an ontological potentiality, becomes the criterion and referent of human behavior. Gone is the inscrutable, theistic tyrant who deprives man of his subjectivity. Henceforth, man has the good conscience to plead that he is innocent of the absurdity of the world. Yet, he has the existential possibility of doing something about it. Through stoic, ecstatic and Christian striving, man *may* be able to effect a kairos.

Fifth, Tillich exhibits great catholicity in admitting figures to his pantheon of sources (his "host of ancestors"). Voluntarism and/or romantic naturalism are found in Nietzsche (whom he designates as an atheist) and in Schelling, as well as in apologetic theologians. Sixth, Tillich's naturalism assumes the universal availability of the inspiration and courage which man draws from the *depths*, or from the Unconditioned. This is the case whether one traces the conceptual lineage of this notion through the metaphysical visions of Nietzsche, Hegel, Schleiermacher, Spinoza, or of Jacob Boehme. Seventh, this naturalism legitimatizes and blesses human reason in the spatio-temporal dimension of reality. Like Schleiermacher's *Christian Faith*, it tends to identify divine and human reason—for all practical purposes in man's cognitive endeavors. Tillich broadens this viewpoint in his reinterpretation of the Protestant principle and the doctrine of justification by faith. Intellectual doubt is "justified" if it occurs under the aegis of ultimate concern. Certain epistemological methods of naturalism are thereby sanctioned. Hence, it is not surprising to find Tillich frequently acknowledging his indebtedness to the two hundred years of "scientific" research which culminates in the demythologizing work of Schweitzer and Bultmann. The degree of continuity and intelligibility between autonomous and theonomous reason makes him free to employ the scientific principle of continuity for demythologizing in history, scripture, and in physical reality. At the same time, re-mythologization occurs on the ontological level—beyond the danger of objectification which is associated with the categories of finitude. In fact, the ontology as such constitutes a process of transcendental re-mythologizing.

Eighth, the principle of discontinuity is so employed that the Unconditioned, and the ontological dimension of reality, metaphorically perform many of the functions and enter into many of the relations which would be expected only in a fully hypostatized dualism. And yet, since hypostatizing is technically excluded, the entire procedure involves what Kierkegaard might call a "revocation" of the supranatural into the natural. The metaphorical language echoes Plato's notion of essence but it rejects his objective dualism. It also echoes selected aspects of Kantian transcendentalism. Tillich's special theological category of essentialism is "directive" and regulative—when viewed from an ontic, psychodynamic and moral perspective. However, from an ontological perspective it is constitutive. Both perspectives are real and true because the mystical unity of reality is predicated upon a primordial unity of *thinking, being and nature*. Voluntarism, idealism and naturalism are blended into a single all-embracing category. Reflection upon this cluster of concepts and postulates in Tillich's worldview provides a provocative comprehension of the impact and implications of the naturalistic elements which have been incorporated in his system.

Nothing is more fundamental in the schematism of Tillich's ontological naturalism than the dialectical tension and interplay between the principles of continuity and discontinuity. These principles are his major instruments and criteria for making intelligible his existentialism, the role of the unconditioned, the horizon between ontological and ontic reality, and his attempt to overcome reductive forms of naturalism. Consequently, despite appearance to the contrary, the supposedly well-defined positions of idealism, naturalism, theological theism, essentialism, etc., are not the ultimate objects of his theological and philosophical polemics. They simply function as variant and influential embodiments of reductive thinking. His basic concern is directed toward any principle, procedure, or concept which tends to have *reductive consequences* for man, or for ultimate reality. From his perspective, either continuity or discontinuity, monism or dualism, can be reductive and demonic if employed exclusively and incorrectly. In terms of the abstract structure of his conceptual apparatus, one real key to his method is the achievement of the required dialectical equilibrium in the relation of these two principles. Discontinuity and subject-object structure are both derivative and hence transient in Tillich's system. However, while there is *existence*, both discontinuity and continuity must be granted almost equally radical seriousness and validity. On the other hand, the controlling categories of the system suggest that Tillich ultimately seeks not a genuine discontinuity, but a dialectical discontinuity *within* mystical continuity.

It can also be observed that, though Tillich chooses the non-methodical line of philosophy, his is an extremely methodical (i.e., rationalistic) form of non-methodical thinking. Admittedly, he employs a dialectical as well as a formal system of logic; also, he employs dynamic, fluid semantics and categories. Nevertheless, the architectonic interrelatedness of the entire intellectual edifice bears the splendid trademark of German rationalism: everything must be systematized. Only the Unconditioned is outside the perimeter of rational analysis. However, it too is conceived within the framework of an ultimate and natural monism. Though non-rational, the Unconditioned is the depth of reason. And as indicated above, it does not violate the rational, structural integrity of reality. Consequently, Tillich remains on the boundary, even in his choice of the lines of philosophy.

In concise summary, this paper has argued the following points: First, Tillich telescopes the voluntaristic form of naturalism into his ontology. Thus nature and idea, thinking and being, tend to become dialectically identified in mystical unity. Dualism and all supernaturalism are rejected. Second, Tillich is committed to a principle of primordial continuity, a principle which emerges naturally out of the notion of the identity of thinking and being. However, he qualifies continuity with a derivative structure of dialectical discontinuity. This structure provides the basis for subject-object relations in ontic reality; for the gap between essence and existence; and, hence, for his existential reinterpretation of the myth of the Fall. Third, the first and second notions just cited enable Tillich to achieve his basic goal in relation to traditional naturalism: to function as a nature philosopher and yet to eliminate all traces of the reductionism which has allegedly been inherent in naturalism.

The non-reductive thrust of Tillich's self-transcending naturalism results in an indirect celebration of the ultimate worth of man. That is, an important element of humanism emerges in the non-reductive enterprise. Blending transcendental ontology and creative rationalism, he projects himself to a point of observation which is beyond nature as such. He thereby achieves an enrichment of the human situation—not because the ecstatic projection postulates objective theocentricity, but because it avoids reduction to the bland anthropocentricity of everyday life.

Part II
TILLICH
AS A
SYSTEMATIC
THEOLOGIAN

From System to Systematics: The Origin of Tillich's Theology

PAUL WIEBE

In his later years, Paul Tillich viewed his first large book, *The System of the Sciences*,[1] with some ambivalence. He explained the fact that the book had "remained without an extensive influence" by pointing out that it is "an outline, which attacks an enormous topic with limited means"; but he acknowledged that the writing of the book had been an important event in the development of his thought, because for him "it was a first orientation in the confused variety of scientific operations, and the way to establish the place of theological work" within the whole of science.[2] He also reported that the volume represented his "first and rather insufficient step" toward his later definition of theology and theological position; he

---

[1]*Das System der Wissenschaften nach Gegenstaenden und Methoden* first appeared in 1923 (Göttingen: Vandenhoeck & Ruprecht); it has been republished in Tillich's *Gesammelte Werke*, ed. Renate Albrecht, Band 1: *Fruehe Hauptwerke* (Stuttgart: Evangelisches Verlagswerk, 1959). Subsequent citations of this work will refer to this latter publication; all translations are mine.

[2]"Vorwort" to *Gesammelte Werke*, Band 1, 9.

nevertheless recognized that many of the ideas contained in the book had remained with him. [3]

To the extent that they disparage *The System of the Sciences*, these remarks would appear to justify its common neglect by Tillich's English-speaking interpreters. When taken in their entirety, however, the remarks actually point to the seminal importance of the work for the further development of Tillich's thought. In this essay, I wish to maintain that the early Tillich helps to explain some of the features of the later, mature Tillich—more precisely, that "Tillich I" (in *The System*) is a natural key for interpreting much of "Tillich II" (especially *Systematic Theology*). The thinker himself once said that *Systematic Theology* requires some knowledge of some concepts and arguments that had been treated in other places. [4] Though there can be no question here of arguing the point in detail—I will be content to give brief indications—a most important "other place" is *The System*. Thus in the first part of this essay, I will recount the nature and structure of this early work. In Part II, I will sketch the itinerary of Tillich's theological thought, in preparation for a description, in Part III, of the main features of the relationship between *The System* and *Systematic Theology*.

I

The System of the Sciences is an attempt to systematically understand the relationships among the various cognitive disciplines. There are at least three motives behind Tillich's construction of this system: (1) to view the entire world of science as a coherent whole (this is, of course, the obvious and immediate motive); (2) to state the relation between the human sciences (the *Geisteswissenschaften*) and the natural sciences; and (3) to establish the place of theology within the totality of the modes of knowing (this is Tillich's mediate motive). Each of these strands falls within a historical tradition.

The first tradition within which this work stands is suggested by the name of the book itself. The tradition of attempts to organize the various

---

[3]"Author's Introduction," *The Protestant Era*, trans. James Luther Adams, abr. ed. (Chicago: University of Chicago Press, Phoenix Books, 1957) xxii. See also Tillich, *On the Boundary: An Autobiographical Sketch*, rev. ed. (New York: Charles Scribner's Sons, 1966) 55-57.

[4]"Autobiographical Reflections," *The Theology of Paul Tillich*, ed. Charles W. Kegley and Robert W. Bretall (New York: Macmillan Co., 1961) 15.

cognitive disciplines into a coherent whole extends from the Greeks to the German idealism of which Tillich himself is a late product;[5] it includes both the systems constructed by individual thinkers and the various forms of curricular organization within the academy. Another part of the historical background of Tillich's ambitious outline is the extended German discussion of the relation between the human sciences and the natural sciences. This discussion was pursued by such thinkers of the late nineteenth and early twentieth centuries as Dilthey, Windelband, and Rickert, who were concerned to distinguish between these two basic forms of knowledge in order to secure the human sciences as ways of cognition that are as legitimate as those of the established natural sciences. A third tradition is the tradition of concern, in nineteenth- and twentieth-century Protestant theology, with the question of the very possibility of theology, a question that includes both the question of the rationale for theology and that of whether theology is even a legitimate cognitive endeavor.[6] Schleiermacher's entire theological programme can be seen as an attempt to answer this question. By discovering the location of theology within the totality of the sciences, Tillich's system in effect both determines the nature of theology and demonstrates its right to exist alongside the other sciences.

For Tillich, the principle that determines the systematic classification of the sciences is the idea of science itself. Accordingly, the basic division is determined by an analysis of the knowing act. When this act is considered apart from all contents, it can be seen to be constituted by both the act of intention and what is intended, or thought and being. "Thought" is not the psychological phenomenon of reflection, and "being" does not refer to anything in existence. Tillich is only interested in the pure elements of the act of knowledge, so thought in its purity is defined as the act that is directed toward being; conversely, being is simply defined as that to which thought is directed. The two are the original elements of science, for they constitute the essence of knowledge itself.[7]

---

[5]The models for Tillich's own construction appear to have been Fichte's *Theory of Knowledge* and Hegel's *Encyclopedia*.

[6]See Claude Welch, *Protestant Thought in the Nineteenth Century* 2 vols. (New Haven: Yale University Press, 1972) 1:4-5.

[7]*Das System der Wissenschaften*, 117-18. It should be clear that the term "being" in this work is not to be confused with the term "being-itself," which appears in *Systematic Theology*.

From this analysis of the act of knowledge into its constituent elements, Tillich derives his tripartite division of the sciences into the sciences of thought, of being, and of spirit. In each of the first two kinds of knowledge, thought directs its attention to one of the basic elements of the cognitive act. In the sciences of thought, or the formal sciences, the goal is a knowledge of the pure forms of thought itself, considered in abstraction from their relation to being. In the sciences of being, or the empirical sciences, man seeks to know the existents within the realm of being. But how can the sciences of spirit, the human sciences, be derived through the analysis of the idea of knowledge? Tillich attempts to effect such a deduction by understanding the area of the human sciences as that area in which thought is directed to spirit (*Geist*) and by viewing spirit as a third, synthetic element alongside thought and being—an element dependent upon these prior constituents for its definition, but one that nonetheless enjoys a status equal to theirs. Spirit is thought within the realm of being; spirit is existing thought. This means that the area of spirit is that area in which thought forms being, in which spiritual (i.e., cultural) creativity occurs, in which such things as paintings, laws, and metaphysical systems appear.[8]

The sciences of thought are composed of two disciplines: logic and mathematics. These formal sciences deal with the pure and universal forms inherent in thought itself. Such forms are like the Kantian categories in that they are the necessary preconditions of any knowledge of being; every existent must be thought under them. The demonstration and deduction of these forms depend upon definition, so the degree of certainty attainable in these sciences is one of axiomatic certainty.[9] In the empirical sciences, thought turns its attention toward being, which is infinite for thought. In order to effect a union with objective being, thought creates a variety of frameworks. These frameworks strive for universal applicability, but they can never claim the necessity of the logico-mathematical forms. This explains why the only degree of certainty possible for empirical knowledge is that of probability. These sciences are themselves divided into three groups: the physical sciences of law (including mathematical physics and chemistry), the gestalt sciences (biology, psy-

---

[8]Ibid., 118-21, 210-11.

[9]Ibid., 124-32.

chology, and sociology, with their technological applications), and the historical sciences.[10]

The human sciences are organized into a subsystem of sciences, which includes the theory of knowledge, aesthetics, metaphysics, the science of law, the theory of community, ethics, and the science of religion (though religion for Tillich is not one cultural sphere alongside the others, but is an attitude within them). These disciplines are normative sciences, in the sense that they provide guidance for the cultural process within the spheres of knowledge, community, religion, and the other areas. To say that the theorist creates norms for these spheres is to deny that he discovers them. Norms are not given; they are created by individuals standing within history. So the degree of certainty possible in the human sciences is one of conviction, which is a function of the standpoint of the theorist who is creating the norm. The construction of a norm in each of the cultural spheres involves three consecutive subdivisions of the science. The philosophy of the sphere (e.g., the philosophy of art, of community, of religion) has the task of determining the essence or nature of that sphere; the spiritual history of the sphere develops the types in which this essence has been historically realized; and the systematics of the sphere synthesizes these types into a norm, or normative type.[11]

Now, each of the cultural spheres has a science corresponding to it, a science that can be divided into the three subdivisions. The science of religion is no exception to this statement. The science of religion (*Religionswissenschaft*) is composed of the philosophy of religion, the spiritual history of religion, and theology. So theology, or the systematic element in the science of religion, is the subdiscipline that synthesizes the types that have been constructed by the history of religion into a normative type, a religious norm. Theology, then, is indeed a member of the total world of cognitive disciplines: it is the systematic or norm-constructing element within the science of religion.[12]

II

The question of the significance of Tillich I for Tillich II can best be approached by placing *The System of the Sciences* within the chronological

---

[10]Ibid., 135-209.

[11]Ibid., 210-71.

[12]Ibid., 271-83.

framework of the development of his theological thought. There are two
distinguishable moments in this evolution. The first moment is one of work
on justifying theology as a science by placing it within a systematic classification of the sciences, thereby establishing the very nature of theology.
This period extends from 1919 to 1925. Tillich began work on this task in
his long 1919 essay, "On the Idea of a Theology of Culture,"[13] which contains a few of the seeds that bore fruit in *The System*; he continued this
inquiry in a short essay, "Theology as a Science" (1921),[14] which indicates
the major thrust of his interest during this period. *The System of the Sciences* (1923) itself is the culmination of this period, but it was followed, in
1925, by a work that is an extension of *The System*, entitled *The Philosophy
of Religion*.[15] Though *The System* had been primarily concerned with the
placement of theology within the systematic whole of the sciences, it had
not singled out either the science of religion generally, or theology specifically, for special treatment. But *The Philosophy of Religion* provides an extended treatment of the science of religion, thus revealing the direction of
his basic interest. Building upon the edifice already established in the tax-
onomy of the sciences, this work focuses on the sphere of religion. More
specifically, it contains a thorough exposition of the fundamental element
within the science of religion, the philosophy of religion. But since this element cannot be viewed in isolation from the other two, theology and the
history of religion are also treated, though not in detail. In the final sentence of this work, however, he points ahead: he has created a philosophy
of religion to which a theology can be attached as a concrete realization
and fulfillment.[16]

The second moment in Tillich's development is constituted by the various drafts of the theological system proper, from 1925 to the completion
of *Systematic Theology* in 1963. As Tillich himself later acknowledged,
work on his theological system began in 1925[17]—immediately after the

---

[13]An English translation of this essay, by William Baillie Green, appears in Tillich, *What
is Religion?*, ed. with an introduction by James Luther Adams (New York: Harper & Row,
1969) 155-81.

[14]In *Vossische Zeitung* 512 (1921): 2-3.

[15]The English translation of this work, by James Luther Adams, Konrad Raiser, and
Charles W. Fox, appears in *What is Religion?*, 27-121.

[16]Ibid., 121.

[17]*Systematic Theology* 3 vols. (Chicago: University of Chicago Press, 1951-1963) 3:7.
See also ibid., 1:xi.

completion of *The Philosophy of Religion*! His lectures on "The Doctrine of Faith" were presented in that year.[18] After his move from Germany to the United States, with its inevitable problems of relocation, Tillich continued his work on the theological system in the form of the lectures on "Systematic Theology" he delivered at Union Theological Seminary.[19] The final draft is, of course, the finished version of *Systematic Theology* (1951-1963).

III

This abbreviated sketch of Tillich's theological development would seem to suggest that *The System of the Sciences* is of utmost importance because, through *The Philosophy of Religion*, it provides the foundation for *Systematic Theology*. But it would be wrong to suppose that the material theological work he began in 1925 was merely the continuation of his earlier methodological work, that the completed theological system is merely the logical result of his prior systematization of the sciences and his foundational work in the philosophy of religion. Any comprehensive comparison of *Systematic Theology* with *The System* and *The Philosophy of Religion* would yield this judgment, for the former does not simply follow through in the direction prescribed by the latter two. The finished system is not merely the completion of a pre-established task along lines that had already been determined.

Certainly the system Tillich had been ready to write in 1925 came into being; but it was a somewhat different system than the one he had foreseen in the closing sentence of *The Philosophy of Religion*. *Systematic Theology* is a different system: this is to say that there are discontinuities between the thought structure expressed in the finished system and that presented in the earlier two works; this accounts for Tillich's later detracting remarks about *The System*. But it is only somewhat different: there are also continuities between the two thought structures; and this fact justifies the claim that *The System* is a significant moment within the evolution of Tillich's theology, and that therefore it is important for an understanding

---

[18]Tillich Archive, Andover-Harvard Theological Library, Cambridge MA. A.1 (25-42). The handwritten notebooks containing these lectures on the "Glaubenslehre" are marked: "1925/26, Dresden."

[19]Mimeographed copies of the substance of these lectures are located in the Tillich Archive. C.4 (1-16).

of the completed theological system. Both, discontinuities as well as continuities, need to be explicated.

The crucial discontinuity between the early and the late systems concerns both the placement of theology on the map of the cognitive disciplines and the very conception of theology this placement involves. Tillich's primary interest in *The System of the Sciences* had been to find a place for theology among the other modes of knowledge: theology, as one of the three elements constituting the science of religion, was placed in a direct relationship to the other spheres of human science, and so in an indirect relation to the formal and the empirical sciences. But in *Systematic Theology*, this elaborate placement is completely abandoned; instead, the problem of the relationship of theology to the other sciences is treated briefly, efficiently, and differently. Tillich establishes a distinct hiatus between theology and all other sciences, stating that theology is that science whose object is what concerns us ultimately, while the objects of the rest of the sciences are those matters that concern us only in a preliminary way. But he also sees a positive relationship, for both the sciences and theology make ontological assumptions; so, since the point of contact between theology and the special sciences lies in their common ontological element, he merges the problem of their relation into the question of the relation between theology and philosophy.[20] Accordingly, Tillich's view of the nature of theology underwent a decisive reorientation between the period of his system of the sciences and the publication of his major work. A structural comparison of the two conceptions reveals that this shift was from a cultural conception, in which the task of the discipline is to construct a norm for religious creativity, to a soteriological conception, in which theology, as the science of ultimate concern, has the task of discovering how our being—that about which we are ultimately concerned—can be threatened, lost, or saved.[21]

If this discontinuity were decisive, the close study of Tillich could well dispense with an investigation of *The System of the Sciences*. But it is balanced by a number of continuities. There are obviously vestiges of *The System* in the mature period. For example, just as Tillich had earlier pos-

---

[20]*Systematic Theology*, 1:11-15, 18-21.

[21]It is interesting to note that this change in the conception of theology was apparently already beginning to occur in 1925. In Tillich's "Doctrine of Faith," theology is defined as "scientific speech about that which concerns us ultimately."

tulated the several functions of meaning within the human sciences (knowledge and art in the theoretical sphere, law and community in the practical, with metaphysics and ethos as their respective foundations), so in *Systematic Theology* he constructs a similar scheme for organizing the rational functions of the human mind: the grasping or receptive functions of *theoria* are the cognitive and the aesthetic, while the shaping or reactive functions of *praxis* are the legal and the communal. [22] This structure is patently a survival from the earlier system; even the religious "function" is still evident as the "depth" of the various functions of the mind. And when Tillich considers the idea of God in *Systematic Theology*, he does so, not by giving a survey of its history, but in a thoroughly typological way, showing how the concrete element in man's ultimate concern drives him toward polytheistic, the absolute element in this concern drives him to monotheistic, and the requirement of a balance between the two elements impels him toward trinitarian, structures. [23] This and other typological constructions within the later system are reminiscent, of course, of his procedure in *The System*, where he treats the materials of the history of religion in a typological way, with a view to the normative synthesis to be constructed by the theologian.

But there are more profound and significant continuities between Tillich I and Tillich II than these. One of them is the continuity between the primordial epistemological situation analyzed in *The System* and the primordial ontological situation described in *Systematic Theology*. We have seen that the foundation of the classification of the sciences is the thought/being structure of the cognitive act. In the mature theological system, a similar structure is regarded as ontologically, and therefore epistemologically, fundamental. The basic ontological structure is the self/world structure of human being, where "self" is a structure of centeredness and "world" is the structured whole that stands over against the self. And this structure is more precisely specified in the polar elements that constitute the self/world structure. What is more, this structure is the basis of the subject/object structure of reason with which epistemology is concerned. [24] It is clear, then, that Tillich's later ontological analysis has its

---

[22]*Systematic Theology*, 1:72, 76-80; 3:57-68.

[23]Ibid., 1:218-30.

[24]Ibid., 1:71-79, 164-65.

roots in the similar philosophical system of the early book, though a close comparison would undoubtedly yield differences in the details of the two structures.

Probably the most important continuity between the two moments in Tillich's theological life is the enduring position that theology is involved in the task of constructing a norm. Though his conception of theology underwent a transformation from a cultural to a soteriological conception, there was no change in his view that theology is a normative discipline. For the early Tillich, theology creates a religious norm within the historically conditioned place of a religious community. The construction of this norm requires the help of the philosophy and the history of religion; it is a matter of conviction, not of either certainty or probability. This norm is then used to interpret the symbols of the religious community.[25] This view is again expressed in *Systematic Theology*, where it shapes the entire theological method. For Tillich II, theology requires a norm to govern the use of the sources—that is, to interpret the Christian symbols. The fashioning of such a norm requires a dialectic between ontological analysis, which asks "questions" by describing the ontological polarities in the state of disruption, and theology itself, which furnishes "answers" to these questions by describing the synthetic resolution of these polarities in the form of the theological norm of New Being. And the later doctrine of the theological circle holds that the Christian theologian must always construct his norm within the confines of his "circle" (the Christian church); he therefore cannot establish the truth of this norm in either a deductive or an empirical way, but must proceed from personal commitment, so that he is continually involved in "circular" reasoning.[26] Though there are some differences between these two methodological statements, especially in the matter of how the norm is constructed, there are clear similarities. The later complex method appears to be already contained in the earlier and simpler statements of theological procedure.

IV

The System of the Sciences can be valuable in several ways. It is a source for historians of thought, of course. More important, it is a text for

---

[25]*Das System der Wissenschaften*, 276-77.

[26]*Systematic Theology*, 1:8-11, 47-52, 107; 3:201.

systematic thinkers who want to rethink the problems of the organization of the sciences, the character of the human sciences, and the nature of theology. But it is also a necessary aid to a full grasp of Tillich's completed theological system. Certainly Tillich's mature theology is more interesting and valuable than is his early systematic thought, but Tillich II can be completely understood only in the light of Tillich I. It is possible to use the early Tillich as an interpretive guide to the latter because, though there is a basic discontinuity between the initial conception of theology and the systematic theology actually executed, there are also firm and basic continuities between the two. It is necessary to proceed in this way because many of the arguments and positions presented in the finished system presuppose their fuller treatment in the earlier German book.

So far, however, few of the many interpreters of Tillich have concerned themselves with *The System* at all, and even fewer have used it in any way as an exegetical guide for reconstructing the meaning of *Systematic Theology*. Future Tillich scholarship cannot perpetuate this omission.

Questioning, Answering, and Tillich's Concept Of Correlation

JOHN P. CLAYTON

In *Systematic Theology* and elsewhere, Tillich frequently endeavoured to explain the relationship between the "the human situation" of "the cultural context" and "the christian message" by suggesting its similarity to the relationship between "questions" and "answers." This metaphor is perhaps most frequently associated with the so-called "method of correlation." It is not always sufficiently appreciated, however, that Tillich's usage of "questioning" and "answering" as an apologetic technique quite considerably predates the emergence of his method of correlation. Drawing in many cases upon unpublished or only recently published material, I propose to trace some of the changing uses of questioning and answering in the development of Tillich's thought with a view toward determining the role of that metaphor in the formation of his concept of correlation. In this article, I shall be dealing principally with the period prior to Tillich's emigration from Germany.

In order to understand why Tillich came to speak of the relationship between "message" and "situation" in terms of this metaphor, it is useful to consider his attempt almost from the beginning to construct a genuinely dialectical theology, a theology in which "question" and "answer," "yes" and "no" stand in a strictly correlative relationship.[1] Nor can there be any serious doubt that the subsequently articulated "method of correlation" was intended by Tillich to furnish the methodological underpinnings for what he once termed his "neo-dialectical" theology, a theology which in contrast to the "supernaturalism of later Barthianism" was claimed by Tillich to be thoroughly and truly dialectical.[2]

The restriction of the criticism to *later* Barthianism is not altogether inappropriate. For Tillich had been early attracted to the views of Barth and had for a time regarded him as an ally in a common cause.[3] Indeed, about the time that the second edition of the *Römerbrief* had appeared, Tillich is reported to have told Barth that he regarded that commentary as a "genuine symptom" of the dawning of a new age of theonomy.[4] It is not clear that Barth altogether shared that estimate.

Tillich and Barth met, though possibly not for the first time,[5] at Göttingen in the spring of 1922. Their meeting was arranged—and, in view of later events, ironically—by Emanuel Hirsch, who was at the time the most senior and most well-established of the three.[6] Barth's contemporary account of that meeting has long been available in the Barth-Thurneysen correspondence. However, it has not been widely known that Tillich, too,

---

[1]Strictly speaking, these pairs of terms—"question and answer," "yes and no"—are not parallel. They are nonetheless typically used by Tillich as if they were. Cf. "Autobiographical Reflections," *The Theology of Paul Tillich*, ed. C. W. Kegley and R. W. Bretall (New York: The Macmillan Company, 1952) 15f, and *Gesammelte Werke*, Vol. VII: *Die Protestantismus als Kritik und Gestaltung* (Stuttgart: Evangelisches Verlagswerk, 1962) 247ff.

[2]*The Protestant Era* abr. ed. (Chicago: University of Chicago Press, 1957) xxiv, xxii.

[3]Cf. *Gesammelte Werke*, VII:254.

[4]J. D. Smart, ed., *Revolutionary Theology in the Making: Barth-Thurneysen Correspondence*, 1914-1925 (London: Epworth Press, 1964) 95.

[5]Kenneth Schedler suggests that they had met as early as 1919 through their association with the religious socialist movement. *Natur und Gnade: Das sakramentale Denken in der fruhen Theologie Paul Tillichs*, 1919-1935 (Stuttgart: Evangelisches Verlagswerk, 1970) 150ff.

[6]Though two years younger than Tillich and Barth, Hirsch had been *Ordinarious* at Göttingen since 1921. Tillich did not become *Ordinarious* until his call to Dresden and Leipzig in 1925, the same year that Barth became *Ordinarious* at Munster. At Göttingen, Barth had been "honorary professor" since 1921, but he was listed as being "außerhalb der Fakultät" from 1921 to 1924. See Wilhelm Ebel, *Catalogus Professorum Gottingensium*, 1734-1962 (Göttingen: Vandenhoeck & Ruprecht, 1962). I am very grateful to my colleague, Dr. James Richmond, for having called my attention to this useful volume.

recorded his immediate impressions of the occasion in a private and as yet unpublished letter.[7]

Tillich's account agrees in substance with Barth's, especially as regards Hirsch's persistent attempts to polarise the two. Any sign of agreement between them on this or that point would appear to have much distressed their host. It was apparently possible for them to have a serious discussion only when they managed to get away from Hirsch for a private talk together. They talked mainly about philosophy of history, though Tillich confesses—and in his letter Barth concurs—they found little about which to agree; as a "supranaturalistic eschatologist," Barth was judged to have had no interest in history and was said to have found dangerous Tillich's notion of "theonomy." If that be the case, Tillich reportedly countered that Barth's own notion of an "act of faith" must be regarded as equally dangerous—a point which, Tillich implies, Barth conceded.[8] "Finally," he reports, "we made the following pact: he will endeavour to rationalise his supranatural formulae and I shall endeavour to balance [kompensieren] my rational formulae with supranatural ones. He will proclaim the reality of the Unconditioned as a biblical theologian, and I shall do so as a cultural theologian."

"Die Überwindung des Religionsbegriffs in der Religionsphilosophie" appeared later that year in *Kant-Studien*.[9] It might be thought that in it Tillich was upholding his end of the bargain by arguing, among other things, that "God is known only through God!"[10] Tillich also went out of his way in that article to call attention to the similarities which he thought obtained between his own views and those of Barth and Gogarten.[11] This act of generosity possibly had the unintended effect of leading Harnack to

---

[7]The letter was written to Tillich's close friend and brother-in-law, Alfred Fritz. It is marked only as having been written "near Goslar in railway dining car. Sunday afternoon." From internal evidence, and in comparison with a letter from Barth to Thurneysen regarding Tillich's visit to Göttingen [*Revolutionary Theology in the Making*, 95-97], it can be precisely placed as having been written on Sunday, 2 April 1922.

[8]Cf. *Gesammelte Werke*, Vol. XII: *Begegnungen* (Stuttgart: Evangelisches Verlagswerk, 1971) 191f.

[9]Vol. XXVII (1922): 446-69. Reprinted in *Gesammelte Werke*, Vol. I: *Frühe Hauptwerke* (Stuttgart: Evangelisches Verlagswerk, 1959) 367-88.

[10]Ibid., 388.

[11]Ibid., 367f.

count Tillich among those theologians "who are contemptuous of academic theology"![12] In any case, Tillich's article originated as an address to the Berlin chapter of the *Kant-Gesellschaft* on 25 January 1922 and was, therefore, written well before the meeting with Barth in Göttingen. It is in fact evidently the "unpublished address" mentioned by Barth and Tillich alike in their respective letters. In view of the highly dialectical and even paradoxical formulations in that article, it is perhaps not surprising that Barth could, for a time at least, have regarded Tillich as a comrade in a common fight and could even have commended Tillich's forthcoming book on philosophy of religion to his own publisher, Chr. Kaiser, so as to show Tillich's connection with the dialectical theologians.[13]

The pact was short-lived, however, and Tillich's book was published instead by Vandenhoeck and Ruprecht of Göttingen. Nor has *Das System der Wissenschaften*, in which Tillich self-consciously appropriated for himself the mantle of Troeltsch, generally been interpreted as having demonstrated Tillich's close links with the views of Barth![14]

The very next year Tillich began contrasting his own use of dialectic with Barth's usage and, in return, Barth politely protested that he did not really understand what Tillich was talking about (!) and then proceeded "to understand Tillich better than he understands himself."[15] At the end of his riposte to Barth, a reply which Barth scathingly dismissed in a letter to Thurneysen,[16] Tillich expressed the fear that the way Barth and Gogarten use dialectic "leads unintentionally beyond the dialectical position to a very positive and very undialectical supranaturalism, that from the 'yes' and 'no' of relations between God and world which are essential to every dialectic emerges a simple 'no' against the world, whose destiny it is most

---

[12]Cf. Harnack's "postcard" to Barth which is reprinted in *Revolutionary Theology in the Making*, 127-28.

[13]Ibid., 96.

[14]*Gesammelte Werke*, I:112: "Während der Drucklegung traf mich die Nachricht von dem plötzlichen Tode Ernst Troeltschs. Sein leidenschaftliches Streben war es, zum System zu kommen. Dem Dank, den ich ihm schulde auch für die Wirkung, die seine Arbeit auf die geistigen Grundlagen dieses Buches gehabt hat, möchte ich dadurch Ausdruck geben, dass ich das Buch seinem Andenken widme."

[15]Reprints of the texts of the debate between Tillich, Barth, and Gogarten on the nature of "paradox" are available in various places, including *Gesammelte Werke*, VII:216ff.

[16]*Revolutionary Theology in the Making*, 160.

definitely always to remain impracticable and at some point to be transformed unexpectedly into an all the more positive and undialectical 'yes.'"[17]

As Barth turned increasingly to the production of his dogmatics, first
"christliche" and then "kirchliche," Tillich felt that his early suspicions had
been confirmed. Soon after his emigration to the United States, he wrote
an appreciative but nonetheless damagingly critical article about Barth under the title, "What is Wrong with the 'Dialectic' Theology?"[18] In it Tillich
argued that the "dialectical" theology is not really dialectical at all: it is,
rather, supranaturalistic and paradoxical. Throughout that particular article, as well as elsewhere, Tillich regularly contrasted Barth's so-called
dialectical theology with his own theology, which was—of course—*really*
dialectical. In the introduction to the collection entitled *The Protestant
Era*, Tillich defined dialectics as "the way of seeking for truth by talking
with others from different points of view, through 'Yes' and 'No,' until a
'Yes' has been reached which is hardened in the fire of many 'No's' and
which unites the elements of truth promoted in the discussion."[19] Tillich
then added, in clear if somewhat unfair reference to Barth, "It is most unfortunate that in recent years the name 'dialectical theology' has been applied to a theology that is strongly opposed to any kind of dialectics and
mediation and that constantly repeats the 'Yes' to its own and the 'No' to
any other position." Yet, the pages which follow make it clear that Tillich
still wished his own thought to be described as in some sense dialectical.

Tillich's thought was from the beginning "in some sense dialectical."
His first tentative sketch of a systematic theology is dialectical in the sense
that that term is popularly, if misleadingly, identified with Hegel: namely,
thesis, antithesis, synthesis.[20] That sketch is developed from an argument
begun in its first section (fundamental theology) to the effect that the necessary conflict or contradiction which is said to arise between what is
there termed "the absolute standpoint" or *intuition* (§§1-15) and "the relative standpoint" or *reflection* (§§16-21) is resolved only within "the theo-

---

[17]*Gesammelte Werke*, VII:243.

[18]*The Journal of Religion* XV:127-45 (1935).

[19]P. ix.

[20]Originally written in December 1913, this unpublished "Systematische Theologie"
consists of seventy-two theses. Some marginal notes were added to Tillich's manuscript
in 1965 by his close friend, Richard Wegener.

logical standpoint," based as it is in the *paradox* (§§22-28). This process is explained by Tillich in the following way:

> The absolute and the relative standpoints are related to one another in such a way that the relative standpoint is both produced and destroyed by the absolute standpoint. This contradiction demands to be resolved for the sake of the absoluteness of the absolute standpoint. For it can only prove itself to be absolute by showing that it does not go on endlessly producing and negating its contradiction; it must show that it takes the contradiction up into itself positively, yet without depriving itself of its dialectical independence. The absolute standpoint must therefore without prejudice to its absoluteness lower itself to the relative standpoint and raise the relative up into itself. Intuition must enter into the sphere of reflexion, of particularity [*Einzelheit*], of contradiction, in order to guide reflexion out through itself beyond itself. (§22)

Tillich makes it emphatically clear in the second and more doctrinal part of his earliest "systematic theology" that the theological paradox is to be understood christologically: "In Jesus of Nazareth the theological paradox—that is, the unity of the absolute and the relative in the sphere of the relative—is realised in a single individual." (§37) This paradox, actualised as it is in the symbol of the cross (§§39-42), is the criterion by which the work of the theologian, no less than the rest of the cultural sphere, is measured. Here, as later, Tillich stresses that "the theological system itself is brought under the paradox, which is established by it and realised in it. But the theological system is not the absolute system, no more so than is the system of the sciences out of which it proceeds and to which it returns again. . . ."(§72) Thus, from the outset, Tillich had a strong sense that God is in heaven and man is on earth, even when he is a theologian![21]

There are still other ways in which Tillich's earliest theological thinking was intrinsically dialectical. In 1912, when he was examined for his *Licentiat* in theology, he defended ten theses, the last of which constitutes perhaps his first formulation of the kind of relationship which he envisaged between "message" and "situation":

> The church can faithfully fulfill its apologetic task to the cultured only to the extent that it aspires neither to the vindication and defense of the church's teachings nor to the definition and control of boundaries between faith and knowledge, but aspires rather to exposing the living and dialectical relation of the present cultural situation to christianity.

---

[21]Cf. Karl Barth, *Der Römerbrief* (Zurich: EVZ Verlag, 1967) xiii.

Curiously linked here are the notion of the dialectical interplay between christianity and culture and the apologetic task of the church. At first glance, apologetics and this sort of dialectics would not seem to be wholly compatible, for the usual meaning of *apologetics* is, as in an adversary system of justice, the defense of a particular position in the face of an accusor. The usual meaning of *dialectics* is "a co-operative inquiry carried on in conversation between two or more minds that are equally bent, not on getting the better of the argument, but on arriving at the truth."[22] Even so, apologetics and dialectics are from the beginning closely intertwined in Tillich's methodology. How, then, does he propose to hold the two motives together?

The very structure of *Systematic Theology* suggests the way he eventually came to regard the connection between the two, for each of its five parts consists of the analysis of certain "questions" implied in the human situation and the corresponding "answers" implied in the christian message. Correlation is defined by Tillich principally, though not altogether exclusively, as the sort of relation which ought to obtain between those questions and their answers. Tillich would want us to conclude that this structure reflects a genuinely dialectical process: "Question and answer, Yes and No in an actual disputation—this original form of all dialectics is the most adequate form of my own thinking."[23] Yet, the three volumes of *Systematic Theology* are judged by many not to record the give and take of "an actual disputation." There, questioning and answering are sometimes adjudged as being undertaken in almost total isolation from any real engagement between the apologist and the "cultured," or even between theologians and philosophers generally. Nor could one acquit the author of *Systematic Theology* of the charge that it is more characteristically philosophy and theology, than philosoph*ers* and theolog*ians* who are made to "converse" with one another in that work, with Tillich manipulating the abstractions in such a way that they move inexorably toward "the christian answer" in every case. It is, therefore, little wonder that many critics— and not only those who would discredit him—have accused Tillich of hav-

[22]F. M. Cornford, *Plato's Theory of Knowledge* (London: Routledge & Kegan Paul, 1960) 30.

[23]Kegley & Bretall, eds., *The Theology of Paul Tillich*, 15f.

ing subordinated dialectics "in its original form" to apologetics in the pejorative sense of that term. His usage of the question-answer schema is
most usually cited as the basis for the charge. Yet surprisingly little attention has been given to the role of questioning and answering in the course
of Tillich's development of what is eventually called the method of correlation. Sufficient evidence is now available to allow a reappraisal of this aspect of Tillich's methodology, a reappraisal in which the metaphor of
questioning and answering may fare somewhat better than it has tended
to do in the past.

In the form used in *Systematic Theology*, the question-answer schema
is a fairly late addition to Tillich's methodological apparatus. The concept
of correlation, though used by Tillich as early as 1924,[24] is not explained
specifically in analogy with questioning and answering until 1935.[25] Nor
does Tillich seem even then to have been entirely certain as to the precise
status of "questioning" and "answering," which he introduced tentatively
as "a simile which, I think, is more than a simile."[26] Whatever his doubts
at that stage, questioning and answering, or "dialectics," as an apologetic
technique is nonetheless rooted in Tillich's earliest sustained reflections
on the theological task as recorded in the only recently published *Kirchliche Apologetik,*[27] a document which—having been prepared in 1912-
1913—substantiates in some respects Tillich's later claim that his own
"dialectical" position had been arrived at independently of any contact with
Barth.[28] There is another striking feature of the *Kirchliche Apologetik*
which should not go unmentioned in view of the not uncommon opinion that
Tillich's earliest interests were more nearly philosophical than theological,
and theoretical than practical: namely, the concern exhibited in that work
for the life of the church and the church's mission.[29] But our main interest

---

[24]Cf. *Gesammelte Werke*, Vol. IX: *Die religiöse Substanz der Kultur* (Stuttgart: Evangelisches Verlagswerk, 1967) 32.

[25]In "Natural and Revealed Religion," *Christendom* I:159-70 (1935).

[26]Ibid., 168f.

[27]*Gesammelte Werke*, Vol. XIII: *Impressionen und Reflexionen* (Stuttgart: Evangelisches
Verlagswerk, 1972) 34-63.

[28]*Gesammelte Werke*, I:368.

[29]See *Gesammelte Werke*, XIII:59ff; cf. also I:543ff.

in that work lies elsewhere, in what is there termed by Tillich simply "the dialectical method."[30]

What could be described as the conversational or dialogical character of apologetics is in the main stressed in *Kirchliche Apologetik*. There the apologist is said not to be an authoritative schoolmaster tutoring ignorant pupils;[31] possessing truth only in a relative way, he enters discussion with the "cultured" as a partner, as a fellow-seeker after truth.[32] With truth alone as the object of the apologist's "dialogue," he stands ready to rethink and to modify his own position, as well as critically to test the position of his discussion-partner.[33] He is able to enter the conversation as a partner, rather than as a teacher, because of his realisation that truth is not his private possession and because of his conviction that no truth is ultimately incompatible with christianity.[34] So, according to this early "dialectical method," a final affirmative "Yes" emerges through the give and take of mutual criticism. Tillich does not doubt that this final "Yes" will be an affirmation of christianity, and he is firmly convinced at this point that all spiritual or cultural tendencies must finally find their goal in christianity,[35] which alone is said to have power to give unity to a fragmented culture.[36] Considerable difficulties are created by these final remarks, for they seem not only to beg the important issues but also seriously to undermine the force of Tillich's brave words about the christian apologist's being simply a partner in the mutual search for truth.

There is in fact a certain amount of unresolved tension between the dialectical and apologetic motives within "the dialectical method" as it is presented in *Kirchliche Apologetik*. Two basically different and ultimately competing views of "dialectic" are intertwined in that work. The first sense of dialectic may be termed *dialectic as reciprocal influence*, because the two coequal discussion partners are said mutually to influence one another in the "dialogue" between christianity and culture, between the

---

[30]Ibid., 40.

[31]Ibid., 39.

[32]Ibid., 40-41.

[33]Ibid., 40.

[34]Ibid., 41-42.

[35]Ibid., 41. Cf. *Gesammelte Werke*, XII:96.

[36]*Gesammelte Werke*, XIII:36ff, esp. 38.

apologist and the cultured. This is the sense of dialectic which is in the main stressed in *Kirchliche Apologetik*. And it would not be inaccurate to suggest that this sense of dialectic is most nearly commensurate with what Tillich, beginning in 1919, would refer to as "cultural theology":[37] in both cases the theologian could be said to act as a free agent, so that the discussion would be entirely open-ended and there would be no sure way to predict beforehand where it would lead. Any procedures in which this sense of dialectic was employed would surely afford a thorough going reciprocity between the two partners, yet, it would provide no clear guidelines, much less criteria, for the direction and goal of the "conversation."

Yet there is also another sense in which "dialectic" is employed in *Kirchliche Apologetik*. This second sort of usage can be called the *didactic use of dialectic* since one partner assumes the role of teacher and leads the other to knowledge which is either not otherwise available to him or which, as tends to be the case in *Kirchliche Apologetik*, is extracted from him by socratic midwifery, so that the discussion partner comes to see that he has been "really" religious all along.[38] According to this second use of dialectic, the apologist may be seen as one who skillfully and patiently leads the cultured despiser of religion from one way of seeing things to another, though with his consent at every stage. But, in any case, the apologist speaks from a specific if unacknowledged standpoint and to a definite if undeclared end, namely the persuasion of the other person. This use of dialectic, which is arguably more susceptible to Barth's well-known critique of the ethics of apologetics than is the other sense, corresponds roughly to that which would be appropriate to what Tillich early termed "church theology."[39] Here a definite shape is given to the discussion between the apologist and the cultured, but the element of reciprocal influence is as a consequence greatly diminished, if not largely eliminated. This is hardly the sort of relationship between "question and answer, yes and no in an actual disputation" involving two discussion partners equally bent only on arriving at the truth, regardless of the consequences for their individual positions.

---

[37]See *Gesammelte Werke*, IX:19ff, esp. 28f.

[38]*Gesammelte Werke*, XIII:49.

[39]See *Gesammelte Werke*, IX:27ff.

Fortunately, however, this second sense of using dialectics as an apologetic technique is largely absent from Tillich's early writings which appeared in the years following the first world war. Even though he does not in them continue to talk much of questioning and answering as such,[40] it would not be inappropriate to suggest that most of Tillich's writings from that period presuppose this "conversational" conception of the dialectical character of the theological task. It is precisely this questioning and being questioned, answering and being answered, which gives vitality—as well as persuasiveness—to many of Tillich's writings in the 1920s, produced as they were from the "boundary" between religion and the other spheres of culture.[41] One thinks especially of his essays on religious socialism in which Tillich submits christianity to the radical critique of marxism without allowing marxism itself to go unchallenged by an equally radical critique.[42] And, indeed, the truly dialectical character of his thought is more easily seen when he is dealing concretely with such issues than when, as so often seems in *Systematic Theology*, he simply manipulates abstract concepts such as philosophy and theology.

Questioning and being questioned; answering and being answered— this is the essence of the sort of dialectical method which, from the outset, Tillich intended to follow. The real problem with this sort of usage of the metaphor of questioning and answering is not (as is often supposed) its rigidity, but rather its shapelessness. A vague and even question-begging appeal to "truth" is hardly a sufficient means of protecting (from the theologian's side) the specifically christian character of christianity. This, however, is an issue to which Tillich would later turn his attention.

Even so, this early "dialectical method" can be regarded in an important sense as a first step in the direction which would lead eventually to the method of correlation. There are of course intermediary steps and, as we shall see, not all in the same direction! For it would be just as much a distortion to assert that the sort of questioning and answering formalised in the method of correlation is entirely continuous with this early dialectical method as it would be to deny that there is any connection whatever be-

---

[40]But see *Gesammelte Werke*, Vol. II: *Christentum und soziale Gestaltung* (Stuttgart: Evangelisches Verlagswerk, 1962) 96.

[41]*Religiöse Verwirklichung* (Berlin: Furche, 1930) 11ff.

[42]See *Gesammelte Werke*, II:91ff, 159ff, 219ff.

tween them. There is a gradual but unmistakable modification in the application of the dialectical principle in Tillich's writings subsequent to his brief and only reluctantly accepted appointment as *Extraordinarius* at the University of Marburg in 1924-1925. Two factors may have played a special part in this process: first, the opportunity to offer for the first time courses specifically in christian theology and, second, the contact there with a new style of philosophising.

Tillich's having begun lecturing specifically on systematic theology first at Marburg helps account for one major shift of emphasis in many of his writings in the late 1920s and the early 1930s. For thereafter Tillich tended to write increasingly explicitly as what he would no doubt earlier have termed a "church theologian." This is not to say that he wrote correspondingly less explicitly as a cultural theologian. Rather, it is more accurately the case that after about 1926, in addition to his characteristic themes in cultural theology, one begins to encounter for the first time in any writings after the first world war a sustained discussion of more specifically doctrinal themes, at times in conjunction with and as an extension of long-standing topics, such as *kairos*. Given that the concept of correlation is presented in *Systematic Theology* principally as a means of relating within the context of church theology the christian message and modern culture, such a shift of emphasis is of considerable importance for our understanding of the development of Tillich's concept of correlation.

That such a shift in fact occurred is supported in part by Tillich's tendency in his writings between 1927 and 1933 to lay greater stress upon christology than he had done in those published between 1919 and 1926. This is significant for our purposes in that a specifically christological norm is later employed by Tillich to provide the sort of criterion which is so obviously absent from his earlier usage of the metaphor of questioning and answering. As we have already seen, a similar sort of norm had been a feature of his first sketch of a systematic theology prepared in 1913. So, there is a sense in which this "shift" represents a return to an earlier emphasis. Was there then no "shift" at all?

More surprising than the reintroduction of the christological motif in writings after 1926 is its virtual absence in those which appeared between 1919 and 1926. This motif is perhaps most noticeably absent from the various essays on the concept of *kairos* which were published in the early

1920s. This includes not only the article on "Kairos und Logos,"[43] but also the much cited article entitled "Kairos" which appeared originally in an issue of *Die Tat* which was devoted entirely to the religious socialist movement.[44]

Some readers of *The Protestant Era* might be expected at this point to protest that the essay entitled "Kairos" is shot through with references, both direct and indirect, to christological themes. They might well call attention to the passage in which Tillich distinguished three senses of *kairos*:

> Kairos in its *unique* and universal sense is, for Christian faith, the appearing of Jesus as the christ. Kairos in its *general* and special [*sic*] sense for the philosopher of history is every turning-point in history in which the eternal judges and transforms the temporal. Kairos in its *special* [*sic*] sense, as decisive for our present situation, is the coming of a new theonomy on the soil of a secularized and emptied autonomous culture.[45]

In the ensuing paragraphs it is even made clear that the christological *kairos* is to be regarded as the criterion in terms of which the other *kairoi* are measured.

These words certainly stand in the article which was printed as "Kairos" in *The Protestant Era*, and they also stand in the German translation of the same article which was published in *Gesammelte Werke*.[46] But they do *not* appear in the original version of the article on "Kairos" which was published in *Die Tat* in 1922. Virtually the whole of the section in which the words cited above would be wrongly thought to have appeared had been subsequently rewritten by Tillich in order to accommodate later developments in his thought, including the increasingly close identification of "kairos in the unique and general sense" with the appearance of Jesus as the Christ. As it happens, Jesus Christ is hardly mentioned at all in the 1922

---

[43]The subtitle more precisely defines the object of this article: "eine Untersuchung zur Metaphysik der Erkenntnis." Reprinted in *Gesammelte Werke*, Vol. IV: *Philosophie und Schicksal* (Stuttgart: Evangelisches Verlagswerk, 1961) 43-76.

[44]*Die Tat* XIV (1922): 330-50.

[45]*The Protestant Era*, 46f.

[46]*Gesammelte Werke*, Vol. VI: *Der Widerstreit von Raum und Zeit* (Stuttgart: Evangelisches Verlagswerk, 1963) 24.

version of that article, and then only once in passing at the beginning of section one.[47]

Far from constituting a damaging counterexample, the "Kairos" article of 1922 substantiates my point dramatically. The very fact that Tillich felt compelled to rework extensively that article before allowing it to be "reprinted" in *The Protestant Era,* and to rework it in this particular way, helps corroborate the thesis that christology gains an importance in Tillich's later thought that it did not have in his earlier writings on the philosophy of history and culture.[48] But, when did the shift occur?

That a shift of some such sort is under way might be suspected from a little-known address on "Gläubiger Realismus" which was delivered to a youth group in 1927.[49] Yet, one would have to read with that article at least one other published during that year in order to get a more clearly defined picture of the christological character of that shift. In the article on "Die Idee der Offenbarung," Tillich relates his already familiar views on the "breakthrough" of the unconditioned specifically to christology in a way that he simply never did in his earlier writings.[50] While most assuredly built upon foundations laid in his earlier writings, this specifically christological application nonetheless represents a significant movement toward explicitly doctrinal themes—and toward a more explicitly church theology.

This shift in emphasis was firmly and unmistakably established when, in an article written especially for his collection published in 1930 as *Religiöse Verwirklichung,* Tillich asserted that no one can deal adequately with the main issues of a philosophy of history without dealing with the christological issue.[51] In weighing the significance of this shift, one must bear in mind that Tillich himself had been writing not a little since 1919 on philosophy of history with hardly any direct consideration at all of the chris-

---

[47]"Kairos," *Die Tat,* 330.

[48]Theodor Mahlmann is near the truth when he argues that from the time Tillich came to reorientate his doctrine of *kairos* so that it is identified with the appearance of the christ, he can be said to have become a "church theologian," *ein Theologe der Kirche.* "Eschatologie und Utopie in geschichts-philosophischen Denken Paul Tillichs," *Neue Zeitschrift für systematische Theologie und Religionsphilosophie* VII (1965): 364-65.

[49]Reprinted in *Gesammelte Werke,* IV:77-87.

[50]See esp. *Gesammelte Werke,* Vol. VIII: *Offenbarung und Glaube* (Stuttgart: Evangelisches Verlagswerk, 1970) 36.

[51]*Gesammelte Werke,* VI:83.

tological question! In those writings, it was not so much the *kairos* in the distant past as the present *kairos* which had so obviously caught his imagination. Indeed, Tillich had in those writings—following perhaps Troeltsch—quite explicitly rejected any notion of a *Heilsgeschichte*. So it is not an inconsiderable reversal when in this piece on "Christologie and Geschichtsdeutung" Tillich came to describe Jesus Christ as the centre of history from which the whole of history gets its meaning.[52] This new centre of Tillich's philosophy of history gains fresh significance when, in his open letter to Hirsch in 1934, he speaks of Jesus Christ as the final criterion against which every other historical moment is to be measured.[53] Jesus Christ subsequently comes to be identified by Tillich as the *kairos* in relation to which all other *kairoi* are to be assessed.[54] It is clearly only a short step beyond such statements to say, as he did in *Systematic Theology*, that Jesus Christ—or, perhaps more accurately, the symbol "Jesus as the christ"—is the content of the christian faith, or that the kerygma is the substance and criterion of all theological statements.[55] This new factor in Tillich's thought is a necessary component of the method of correlation, but it is not on its own sufficient to explain the changing role of questioning and answering in his thought.

A second factor in this change may have been Tillich's having come into contact at Marburg with the work of Martin Heidegger, who was at the time preparing to publish his *Sein und Zeit*, the first and only volume of which appeared in the spring of 1927. Some years later Tillich would list that work as being among the ten books which most influenced the formation of his thought.[56] There is, nonetheless, no ready consensus in the literature as to the exact extent of Tillich's intellectual indebtedness to Heidegger. Without denying that he was measurably influenced by Heidegger, it must be remembered that behind the work of both men there stands a common philosophical heritage and a similar reading of that heritage which

---

[52]Ibid., 87f, 93f.

[53]"Die Theologie des Kairos und die gegenwärtige geistige Lage," *Theologische Blätter* XIII (1934): cols. 318-19.

[54]See *Gesammelte Werke*, VI:137-39; *Systematic Theology* (Chicago: University of Chicago Press, 1963) III:369-72.

[55]*Systematic Theology* (Chicago: University of Chicago Press, 1951) I:7.

[56]*Gesammelte Werke*, Vol. XIV: *Register and Bibliographie* (Stuttgart: Evangelisches Verlagswerk, 1975) 222.

predates Tillich's having come into contact, however indirectly, with Heidegger and his students in 1924-1925. To make the point, one need only recall the impact upon each independently of the pre-Socratics, the medieval mystics, Schelling, Kierkegaard and Nietzsche, not to mention Kant and Hegel. Even so, Tillich did more than once explicitly acknowledge his debt to Heidegger.

Whatever the precise extent of Tillich's indebtedness to Heidegger generally, a simple fact cannot be allowed to go unnoticed: the activity of "questioning" and "answering," although surely grounded in Tillich's earliest methodological reflections, gains a new and different significance in his work after the time spent at Marburg. I suggest that it is at least possible that this different significance, which was in any case a gradual development, reflects one aspect of Heidegger's influence on Tillich. It will be remembered that Tillich implies he came to a different understanding of the relationship between philosophy and theology as a result of his contact with Heidegger.[57] The method of correlation was one consequence of that "new understanding."

So far as I have been able to determine from the material at my disposal, whether published or unpublished, the first example of this new use of "questioning" and "answering" after Tillich left Marburg occurs in the prologue to his lectures on epistemology which were delivered at the Technological Institute in Dresden, where Tillich had become *Ordinarious* in 1925. No full manuscript of these lectures exists, but the partial typescript from which Tillich lectured is in the Tillich archive in Germany under the title *Die Gestalt der religiösen Erkenntnis*. It consists of the prologue, an outline of the course and a set of propositions which, as was the custom at that time, Tillich dictated to his students.

In what is available of that series of lectures, one becomes clearly aware that Tillich is in the process of modifying his earlier "dialectical method" so as to accommodate his new understanding from Heidegger of the object of philosophy as the clarification of the question of being. Even so, the role of "questioning" and "answering" had not by then become sufficiently regularised for one to be able yet to speak of "the method of correlation." That degree of standardisation would not be reached until several years later, not until after Tillich's emigration from Germany. That

---

[57]*Gesammelte Werke*, XII:36.

its development had already been begun in earnest, however, is clear from the Dresden lectures.

Tillich's lectures on *Die Gestalt der religiösen Erkenntnis,* which were delivered in 1927-1928, invite brief comparison with his only slightly earlier essay on the philosophy of religion which appeared in Dessoir's *Lehrbuch der Philosophie.*[58] For both in that article and in his lectures on epistemology, Tillich addresses similar issues, including the nature of the boundary line beyond which ontology or metaphysics would pass over into theology and vice versa. Even though the subject matter is similar, the perspective in each is quite different. The notion of philosophical "questioning" and theological "answering" which, as we shall see, is so central in the Dresden lectures, is totally absent both from the article on the philosophy of religion and from *Das System der Wissenschaften,* in each of which the relationship between theology and philosophy is worked out primarily in terms of the dialectic of form and *Gehalt* and the dialectic of autonomy-theonomy. In those works the point at which philosophy passes over into theology and theology into philosophy is the point at which the two are synthesised: "There is both in the doctrine of revelation and in philosophy a point at which the two are one. To find this point and from there to create a synthetic solution is the decisive task of the philosophy of religion."[59] The location of that point is to be determined by an analysis of the place of philosophy and the place of theology in the general system of the sciences. Such an analysis reveals that philosophy's extremity is the point at which it is one with theology so that it is possible for Tillich to speak there of theology as a special sort of metaphysic, a metaphysic which expresses the power and unity of meaning, a metaphysic in touch with its depth, a theonomous metaphysic.[60]

The character of the "boundary" between philosophy and theology is of a very different sort in the Dresden lectures. Tillich there addresses the problem of the transition from philosophy to theology in terms of the transition *from raising ontological questions to receiving theological answers.* Man necessarily asks the question of the meaning of his existence. Implied in this question, however, is the question of being-as-such. This, says Til-

---

[58]Reprinted in *Gesammelte Werke,* I:297-364.

[59]Ibid., 299.

[60]Ibid., 251ff, 278ff.

lich (perhaps following Heidegger), is the question addressed by the philosopher. But, he continues, this time in contradistinction to Heidegger, to ask the question of the meaning of being also inevitably raises the question of that which lies beyond or transcends being, the question of *das Jenseits des Seins*. Although the philosopher can, and even must, raise this question, it is not within his power to form an answer. The philosopher qua philosopher can lead from the ontological analysis of being-as-such to the point where the question is asked as to that which transcends being, but he can go no further without ceasing to be a philosopher. He cannot transgress "the bounds of sense," cannot pass from the phenomenal to the noumenal. When confronted with the question of *das Jenseits des Seins*, the philosopher qua philosopher must remain silent. If he does not remain silent, he ceases to be a philosopher and becomes instead a theologian. That is to say, he can address that question only upon the basis of a disclosure of that which transcends being, or what Tillich later called the power and ground of being. For Tillich, as for Heidegger, the "answer" to the question of the meaning of being cannot be deduced from the analysis of human existence: it must disclose itself. On this account, if no other, one must conclude that the complaint made by many to the effect that Tillich distinguishes philosophy and theology merely by definition is to some extent misdirected. This is not to say, of course, that there are consequently no difficulties whatever in Tillich's attempt to distinguish between them!

The problem arises as to how the philosopher can even broach the question of the transcendent if the answer to that question can come only from something which lies beyond the grasp of man, from *Jenseits des Seins*. Tillich's reply to this question is instructive and, although a full consideration of it is beyond the scope of this article, should be cited:

> Man can ask in earnestness for the transcendent only if the transcendent has already spoken. The voice may be faint, but it is nonetheless operative in ontology at every point. . . . And that means that, rather than the theological's being grounded in the ontological, the ontological is grounded instead in the theological. . . . For it is neither being-as-such nor human existence as such which is primary, but rather that which transcends being.

Despite Heideggerian echoes in this quotation from *Die Gestalt der religiösen Erkenntnis*, Tillich's critique of Heidegger is implicit especially in the last sentence. According to Heidegger, the existential is grounded in the ontological. According to Tillich, however, the ontological in which the existential is grounded is itself grounded in the theological. As he had done earlier with Marxist philosophy, he has now taken Heideggerian philosophy and turned it back upon itself. He has with Heideggerian tools criticised Heideggerian philosophy, thereby carrying through with "socratic irony"[61] the programme projected first in *Kirchliche Apologetik*. Even so, these lectures mark the beginning of an important revision of that earlier dialectical principle, a revision the magnitude of which does not become evident in Tillich's published writings until well after his emigration.

Indeed, were it not for the existence of this partial manuscript of Dresden lectures, it would not be known for certain that Tillich had entertained such ideas as early as 1927, though there are possibly indirect hints in his writings from as early as 1925. For instance, in a lecture delivered first to a group of Marburg students in December 1924, Tillich developed the theme of apologetics as the art of "answering,"[62] a theme which became a leading motif in subsequent writings, including his *Systematic Theology*.[63] In addition, the "boundary" theme is introduced in his collection of essays entitled *Religiöse Verwirklichung* and developed extensively especially in the first essay entitled "Die protestantische Verkundigung und der Mensch der Gegenwart," in which is stressed the limits of human possibility owing to the brokenness of his existence.[64] And, in one of the articles contributed by Tillich to the second edition of *Religion in Geschichte und Gegenwart,* he lays stress on the importance of radical questioning in philosophy,[65] while in another he remarks that philosophy asks the radical question, *die Frage nach der Frage*.[66] Yet, in the latter case, his account of dialectical relations between philosophy and theology is substantially more similar to the 1925 article in Dessoir's *Lehrbuch* than to that exhibited in the Dresden lectures. Nonetheless, in the chapter entitled "Christologie und Geschichtsdeutung" in *Religiöse Verwirklichung,* Tillich wrote in words that clearly anticipate later developments: "Geschichte und Chris-

---

[61]Cf. *Gesammelte Werke*, XIII:40.

[62]*Gesammelte Werke*, XII:81ff.

[63]*Systematic Theology*, III:195.

[64]*Religiöse Verwirklichung*, 25-42.

[65]Hermann Gunkel and Leopold Zscharnack, eds., *Religion in Geschichte und Gegenwart* 2d ed. (Tübingen: J. C. B. Mohr, 1930) IV, cols. 1198-1204.

[66]Ibid., col. 1231.

tologie gehören zusammen wie Frage und Antwort. Wir wollen darum so vorgehen, dass wir zunächst die geschichtsphilosophische Frage entfalten, um dann den Sinn der christologischen Antwort auf zuweisen."[67] This is, so far as I know, the first time that this particular sense of "questioning and answering" appears in Tillich's writings. There is some evidence that at this time Tillich himself was not entirely clear which way such thoughts would lead.[68]

With the benefit of hindsight, *we* know that the method of correlation would not be long coming.

---

[67]*Religiöse Verwirklichung*, 111.

[68]Cf. *Religion in Geschichte und Gegenwart*, vol. IV, col. 1233.

Creation, Fall, and Theodicy in Paul Tillich's *Systematic Theology*

JOEL R. SMITH

Introduction

Paul Tillich states that the distinction between essence and existence is central to his *Systematic Theology*:

> A complete discussion of the relation of essence to existence is identical with the entire theological system. This distinction between essence and existence, which religiously speaking is the distinction between the created and the actual world, is the backbone of the whole body of theological thought. It must be elaborated in every part of the theological system.[1]

While we cannot trace the role played by this distinction throughout Tillich's entire system, we shall focus on its use in one particularly important

---

[1] Paul Tillich, *Systematic Theology* 3 vols. (Chicago: University of Chicago Press, 1967) I:204.

and problematic area of Tillich's theology: the doctrines of Creation and
Fall.

The problem which we shall explore is whether or not the Fall is necessary for the fulfillment of Creation. Tillich himself comes closest to stating that the Fall is necessary for the fulfillment of Creation in the following
passage: "Creation is fulfilled in the creaturely self-realization . . . through
a break between existence and essence."[2] In exploring what Tillich means
by this passage, we shall find that Tillich argues against the idea that the
Fall is necessary for the fulfillment of Creation. His argument rests upon
two key points: the ontological coincidence of Creation and Fall, and the
tragic destiny of human freedom. Tillich holds that these two points are
crucial for any theologian who honestly faces the problem of the relation
between Creation and Fall:

> Every theologian who is courageous enough to face the twofold truth that nothing
> can happen to God accidentally and that the state of existence is a fallen state must
> accept the point of coincidence between the end of creation and the beginning of the
> fall.[3]
> Creaturely freedom is the point at which creation and the fall coincide.[4]

After exploring Tillich's treatment of this problem, and analyzing specific points to show that his view is not entirely satisfactory, we shall turn
to Tillich's discussion of the questions raised by theodicy. We shall contend
that Tillich's view is not satisfactory here either. The problems brought to
light in these two areas—the coincidence of Creation and the Fall, and theodicy—reveal a background tendency in Tillich's system which implies the
Fall *is* necessary for the fulfillment of Creation. We shall suggest that this
problematic tendency raises serious questions about Tillich's theological
method. We shall suggest that Tillich's thinking occurs under the shadow
of Hegel as well as under the shadow of Christian revelation. Consequently,
philosophy and Christian revelation exist in tension in Tillich's theological
method, rather than in correlation.

---

[2] Ibid., I: 256.

[3] Loc. Cit.

[4] Loc. Cit.

The Coincidence of Creation and the Fall

In defining "essence" and "existence," Tillich points to a basic ambiguity in both terms which is justified by the ambiguous nature of existence itself:

> Essence as the nature of a thing, or as the quality in which a thing participates, or as a universal, has one character. Essence as that from which being has "fallen," the true and undistorted nature of things, has another character . . . the ambiguous character of existence . . . expresses being and at the same time contradicts it—essence as that which makes a thing *what* it is (*ousia*) has a purely logical character; essence as that which appears in an imperfect and distorted way in a thing carries the stamp of value. Essence empowers *and* judges that which exists. . . . Whatever exists, that is, "stands out" of mere potentiality, is more than it is in the state of mere potentiality and less than it could be in the power of its essential nature. [5]

The relation between essence and existence is expressed religiously as the relation between the created world and the actual world. Thus Tillich uses the transition from essence to existence to "half-way demythologize" the Christian symbol of the Fall. The Fall is the transition from the essential goodness of creation to the distortion of estranged existence. Yet the logical difference between creation and the fall allows an ontological coincidence between them:

> Creation and the Fall coincide in so far as there is no point in time and space in which created goodness was actualized and had existence. . . . Actualized creation and estranged existence are identical. . . . Creation is good in its essential character. If actualized, it falls into universal estrangement through freedom and destiny. [6]

Tillich wants to hold that existence is estranged while holding that God's creation is good. To do so, he maintains that creation qua essential is good while creation *qua* actualized is estranged. So only unactualized creation is good and created goodness never "existed." Yet to speak of unactualized creation is strange. Creation has the basic sense of "bringing into existence" and so is intimately bound up with some sort of spatio-temporal existence. Creation that is merely "essential" and not actualized in existence would violate all ordinary meanings of the word. Tillich might re-

---

[5]Ibid., I:202-203.

[6]Ibid., II:44.

ply that creation means "bringing into essential being" here rather than "bringing into existence." But by "essential being" Tillich usually means "potentiality,"[7] so creation would then mean "bringing into potentiality." Creation usually involves a transition from potentiality to actuality, so this interpretation sounds strange also. Tillich might reply that potentiality is created out of nothing. God's creation, then, consists of bringing essential or potential being out of nothing. Essential being, in this interpretation, would have a kind of intermediary status between nothingness and existence. It seems that this move would help make sense of Tillich's notion of unactualized creation, yet it remains unsatisfactory. The ontological status of essential being which subsists between nothingness and existence remains problematic. Moreover, creation would still not carry the full meaning that it has ordinarily within the Christian tradition.

We are left, then, with the view that creation requires actualization in order to be creation in the full sense. Tillich seems to agree with this when he says: "Existence is the fulfillment of creation; existence gives creation its positive character."[8] Moreover, in Tillich's explanation of essence and existence quoted on a previous page, he says that whatever exists is not only less than its essential nature but also "*more* than it is in the state of *mere* potentiality" (emphasis added). The implication here would also seem to be that actualization in existence fulfills creation by completing it and giving to it a positive character. Finally, Tillich seems to admit that creation involves actualization in existence when he says: "If God creates here and now, everything he has created participates in the transition from essence to existence."[9] But if creation requires actualization in existence, and existence is estranged, is creation not fulfilled by estrangement? In a reply to Reinhold Niebuhr and two other critics, Tillich modifies his choice of words somewhat:

> . . . the fulfillment of creation and the beginning of the fall are, though logically different, ontologically the same. Perhaps I should have said "actualization" instead of "fulfillment." "Fulfillment" seems to connote that an unfinished creation has been finished in an evil way. This, of course, is not my idea. The fall is the work of finite

---

[7] Tillich most clearly uses "essential" and "potential" interchangeably in the following places: Tillich, II:35, 91, 148; III:12, 113.

[8] Ibid., I:203-204.

[9] Ibid., II:44.

freedom, but it happened universally in everything finite, and therefore unavoid-
ably. . . ."[10]

Here Tillich clearly places responsibility for the fall on human freedom
rather than on God. While creation requires actualization in existence in
order to be creation in the full sense, at the moment of actualization, so to
speak, finite freedom transforms what is essentially good into a distorted
and estranged existence. While actualization in existence does fulfill creation in the sense of giving it a positive character, human freedom's key
role here results in distorted actualization. In this way Tillich holds human
freedom to be responsible for the estrangement of existence while cred-
iting God with a good creation.

We should emphasize here that in our interpretation it is not actualization of creation per se that distorts creation. Creation requires actualization to be creation in the full sense, so its actualization in existence is
essentially good. Whenever actualization occurs, however, human freedom participates and causes the actualization to be an estranged existence. Existence and essence need not be estranged, as the New Being in
Jesus the Christ exemplifies. Both God and man contribute to the actualization of creation. God's contribution is good while man contributes the
estranged character of existence. Actualized creation and estranged existence are identical not because actualization per se results in estrangement, but because human freedom always participates in actualization and
always distorts it. God's creation, as actualized, is estranged because actualization occurs, in part, through human freedom.

Tillich clearly maintains that estrangement occurs through the power
of finite freedom and is not a structural necessity. Yet estrangement always
occurs and so is tragically universal:

> . . . theology must insist that the leap from essence to existence is the original
> fact—that it has the character of a leap and not of structural necessity. In spite of
> its tragic universality, existence cannot be derived from essence.[11]

Tillich's distinction between tragic universality (or universal destiny) and

---

[10]Charles W. Kegley and Robert W. Bretall, *The Theology of Paul Tillich* (New York:
Macmillan, 1964) 342-43.

[11]Tillich, *Systematic Theology*, II:44.

structural necessity is crucial for his view that God is not responsible for estrangement. But what does it mean to assert that something always occurs universally yet is not necessary? It is not enough simply to assert the distinction. Tillich is obligated to explicate it. Yet he allows it to remain a verbal distinction without showing that it expresses any real difference.

When we examine Tillich's description of how the Fall occurs through human freedom, it becomes even more difficult to accept his claim that the Fall is not a structural necessity. The state "before" the Fall—the dreaming innocence of undecided potentialities—drives beyond itself. [12] The possibility of the transition from essence to existence is experienced as a temptation. Finite freedom is aware of itself as finite, as threatened by nonbeing, and so is anxious. This anxiety of freedom is one of the driving forces behind the transition from essence to existence. The very structure of finite freedom, then, includes the "drive" toward actualization. Since actualization and estrangement occur universally, this "drive" is always enacted. Although it is enacted through freedom, since this "drive" (which *is* a structural necessity, I assume) *always* leads to actualization and estrangement, it is difficult to see the difference between the universal destiny of freedom and a structural necessity within freedom.

Tillich speaks to this issue in discussing the reality of Christ's temptations. [13] The desire for finite fulfillment, and so the drive toward actualization, are not bad in themselves and are not incompatible with man's essential unity with God in the dreaming innocence "before" the Fall. The temptation is that this desire will be changed into concupiscence. Concupiscence is the distorted self-transcendence which consists in the unlimited desire to use the power of one's finite freedom for one's self. Yet the same problem arises here for Tillich. In the actualization of finite freedom, desire is *always* changed into concupiscence, so that man's tragic destiny is that he always yields to this temptation. Once again, although desire becomes concupiscence through freedom, it is difficult to see the difference between the tragic destiny of freedom and a structural necessity immanent to freedom.

Tillich focuses the issue most clearly when he speaks of the "double threat" man experiences, which is rooted in the structure of human free-

---

[12]Ibid., II:33-36.

[13]Ibid., II:127-32, especially 129.

dom and expressed in anxiety.[14] In the state of "aroused freedom," man is caught between the desire or drive to actualize his freedom and the demand to preserve the state of dreaming innocence. The dilemma of freedom is that man not only experiences anxiety over losing himself through actualizing his freedom, but also experiences anxiety over losing himself by *not* actualizing himself. Loss of self is possible either way. This dilemma, a kind of "double bind," is characteristic of the structure of finite freedom and so would seem to be a structural necessity. Part of freedom's structure, then, is that it requires actualization in existence in order to avoid loss of self, yet this actualization is always estrangement. Man need not actualize his freedom *if* he wishes to avoid the threat to his being imposed by not actualizing himself. Although it is through the power of his finite freedom that he (always) decides for actualization, the choice is between two anxieties which threaten the loss of self. This dilemma is structurally necessary, it seems, so that a basic ambivalence lies at the heart of human freedom.

Given this double threat and double anxiety intrinsic to the structure of freedom, it is difficult to see how Tillich can call the Fall the "work of finite freedom" without more qualification than he provides. The dilemma of human freedom, as just described, seems to circumscribe man sufficiently so that the Fall can be said to be his "free choice" in only a very attenuated sense. Consider the following simple but instructive analogy. Suppose someone arranges things so that we have only two courses of action. We may lie warm and inert in bed all of our life, or we may get out of bed and live an active life in the cold world beyond our bed. Suppose further that we are aware that to remain in bed is not to actualize important potentialities and so to lose our self. Yet to get out of bed is to actualize our potentialities in such a way that we are estranged from our essential being and so lose our self. If we choose to get out of bed, and by doing so Fall and become estranged, then there is an obvious sense in which someone might say that it wasn't necessary that we get out of bed, but that we did so freely and so we are responsible for our Fall. But there would also be an obvious sense in which our original situation was so severely circumscribed that whoever arranged things for us would share responsibility for our Fall. Why couldn't our original situation have been arranged so that

---

[14]Ibid., II:35-36.

staying in bed would not foreclose important potentialities and so result in loss of self? Why couldn't getting out of bed result in a healthy life without estrangement rather than a Fall? By structuring the situation as he did, whoever arranged the context in which our choice occurred must share partial, if not major, responsibility for the Fall that resulted.

The problem becomes even more difficult for Tillich when we consider God's directing activity. So far we have only argued that God shares some responsibility for the Fall because of the way in which he created the structure of human freedom. But God's directing activity also seems to "direct" finite freedom toward actualization. Tillich makes the general point that the divine creativity drives every creature toward fulfillment, which requires actualization in existence:

> The concept "the purpose of creation" should be replaced by "the telos of creativity"—the inner aim of fulfilling in actuality what is beyond potentiality and actuality in the divine life. One function of the divine actuality is to drive every creature toward such fulfillment.[15]

More specifically, Tillich states that the actualization of finite freedom is required for the fulfillment of God's creation:

> In maintaining that the fulfillment of creation is the actualization of finite freedom, we affirm implicitly that man is the *telos* of creation.[16]

In these passages, we clearly see that actualization is intimately bound up with God's directing activity for creation in general and for man in particular. Both creation and finite freedom would be unfulfilled if they were not actualized in existence. The inner aim of divine creativity would not be fulfilled unless creation and finite freedom were actualized in existence.

The actualization of human freedom is part of the *telos* of divine creativity, yet this actualization universally involves estrangement. We have suggested that the tragic universality of estrangement comes close to being a structural necessity. Even if Tillich is able to maintain his distinction, however, it seems that God's directing activity, and not simply human

---

[15]Ibid., I:264.
[16]Ibid., I:258.

freedom, is at work in the transition from essence to existence. For Tillich says:

> Providence is a permanent activity of God. He never is a spectator; he always directs everything toward its fulfillment. Yet God's directing creativity always creates through the freedom of man. . . .[17]

This means that the Fall is, indeed, the work of human freedom, but that it is also the work of divine creativity, in that God's directing activity is present in the Fall.

It is not the case that divine creativity qua Providence fore-sees and fore-orders estrangement by fore-seeing and fore-ordering the actualization of finite freedom. Tillich clearly holds that creatures are not the sole agents with God as a spectator, nor that creatures are cogs in a machine with God as the sole agent.[18] Rather, mutual activity of creatures and God is involved. But this is precisely our point—the Fall is not simply the work of human freedom, it is the work of human freedom *and* divine creativity. Tillich always emphasizes that the Fall occurs through both freedom and destiny. What he does not usually indicate, which we are trying to bring out, is that the divine creativity bears major responsibility for the role destiny plays in the Fall. The most explicit passage we can find where Tillich recognizes this is the following:

> . . . God's directing activity in the case of man works through his freedom. Man's destiny is determined by the divine creativity, but *through* man's self-determination, that is, through his finite freedom.[19]

God's role in determining the tragic destiny of the Fall is clearest in the double threat and double anxiety of freedom discussed earlier. Human freedom, when it becomes conscious and so is "aroused," is caught between the demand to preserve dreaming innocence and the desire to actualize its freedom. We have now seen that the actualization of human freedom is part of the *telos* of the divine creativity. Human freedom is subject to a kind of "demand" to actualize itself as well as not to actualize itself.

---

[17]Ibid., I:266.

[18]Loc. Cit.

[19]Ibid., II:130.

The desire or drive toward actualization is not merely human in origin, but is also rooted in the divine *telos* for man. It seems that finite freedom always chooses actualization, at least in part, due to the directing activity of God. The choice between dreaming innocence and actualization, then, is not arbitrary, nor equally weighted, nor rooted solely in human freedom. The choice of actualization by human freedom is destined in the sense of being directed by Providence. In fact, it is directed sufficiently so that this choice always occurs. This is not to say that the Fall is completely determined by God, for His directing activity does occur through human freedom. But if our interpretation is correct, then to say that the Fall occurs through freedom and destiny is to say that it occurs through human freedom and the directing activity of the divine creativity.

Does Tillich's view imply that God fulfills creation by directing human freedom to actualize itself in an estranged way? We might defend Tillich by saying that while God directs finite freedom towards actualization, He does not direct it toward estranged actualization. The estranged character of actualization would be due to man, not to God. Yet actualization seems to entail estrangement. Human freedom, in order to actualize what it essentially is, seems to be required to participate in a break between essence and existence. Tillich says:

> Man has left the [divine] ground in order to "stand upon" himself, to actualize what he essentially is, in order to be *finite freedom*. . . . Fully developed creatureliness is fallen creatureliness. The creature had actualized its freedom in so far as it is outside the creative ground of the divine life. . . . To be outside the divine life means to stand in actualized freedom, in an existence which is no longer united with essence.[20]

Human freedom has the choice to preserve innocence or to actualize itself. It does not have the choice to actualize itself in either an estranged or a non-estranged way. To choose actualization is necessarily to choose estrangement. We have seen that although it is technically free not to choose actualization, finite freedom always does choose it because this is necessary to avoid one kind of loss of self, and because the divine creativity directs finite freedom toward actualization in order to fulfill creation and man. God does not will estrangement per se. But we have argued that fulfillment of creation requires actualization, and actualization requires es-

---

[20]Ibid., I:255 (brackets added).

trangement. God does will the fulfillment of creation, and to do so is to will estrangement as a (perhaps unfortunate) consequence. To will the end of fulfillment of creation is to will the means, or concomitant consequences, of actualization and estrangement. In short, Tillich's view implies that God fulfills creation by directing human freedom to actualize itself in an estranged existence.

Let us return to the passage we quoted in the Introduction and which we set out to explicate:

> Creation is fulfilled in the creaturely self-realization which simultaneously is freedom and destiny. But it is fulfilled through separation from the creative ground through a break between existence and essence. Creaturely freedom is the point at which creation and the fall coincide. [21]

We have seen that human freedom is, indeed, the "place" where creation and fall coincide and the locus for both freedom and destiny. However, we have argued that creation and fall coincide in such a way that we cannot simply say, as Tillich usually does, that the fall is the work of human freedom. The way in which human freedom has been structured by God, and the way in which God's directing activity works through human freedom, means that responsibility for the fall must be shared by human freedom and the divine creativity. To say that creation and the fall "coincide," in our interpretation, is to recognize the complex mutual involvement of both man and God in both creation and fall. We have already touched on issues that this interpretation raises for theodicy. We shall now turn to Tillich's theodicy more explicitly and evaluate it in terms of the interpretation offered in the preceding pages concerning the coincidence of creation and the fall.

Theodicy

In order to understand Tillich's theodicy, we must understand more fully how evil is rooted in estrangement. For Tillich,

> . . . estrangement points to the basic characteristic of man's predicament. Man as he exists is not what he essentially is and ought to be. He is estranged from his true being. [22]

---

[21] Ibid., I:256.
[22] Ibid., II:45.

Man's estrangement is both fact and act,[23] both predicament and sin,[24] for it occurs through both personal freedom and universal destiny, as we have seen. The three marks of estrangement are unbelief, concupiscence, and *hubris.*[25]

In essential being, the state of dreaming innocence "before" the Fall, the ontological polarities

> lie within each other, distinct but not separated, in tension but not in conflict. They are rooted in the ground of being, i.e., the source of both of them and the ground of their polar unity.[26]

In contrast, in estranged existence conflict occurs in the ontological polarities so that nonbeing threatens man. Moreover, the categories of finitude are also transformed in estranged existence:

> The structure of finitude is good in itself, but under the conditions of estrangement it becomes a structure of destruction.[27]
>
> The transformation of essential finitude into existential evil is a general characteristic of the state of estrangement.[28]

These passages show Tillich's sharp distinction between finitude and estrangement. Being and nonbeing are both present in the structure of finitude, so anxiety is essential to finitude and not a distortion of it. In estrangement, however, nonbeing predominates over being so that the courage to accept anxiety cannot occur. Estrangement transforms essential finitude into the structure of destruction. Every act of human freedom presupposes the estrangement which it seeks to overcome and so fails to overcome it.[29] One comes to the end of one's possibilities and is driven to despair:

---

[23]Ibid., II:55-58.

[24]Ibid., II:44-47.

[25]Ibid., II:47-55.

[26]Ibid., II:62.

[27]Ibid., II:71.

[28]Ibid., II:68.

[29]Ibid., II:78-80.

Despair is the state of inescapable conflict. It is the conflict, on the one hand, between what one potentially is and therefore ought to be and, on the other hand, what one actually is in the combination of freedom and destiny. The pain of despair is the agony of being responsible for the loss of the meaning of one's existence and of being unable to recover it. One is shut up in one's self and in the conflict with one's self. One cannot escape, because one cannot escape from one's self.[30]

Yet structures of healing and reunion, as we shall see, are also marks of existence, alongside those of destruction.[31]

In estrangement, then, finitude is characterized as evil and as the structure of destruction. For Tillich, theodicy is intimately bound up with the coincidence of creation and the Fall. For evil is a consequence of sin, and sin is the consequence of human freedom:

If one is asked how a loving and almighty God can permit evil, one cannot answer in the terms of the question as it was asked. One must first insist on an answer to the question, How could he permit sin?—a question which is answered the moment it is asked. Not permitting sin would mean not permitting freedom; this would deny the very nature of man, his finite freedom.[32]

In the other passage where Tillich most explicitly addresses the problem of theodicy, he distinguishes moral evil (sin, self-destruction, and such—what is due to human freedom) from non-moral or physical evil (pain, death, and such—what is independent of human freedom):

Physical evil is the natural implication of creaturely finitude. Moral evil is the tragic implication of creaturely freedom. Creation is the creation of finite freedom; it is the creation of life with its greatness and its danger. . . . The creation of finite freedom is the risk which the divine creativity accepts. This is the first step at an answer to the question of theodicy.[33]

Tillich's justification of non-moral or physical evil is much too casual to be entirely satisfactory. We shall grant Tillich's basic point that creaturely finitude, by its very nature, requires physical evil. However, does crea-

---

[30]Ibid., II:75.

[31]Loc. Cit.

[32]Ibid., II:61.

[33]Ibid., I:269.

turely finitude require the degree of physical evil that does, in fact, characterize existence? Certainly we can conceive of a world in which creatures are finite as in this world, and so physical evil is present, yet in which physical evil is not present to the same degree. In such a world, suffering would indeed occur due to non-moral evil, but it would not wreak the incredible toll that it does in this world. We can imagine a world in which natural laws were just different enough so that there were substantially fewer earthquakes, or disease not due to human actions took a substantially smaller toll, and so on. Earthquakes, disease, and so forth would still cause suffering to man due to creaturely finitude. But the world would be better adapted to its creatures so that less suffering occurred. Or creaturely finitude itself could have been created with greater abilities so that man could cope with physical evil better. For example, the advances of medical science which alleviate suffering could come sooner if human intelligence were greater, perhaps. Certainly medical advances have been held back by moral evil as well as non-moral evil. But if human destiny had included greater abilities (although still finite abilities, of course), much human suffering might not have occurred.

A similar argument can be brought to bear concerning moral evil. We grant Tillich's basic point that creaturely freedom requires moral evil. However, does the existence of creaturely freedom preclude limitations being set upon that freedom when a certain level of horror begins to occur? If finite freedom is to be finite freedom, it must be able to sin and do evil to some extent. But would restrictions on human freedom when it reached the level of gross atrocities really deny the nature of man? If Hitler had been prevented from waging the Holocaust, either through limitations inherent to finite freedom or through some kind of presence of divine activity in the world, would the nature of man have been denied? In our interpretation, finite freedom would still be finite freedom if it were allowed to do as it wished up to a point, but not beyond that point. In this way, much suffering due to moral evil would be avoided.

We do not mean to say that the considerations we have raised show that Tillich's view cannot be maintained. His view might well be able to respond adequately to these objections. We do claim, however, that these objections are tenable enough to show that Tillich has not dealt adequately with these areas of theodicy in his *Systematic Theology*. Perhaps he has dealt with them more adequately elsewhere. Even if he has, however, a theological system which does not discuss them more adequately than his system does is seriously deficient.

Whether or not Tillich has adequately justified his view, he does claim that theodicy is not essentially a question about either moral or non-moral evil. The central question of theodicy, rather, is why it seems that some beings are excluded from any kind of fulfillment.[34] Tillich offers two answers based on the principle of participation. Tillich says that questions concerning individual fulfillment must also be questions concerning universal fulfillment. His first solution centers on "representative fulfillment" and "mystery":

> One might speak of a representative fulfillment and nonfulfillment, but beyond this one must refer to the creative unity of individualization and participation in the depth of the divine life. The question of theodicy finds its final answer in the mystery of the creative ground.[35]

Tillich's second solution centers on his claim that the divine life participates in the negativities of existence, even though God as being-itself transcends nonbeing absolutely:

> . . . it is meaningful to speak of a participation of the divine life in the negativities of creaturely life. This is the ultimate answer to the question of theodicy.[36]

Tillich's first solution in terms of "representative" fulfillment through the principle of participation is not developed in Volume I where the passage we quoted above occurs. However, Tillich does develop his idea further in Volume III in terms of "essentialization" and "vicarious" fulfillment. The question of the meaning of distorted forms of life which exclude beings from any kind of fulfillment cannot be answered at all if one assumes separate individual destinies.

> The question and answer are possible only if one understands essentialization or elevation of the positive into Eternal Life as a matter of universal participation: in the essence of the least actualized individual, the essences of other individuals and, indirectly, of all beings are present. . . . And he who is estranged from his own es-

---

[34]Loc. Cit.

[35]Ibid., I:270.

[36]Loc. Cit.

sential being and experiences the despair of total self-rejection must be told that his essence participates in the essences of all those who have reached a high degree of fulfillment and that through this participation his being is eternally affirmed. This idea of the essentialization of the individual in unity with all beings makes the concept of vicarious fulfillment understandable.[37]

Tillich's solution in terms of "representative" or "vicarious" fulfillment seems to us to be less than adequate. Tillich has made fulfillment or nonfulfillment the central question of theodicy. But all theological questions are existential and refer back to the person who asks the question.[38] The person who asks about fulfillment or nonfulfillment is the *total* man *as existing* and it is about himself as concretely existing that he asks. Representative or vicarious fulfillment may offer some consolation, but it does not fully respond to the estrangement and lack of fulfillment experienced by that person. The fact remains that the person has "experienced" fulfillment "vicariously" or "representatively" at best, and this is something less than fulfillment in the complete sense required by the question. Tillich's view helps here, but it is not a complete solution, and the question of theodicy remains to plague his system.

The problem is not only confined to those beings who are excluded from any kind of fulfillment. For all beings in life remain unfulfilled in an important sense for Tillich. Life is based on the transition from essence to existence and so is always an ambiguous mixture of essential and existential elements:[39]

> In all life processes an essential and an existential element, created goodness and estrangement, are merged in such a way that neither one nor the other is exclusively effective. Life always includes essential and existential elements; this is the root of its ambiguity.[40]

Life remains ambiguous as long as there is life.[41]

---

[37]Ibid., III:409.

[38]Ibid., I:269.

[39]Ibid., III:30-32, 96.

[40]Ibid., III:107.

[41]Ibid., II:4.

The experience of estrangement leads to the quest for an unambiguous life which would result in the unambiguous fulfillment of essential being. [42] Yet Tillich points out that

> this quest is for a life which has reached that toward which it transcends itself. . . . [But] the self-transcendence of life never unambiguously reaches that toward which it transcends. [43]
>
> . . . in every act of the self-transcendence of life profanization is present or, in other words . . . life transcends itself ambiguously. [44]

There are, indeed, religious symbols for unambiguous life: Spirit of God, Kingdom of God, and Eternal Life. But the quest for unambiguous life cannot be fulfilled:

> The quest for such unambiguous life is possible because life has the character of self-transcendence. . . . But under no dimension does it reach that toward which it moves, the unconditional. It does not reach it, but the quest remains. [45]

This means that those beings who experience some degree of fulfillment, and not only those who are excluded from any kind of fulfillment, ask the question of theodicy regarding the impossibility of living an unambiguous fulfillment of essential being. The New Being, as exemplified in Jesus the Christ, answers this question for Tillich from another direction. In Jesus the Christ, finite freedom is actualized in existence but without existential disruption. [46] Jesus the Christ exemplifies the essential unity of man and God *in* existence and not merely an essential or potential, as is the case in dreaming innocence. [47] The categories of finitude and the tensions of the ontological polarities are actual in Him and His temptations are real. [48] Jesus the Christ fully participates in finitude, anxiety, and the am-

---

[42]Ibid., III:107.

[43]Loc. Cit. (brackets added).

[44]Ibid., III:87.

[45]Ibid., III:109.

[46]Ibid., II:148, 110.

[47]Ibid., II:150.

[48]Ibid., II:127.

biguities of life, but their actualization in existence does not result in estrangement from God:

> The conquest of existential estrangement in the New Being, which is the Being of Christ, does not remove finitude and anxiety, ambiguity and tragedy; but it does have the character of taking up the negativities of existence into unbroken unity with God.[49]

To put it in other words, ontological anxiety is present in Jesus the Christ, but all forms of despair are absent.[50]

Of course, it is a paradox that Jesus the Christ, the essential unity of man and God, is fully subject to the conditions of existence and yet conquers existential estrangement.[51] And although the New Being is present in Him, it is fulfillment "in principle," that is, the manifestation of the power and the beginning of fulfillment, and so possesses an eschatological dimension.[52] Whoever participates in Jesus the Christ participates in the New Being, but only fragmentarily and by anticipation.[53] The fulfillment exemplified in Jesus the Christ and participated in by those who participate in Him, is "realized eschatology" in that no other principle of fulfillment can be expected and nothing qualitatively new will appear regarding fulfillment.[54]

Tillich's view concerning fulfillment "in principle"—fulfillment which has such a strong eschatological dimension—raises the problem again regarding the adequacy of his answer to the question of theodicy. Once again, it seems to us that the question of theodicy is, indeed, an existential question in the radical sense. It is the existing individual who asks about fulfillment of his essential being and he asks about fulfillment in existence. Fulfillment which is fragmentary and anticipatory may provide some consolation, but it does not adequately solve the existential problem lived by the existing individual, for the individual remains with his quest for unambiguous life with no hope of attaining unambiguous life. Fulfillment of his

---

[49]Ibid., II:34.

[50]Ibid., I:201.

[51]Ibid., II:94, 97, 126, 159.

[52]Ibid., II:119, 164.

[53]Ibid., II:70, 118, 167.

[54]Ibid., II:119.

essential being cannot occur in existence except ambiguously, fragmentarily, and by anticipation. Tillich's view, and perhaps any Christian view, offers a kind of fulfillment and so offers consolation. But the question concerning fulfillment in existence is not answered adequately enough to provide a satisfactory theodicy.

Tillich's claim that Jesus the Christ conquers estrangement "in principle" leads to the second solution of theodicy mentioned previously. The ultimate answer to the question of theodicy is that the divine life participates in the negativities of existence. We have already seen that Jesus the Christ participates fully in the negativities of existence but not in estrangement. Tillich rejects the view that God the Father suffered in Christ, and emphasizes that God as being-itself transcends nonbeing absolutely. Yet one can speak of the divine life participating in the negativities of life in that

> . . . God as creative life includes the finite and, with it, nonbeing, although nonbeing is eternally conquered and the finite is essentially reunited within the infinity of the divine life.[55]

Tillich does not explicate how this provides the "ultimate answer" to the question of theodicy. He may have in mind that the inclusion of the finite and of nonbeing, as conquered, guarantees representative or vicarious fulfillment for all beings. We have already criticized this view. Or he may have in mind that human suffering under the conditions of existence is justified by God's participation in the same conditions of existence. Two objections are in order here. First, presumably the divine life includes the finite and nonbeing but not estrangement. Indeed, to say that nonbeing occurs in the divine life *as conquered* is to say that estrangement is not present there. If this is true, then the divine life does not participate in existence in the same way that finite freedom does. Tillich cannot argue that human estrangement is somehow justified because God also undergoes estrangement, for God does not seem to participate in estranged existence but only in undistorted existence.

Second, even if God were to share man's predicament in the full sense, this would not justify the human predicament. There might be some consolation, or courage, or sense of fellowship to be derived from God's participation in the human situation. But if someone is responsible, in part,

---

[55]Ibid., I:270.

for a situation of estrangement and suffering, that responsibility is not removed simply because the estrangement and suffering are shared. Consider the simple analogy where a father has some kind of complicity for his child's act of blinding himself. If the father were then to blind himself so as to share his son's predicament, the father's initial complicity would not be removed, although father and son might feel consoled or reconciled. At best, then, Tillich's answer to theodicy here helps somewhat, but does not fully answer the radical existential question implied in the problem of theodicy.

All of the solutions to the question of theodicy proposed by Tillich rest, in different ways, on his notion of participation. This notion seems to play a crucial role in his theology, including his theory of religious symbols which we have not discussed. Yet Tillich does not explicate this notion adequately enough. If it is to be strong enough to carry the weight which it needs to in Tillich's thought, it needs to be developed in more depth. Sometimes Tillich seems to appeal to "mystery" as his last defense. In the passage quoted earlier, Tillich says that the final answer concerning theodicy rests in the mystery of the divine ground with its unity of individualization and participation. Tillich also states that the Fall is "irrational":

> . . . the transition from essence to existence, from the potential to the actual, from dreaming innocence to existential guilt and tragedy, is irrational. In spite of its universality, this transition is not rational; in the last analysis it is irrational. . . . It is an undeniable fact which must be accepted, although it contradicts the essential structure of everything created.[56]

We have a mixed reaction to Tillich's ultimate appeal to mystery and the irrational. In one respect it is refreshingly honest, in that it is a kind of admission that Tillich has not satisfactorily answered these questions. In another respect it also seems reasonable to hold that human reason is unable to comprehend and resolve these issues in the final analysis. But in yet another respect, it seems to render Tillich's theology inadequate, in spite of its depth and insightfulness. In a slightly different though related context, when discussing the question of the negative in eternal blessedness, Tillich rejects "escape into the divine mystery," saying: "If theology

---

[56]Ibid., II:91.

refuses to answer such existential questions, it has neglected its task."[57] Tillich has certainly attempted to answer the questions involved in theodicy, and we admire the seriousness and insightfulness of this attempt. But we contend that Tillich has not been successful, in the final analysis, and so his theology, while not neglecting this task, has not accomplished its task.

Conclusion

We would like to conclude with some remarks on more general implications of Tillich's view of the coincidence of creation and the Fall and of theodicy. We do not want to suggest that the interpretation which follows is one that Tillich is logically committed to beyond the shadow of a doubt. Nor do we suggest that this is even the major emphasis that lies in the background of his system. We do contend that the problems we have raised concerning Tillich's views reveal a tendency within his system that should be recognized, and it is a tendency which Tillich and his commentators seldom acknowledge. This tendency in Tillich's system raises serious questions about his theological method.

The basic focus is Tillich's description of how estrangement—the transition from essence to existence—occurs and what meaning it has. In the first section of this essay, we argued in favor of the following points:

(1) Creation requires actualization in existence in order to be creation in the full sense. It could not remain merely essential or potential and still be creation in the full sense.

(2) Tillich does not adequately explicate the distinction between structural necessity and tragic universality. He does not show that a real difference is expressed by this verbal distinction.

(3) The structure of finite freedom includes a "drive" toward actualization. Since this "drive" is always enacted, it is difficult to see how actualization is not a structural necessity.

(4) God's directing activity is present in finite freedom. God directs both creation and finite freedom to their fulfillment through actualization in existence.

(5) Finite freedom is structured so that it is subject to a double threat and a double anxiety; not to actualize itself in existence is to lose itself, yet to actualize itself in existence is to lose itself.

---

[57]Ibid., III:404.

These five points, if they are correct, show that Tillich cannot simply say, as he does, that the Fall is the work of finite freedom. Our interpretation, based on these five points, is that estrangement is determined *by* the divine creativity *through* man's self-determination.[58] This means that the divine creativity and human freedom share responsibility for the Fall— estrangement is the work of both God and man. This is the meaning we feel must be given to the passage quoted at the beginning of this essay: "Creation is fulfilled in the creaturely self-realization . . . through a break between existence and essence."[59]

In the second section of our essay, we examined Tillich's theodicy to see if he was able to answer the question posed by existential estrangement in any other way. We argued in favor of the following points:

(1) Finite freedom can never succeed in its quest for unambiguous life. The unambiguous fulfillment of essential being cannot occur in human existence.

(2) Tillich does not adequately justify the existence of physical evil and moral evil in terms of creaturely finitude and creaturely freedom, respectively. One objection was raised in each case to show that Tillich's discussion needs further development.

(3) Representative or vicarious fulfillment, though helpful, does not provide an adequate answer to the radically existential question of theodicy.

(4) Fulfillment "in principle" and fulfillment in a fragmentary and anticipatory way do not provide an adequate answer to the radically existential question of theodicy.

(5) The divine life's participation in the negativities of existence does not provide an adequate answer to the question of theodicy.

(6) The appeal to the divine mystery as an answer to the question of theodicy is, perhaps, an honest and necessary move, but it prevents theology from completing its task.

If we are correct in the weaknesses we have pointed out in Tillich's view of the coincidence of creation and the Fall and of theodicy, then we must ask if there is any tendency in his system which would explain these weaknesses. Tillich obviously does not want to claim that estrangement is the *telos* of creativity. The aim of the divine creativity is to fulfill creation and to conquer estrangement. Fulfillment of creation includes fulfillment of the finite, as Tillich indicates when he says the New Being does not sac-

---

[58]Ibid., II:130.

[59]Ibid., II:45.

rifice finite being but fulfills it by conquering its estrangement.[60] In using metaphors such as "conquer," "overcome," and "victory" with regard to estrangement, Tillich makes clear that the negative is not absent in the divine life. It is present, but it is present as conquered. Tillich indicates this is true with respect to the New Being as exemplified in Jesus the Christ. Perhaps it is clearest near the very end of his system where he speaks of eternal blessedness:

> It is the nature of blessedness itself that requires a negative element in the eternity of the Divine Life.
> This leads to the fundamental assertion: The Divine Life is the eternal conquest of the negative; this is its blessedness. Eternal blessedness is not a state of immovable perfection. . . . But the Divine life is blessedness through fight and victory.[61]

We suggest that the background tendency revealed by our critique is that the divine creativity fulfills creation *by means of* its conquest of estrangement. We mean this in the strong sense that without estrangement, there could be no fulfillment. Estrangement is the *way* to fulfillment. Indeed, estrangement is required if there is to be fulfillment. At the end of his system, Tillich offers the following general observation:

> Creation into time produces the possibility of self-realization, estrangement, and reconciliation of the creature, which, in eschatological terminology, is the way from essence through existence to essentialization.[62]

The weaknesses we see in Tillich's system suggest that creation is fulfilled *by means of* rather than *in spite of* estrangement. Creation, and most eminently finite freedom, can be both actualized and in unity with God (reconciled) only if it is subject to estrangement which is conquered. The divine creativity directs this process. Reconciliation, not estrangement, is the *telos* of this process. But this *telos* can occur only by way of estrangement.

There are several passages where Tillich hints of this. In a passage which is suggestive but which we do not put too much weight on because

---

[60]Ibid., II:88.

[61]Ibid., III:405.

[62]Ibid., III:422.

it is primarily making a different point and only hinting at our point, Tillich says that "God is creatively working in us—even if his creativity takes the way of destruction."[63] A more significant passage for our interpretation is the following: "He has the character of all life, namely, to go beyond himself and to return to himself."[64] A similar point is made while being qualified in the following:

> . . . the eternal identity of God with himself . . . does not contradict his going out from himself into the negativities of existence and the ambiguities of life. He does not lose his identity in his self-alteration.[65]

The background tendency we are trying to bring out is a quasi-Hegelian dialectic in which actualization occurs through a process of estrangement which culminates in reconciliation. We argued earlier that creation requires actualization to be fulfilled and that actualization brings estrangement as the mutual work of the divine activity and human freedom. Tillich identifies the divine life with the divine creativity, saying that creation is God's destiny as well as His freedom.[66] Although Tillich says earlier that God has no destiny because He *is* freedom,[67] and although these terms must be taken symbolically when applied to God, we suggest that the background meaning of God's destiny is that the creative activity works *by way of* estrangement. God's destiny is His struggle with, and victory over, estrangement. Fulfillment of creation requires actualization in existence which brings with it estrangement. To be Himself qua creative, God must direct creation through finite freedom to actualization, estrangement, and victory over estrangement.

If our interpretation of this background tendency in Tillich is correct, then it raises a basic issue regarding his theological method. Our interpretation would indicate that the philosophical tendency in the system risks gaining ascendency over Christian revelation. The shadow of Hegel would fall over Tillich more strongly than the shadow of Christian revelation, or at least the orthodox interpretation of Christian revelation. Perhaps our

---

[63]Ibid., II:78.

[64]Ibid., II:90.

[65]Ibid., III:405.

[66]Ibid., I:252.

[67]Ibid., I:185.

view would resolve the problems we pointed to regarding the coincidence of creation and Fall and regarding theodicy. Perhaps our interpretation would render Tillich a more consistent philosopher. Yet Tillich would be less of an orthodox Christian theologian, we feel. This suggests that there are tensions in the method of correlation that Tillich does not recognize. The background tendency we have brought out indicates that philosophy and theology exist in tension in Tillich's system, rather than in correlation.

Life and Selfhood
in Tillich's Theology

EBERHARD AMELUNG

"Life" as an Issue in Ethics

Life has become a central issue in ethics. Of course, there is no ethic that does not deal with life when it reflects the course of human action. But "life as such"—considered in the past to a certain degree to be the pre-ethical presupposition of the moral life—has become a moral issue.

But what is life? Ethicists—secular, Catholic and Protestant alike—seem to be rather helpless when confronted with this new focus upon an old issue. Bonhoeffer states in his *Ethics*, "So long as we live, so long as we do not know the boundary of life, death, how can we possibly say what life is in itself? We can only live life; we cannot define it."[1] On the contrary, Eberhard Jüngel asks: "He who wants to speak about death, must understand something of life. Do we understand enough of life in order to be able to speak about death?"[2] We do not. But our time and its problems do not allow us to be silent either.

---

[1] D. Bonhoeffer, *Ethics* (London: The Macmillan Co., 1969⁷) 217.

[2] E. Jüngel, *Tod* (Stuttgart: Kreuz-Verlag, 1971) 25.

PROPOSITIONS CHARACTERIZING OUR TIME. Three basic propositions may characterize our situation. They should define the ethical problem, even the perplexing character of our situation as people living in the Western world, as politicians, as scholars concerned with ethics.

(a) The first proposition: *Growth is dangerous.* In light of numerous reports and studies and a growing body of literature dealing with growth, I do not think that it is necessary to elaborate this proposition. In our context only the background of cultural values needs to be clarified. This proposition signifies that two basic maxims of our Western culture must be defined and limited by a third one. The two are: (1) human life is good, and (2) a better life is better. The third one, however, whose criteria are still open for discussion, may read: Common survival is our only chance. These three maxims determine the character of the proposition: Growth is dangerous.

(b) The second proposition: *In the Western world, the right to live is essential.* We cannot retreat from the conviction that in the broadest sense of the word we must take care of human beings. In this way, our private and public health-services are based on the conviction that human life is good, and that we must do whatever we can in order to protect the right to live.

(c) The third proposition: *The right to live is essential in the third and fourth world.* This proposition is the ethical form of the commandment to preach the Gospel to all the people of the world and it is the simple consequence of everything that was done by Christian missions during the past two hundred years.

If we place these three propositions in the corners of a triangle we find all basic social and ethical problems of our time situated on its sides.

These few remarks, much too briefly presented, may be enough to justify an interest in human life as such.

METHODOLOGICAL PROBLEMS OF THE DEFINITION OF LIFE. But again: What is human life? In trying to find an answer we immediately encounter methodological problems. Bonhoeffer is right when he says: "We can only live life: we cannot define it." And yet, we must define life in order to deal with the social-ethical problems of our days. But because we are living life, its concept cannot be gained in the way we gain other concepts. We live—and we express what life is for us. We actualize life and we are its meaning.

This fact is basic and includes all human beings. In every society, however, some people are called to define life more effectively than others because they determine and control it in a special way. It is their *calling* to determine and control it in a special way. Either society endows them with power to do it or they have received special abilities or education. Such people are mainly doctors and nurses, but also judges, policemen, teachers, and social workers. In different ways, they all interpret for others what life is. In retrospect philosophers, theologians and politicians try critically to conceptualize the meaning of life that others produce through their action. To a high degree, the lives of all of us depend on the ethos created by people in these special groups; therefore, we are interested in the way they fulfill their jobs.

Some Problems in Paul Tillich's Concept of Life

Until Paul Tillich wrote Volume III of *Systematic Theology*, there were very few systematic treatments of the concept of "life." This was one reason why Tillich perceived it to be a risky undertaking. In face of the unnecessary brevity of this paper, I will not be able to delineate Tillich's concept in detail. I must confine myself to some remarks on the conceptual frame of reference and to sketch some problems I find in connection with these frames of reference. Later I would like to develop my own thoughts concerning the concept of life by reflecting upon the implications of the concept of "power of being."

THE BASIC TENSION IN TILLICH'S CONCEPT OF LIFE. I would like to begin with a rather surprising observation. It is surprising that even though Tillich always used his concepts rather freely, laying them aside for a long time and then taking them up again at another time, he never gave reasons why he left them and why he took them up again. The central definition of being as "the power of being" that is all important for Volume I of *Systematic Theology* and for the book, *Love, Power, and Justice*, almost disappears throughout the second and the third volumes of *Systematic Theology*. In the context of the discussion of "life," it does not have any significance at all.

The basic tension is best expressed in the following two quotations from *Love, Power, and Justice*:

The will to power is not the will of men to attain power over men, but it is the self-affirmation of life in its self-transcending dynamics, overcoming internal and external resistance.[3]

Nobody can say where the final limits of human power lie. In his encounter with the universe, man is able to transcend any imaginable limit. But there is a limit for man which is definite and which he always encounters, the other man. The other one, the "thou," is like a wall which cannot be removed or penetrated or used. He who tries to do so, destroys himself. The "thou" demands by his very existence to be acknowledged as a "thou" for an "ego" and as an "ego" for himself. This is the claim which is implied in his being.[4]

The tension I see (and which applies to Tillich's entire anthropology) is found in the following paradox: There is, on the one hand, the power of being, the self-affirmation of life, that overcomes internal and external resistance. There is, on the other hand, the "thou" that definitely limits the "ego" by its very existence as an ego. The question arises: What is the "power of being" when it does not overcome the external resistance exercised by the "thou"? What kind of power is active in the encounter of person with person if it does not touch the "ego" and the "thou" in their very beings? In the following, I would like to analyze this tension as far as possible within the framework of this paper.

The reader of Tillich's writings is confronted with two difficulties as far as the concepts of "life" and "power of being" are concerned: (a) Up to the writing of Volume III of *Systematic Theology*, Tillich does not really differentiate between "being," "life" and "everything real."[5] (b) Life according to Tillich contains essential and existential elements. But often it is difficult to ascertain whether certain statements pertain to the essential or the existential level. This is true particularly for the basic statements on "person" and "personality."

THE THREE FRAMES OF REFERENCE.   There are three frames of reference for the concept of live. The first consists in the basic ontological analysis. In his early paper on "The Idea and Ideal of Personality," Tillich relates personality immediately to being itself.

---

[3]P. Tillich, *Love, Power and Justice* (New York: Oxford University Press, 1954) 37.

[4]Ibid., 78.

[5]Cf. for instance, *Love, Power and Justice*, 54.

> Personality, the possession of control over one's self, is rooted in the structure of being as being. The depth of reality is freedom, the ultimate power of being is power over itself. And the individual personality is the place within the whole of being where this becomes manifest and actual.[6]

From this idea two central aspects of the idea of life are delineated. On the one hand, "power over itself" represents the basis of the concept of the centered self. On the other hand, the presupposition that "personality is that being which has power over its own being . . . leaves two possibilities for any personal life. Either the *power* of being or the power *over* being prevails. In the first case . . . life is kept open. In the second case, the fullness of life, its natural strength, is weakened or completely repressed."[7] These two possibilities are later seen as the basic life processes. But the concept of life in relation to the ontological analysis has not yet been developed by Tillich.

The ontological analysis of being itself is supposed to be the basis of the description of essential life. "Self" and "world" make up the basic structure as delineated in Volume I of *Systematic Theology*. This structure unfolds itself into the polarities of "Individualization and Participation," "Dynamics and Form," and "Freedom and Destiny." The threat of non-being endangers these polarities also and represents the basis of man's ontological anxiety.

> Self-relatedness produces the threat of a loneliness in which world and communion are lost. On the other hand, being in the world and participating in it produces the threat of a complete collectivization, a loss of individuality and subjectivity whereby the self loses its self-relatedness and is transformed into a mere part of an embracing whole. Man as finite is anxiously aware of this two-fold threat.[8]

Thus the ontological elements are not excluded from the basic mixture of essential and existential elements.

In part IV of his system, Tillich deals with the concept of life *in extenso*. Basic for his description are the two possibilities that he attributes to any personal life. They represent the *second* frame of reference. Life as such

---

[6] P. Tillich, *The Protestant Era*, translated and with a concluding essay by James Luther Adams (Chicago: University of Chicago Press, 1957[4]) 118.

[7] Ibid., 119.

[8] P. Tillich, *Systematic Theology* (Chicago: University of Chicago Press, 1959[6]) I:199.

is the going out of a center and the returning to it. Accordingly, Tillich distinguishes three elements in the process of life: self-identity, self-alteration, return to one's self.[9] This dialectic is so important that he can call it the basis of all dialectical thinking.[10]

Tillich combines this dialectical process with the polarity of the ontological elements. Self-integration relates to individualization and participation; self-creativity to dynamics and form; self-transcendence to freedom and destiny. "The three functions of life unite elements of self-identity with elements of self-alteration. But this unity is threatened by existential estrangement, which drives life in one or the other direction, thus disrupting the unity."[11]

The polarities are not only endangered in their essential nature by nonbeing, but also in the process of actualization, for "life is neither essential nor existential but ambiguous."[12]

Tillich, however, is not able to keep up the systematic of this twofold categorization. This, of course, is not a fault as such, for life withdraws from a strict conceptualization. But the way the systematization breaks down is rather significant. There are two interesting points:

(1) The third polarity related to self-transcendence, i.e., to the function of religion, has lost all relationship to the basic movement of life. Tillich does not speak any longer about "the returning to one's self" but about the vertical dimension, about life transcending itself.[13] It is introduced as a special function of life and later related to the postulate of freedom.[14]

---

[9]P. Tillich, *Systematic Theology* (Chicago: University of Chicago Press, 1963) III:30.

[10]Cf. "Man kann von einer Dialektik der Lebensprozesse sprechen, denn es handelt sich um einander entgegengesetzte Bewegungen, um ein Ja und ein Nein wie in einem philosophischen Dialog. Alles dialektische Denken ist nur ein Spiegel dieses Lebensprozesses."

"Die Bedeutung der Gesundheit," P. Tillich, *Gesammelte Werke* (Stuttgart: Evangelisches Verlagswerk, 1967) IX:288. The article is translated from "The Meaning of Health," *Perspectives in Biology and Medicine* (Chicago, 1961) V:1:92-100.

[11]*Systematic Theology*, III:32.

[12]Ibid.

[13]Cf. for instance, *Systematic Theology*, III:31 and 86.

[14]"The polarity of freedom and destiny . . . creates the possibility and reality of life's transcending itself. Life, in degrees, is free from itself, from a total bondage to its own finitude. It is striving in the vertical direction toward ultimate and infinite being." Ibid., 86.

(2) In the argument of part IV only the first element of each polarity is relevant. The function of morality is bound to the concept of individualization, integration, and centeredness. The function of culture depends on dynamics and growth. Participation and form, the other poles of each polarity, are not discussed in this context. Participation, however, receives some emphasis within the context of growth that is dealt with under the heading of the second polarity. Tillich notes:

> Individual life moves within the context of all life; in each moment of a life process, strange life is encountered, with both creative and destructive reactions on both sides. Life grows by suppressing or removing or consuming other life. Life lives on life.
> This leads to the concept of struggle as a symptom of the ambiguity of life in all realms but most properly speaking in the organic realm and most significantly in its historical dimension. [15]

Summing up the argument we may state: the concept of life was developed almost independently from the ontological elements and their polarity. The latter—the polarity—was replaced by the threefold dialectic of integration and disintegration, self-creativity and destruction, self-transcendence and profanization. A further proof of our argument may be found in the article, "The Meaning of Health."[16] Here Tillich presents a short form of his theory of life without any reference to the polarity of the ontological elements and even to the third movement of life. The article was written about the same time as the third volume of *Systematic Theology*.

The *third* frame of reference for anthropological statements is the encounter of person and person. This theme, almost unchanged, runs through all of Tillich's writings. As early as 1926 Tillich wrote: "A person becomes aware of his own character as a person only when he is confronted by another person. Only in the community of the I and the Thou can personality arise."[17] In 1960 he states: "A person becomes a person in the encounter with other persons, and in no other way."[18]

---

[15]Ibid., 53.

[16]*Gesammelte Werke*, IX:287-96.

[17]*The Protestant Era*, 125. Here the English translation of 1948 is identical with the German text of 1926.

[18]P. Tillich, "Existentialism, Psychotherapy and the Nature of Man," *Pastoral Psychology*, II:105 (June 1960): 16.

Little was said by Tillich as far as the character of this encounter is concerned. It raises several problems. The first relates to the quality of the statements on the essential/existential level. This problem was felt by Renate Albrecht, the editor of Tillich's *Gesammelte Werke*, in face of an argument in *Morality and Beyond.* To Tillich's sentence: "The moral imperative is the demand to become actually what one is essentially and therefore potentially,"[19] she asked: " Are 'essential being' and 'to be a person' in this context identical?" Tillich answered the question positively. Her next question reads: "How are the concepts 'essential being' and 'to be a person' related to each other?" The answer: "Every essential being is potential as far as its actualization is concerned. In this regard they are identical. They are different in that which is expressed by the English word 'possible.' 'Possible' is that potential which is actual in existence."[20] In other words: "To be a person" is potential as far as its actualization is concerned. In distinction from "essential being," "to be a person" is actually possible within existence. For Tillich, the following equation is valid: essential being = individual being = centered being = integrated being = to be a person. The Thou, the encounter, are categories of existence by power of which being a person becomes possible, the essential within the realm of existence.

The answers given to the questions of the editor solve one problem but still leave the questions open as to which specific role the encounter of persons or the community of persons take within the process of becoming a person. Tillich may say: "A person becomes a person in the encounter with other persons."[21] In this case, the Thou in the encounter is cooperative in the process of becoming a person. Tillich also says:

> The source of these commands is the moral norms, that is, the essential structures of encountered reality, in man himself and in his world. . . . How does man become aware of the ought-to-be in his encounter with being? . . . "Oughtness" is basically experienced in the ego-thou relation . . . the other self is the unconditional limit to the desire to assimilate one's whole world, and the experience of its limit is the experience of the ought-to-be, the moral imperative. The moral constitution of the self in the dimension of the spirit begins with this experience.[22]

---

[19] P. Tillich, *Morality and Beyond* (New York: Harper & Row, 1963) 20.

[20] *Gesammelte Werke* (1965) III:81.

[21] Cf. Note no. 18.

[22] *Systematic Theology*, III:40.

In this case, the Thou is the source of the moral command, the possible ground of self-realization. The moral act is the self-actualization of the centered self and the constitution of the person as a person. The emphasis is on the self, whereas the Thou receives the function of a revelatory source of an important (or the central) possibility of the self.

What really happens in the encounter of person and person remains open. In part IV of *Systematic Theology*, Tillich states: "It would be possible to continue the discussion of centeredness and self-integration in relation to participation and community, but this would anticipate descriptions which belong to the dimension of the historical. . . ."[23] Unfortunately, in part V, the problem has not been dealt with. We will return to the problem in our concluding remarks.

THE FOURTH FRAME OF REFERENCE.   There is, however, one line of argument in Tillich's thought that begins with the concept of "power of being" and that ends in concrete descriptions of human encounter. Tillich touches on this argument whenever he deals with power as such. In *Love, Power, and Justice* we read:

> In any encounter of man with man, power is active, the power of the personal radiation, expressed in language and gestures, in the glance of the eye and the sound of the voice, in face and figure and movement, expressed in what one is personally and what one represents socially. Every encounter, whether friendly or hostile, whether benevolent or indifferent, is in some way, unconsciously or consciously, a struggle of power.[24]

At many places similar quotations can be found. Dealing with life Tillich argues similarly under the pole of dynamics, growth and participation.[25]

A new problem, however, develops as far as the effects of man's power on man are concerned. In place of many other examples I like to present two quotations from the lecture on "Power" Tillich gave in Berlin in 1953.

> Alles Leben . . . treibt über sich selbst hinaus: es drängt nach vorn, es laüft vorwärts, und wahrend es das tut, begegnet es dem Leben in einem anderen menschlichen Individuum, das auch vorwarts treibt oder sich zuruckzieht oder stillsteht

---

[23]Op. cit., 41.

[24]*Love, Power and Justice*, 87.

[25]Cf. *Systematic Theology*, III:52ff.

und Widerstand leistet. In jedem Falle solcher Begegnungen ist eine andere Konstellation das Resultat. Man zieht eine andere Macht des Seins in sich hinein, und wenn man das tut, wird man entweder gestarkt oder geschacht; man stosst die fremde Macht des Seins voc sich, oder man assimiliert siche vollig in sich; man formt sie um, oder man unterwirft sich ihren Forderungen. Man ist in sie hineingenommen und verliert seine eigene Seinsmacht, oder man wachst mit ihr zusammen und starkt die Seinmachtigkeit beiderseits.

Das Leben hat keinen statischen Charakter. Die Machtigkeit des Lebens, die Seinsmacht, die Fahigkeit, Nichtsein in sich aufzunehmen und zu uberwinden, entscheidet sich in der Begegnung und nur in der Begegnung, sie ist nicht statisch festgelert, und man weiss nicht, wie stark sie ist. Niemand weiss es. Darum muss eine Entscheidung mit Risiken gesucht werden. Risiko heisst, dass die Gewaltanwendung notwendig und zerstorerisch sein kann. Damit sind wir in der tragischen Dimension alles Lebendigen, namlich dass die Selbstverwirklichung des Endlichen zur Selbstzer storung und zur Zerstorung des anderen fuhrt. Ware die Welt statisch, dann ware sie in Wirklichkeit die Welt der reinen Wesenheiten im platonischen Sinne. Aber das ist nicht der Charakter der Welt. Die Welt hat den Charakter der dynamischen Selbstverwirklighung und damit der unendlichen Tragik.[26]

In the first quotation the encounter has possibly positive and negative aspects; in the second the encounter has only tragic consequences. Man exerting power on man can only destroy. The argument relates to our second frame of reference, the line of argument that emphasizes centeredness of the person. Important here is the description of the powerful character of the human encounter. It definitely occurs under the condition of existence; but it is not exclusively a category of estrangement. It seems that the power of being of persons is strengthened in the process of the encounter.

The multidimensionality of Tillich's conceptual apparatus comes to the fore when one discovers that he subsumes the ideas on human encounter also under the concept of "authority in fact." In *Love, Power, and Justice* he states:

> Quite different is the "authority in fact" which is exercised as well as accepted by each of us in every moment. It is an expression of the mutual dependence of all of us on the other; it is an expression of the finite and fragmentary character of our being, of the limits of our power to stand by ourselves. For this reason it is a just authority.[27]

"Authority in fact" as qualification of mutual dependence as an expression

---

[26]*Gesammelte Werke*, IX:210 and 212.

[27]*Love, Power and Justice*, 90.

of power of being has anthropological consequences that I would now like to delineate.

The Context of Controlling and Determining

Tillich points to a fact that is basic for all life and includes his concept of "power of being." Since the day we were born, even prior to our birth, we codetermine the possibilities of life of our fellow men. We cannot withdraw from the necessity of such codetermination. Intersubjectivity and interdependence among men are not an addition but are the substance of human life. We live in such a context that we cannot help controlling and determining each other's life and being controlled and determined by others.

Men have manifold relationships to each other. Within these every existing being has (or much more *is*) the power to change the constellation of the world and between men. I prefer to define "power" in this context with the sociologist Karl Otto Hondrich (Frankfurt/Main) as the chance of units of a social system to satisfy their own needs over and against the needs of others.[28] There are, of course, situations when needs can be satisfied apart from competition with others. But human finitude makes for continuous needs. Here power has its basis. A power-hierarchy develops according to the different chances to fulfill needs.

A THEOLOGICAL ARGUMENT. Anthropological, sociological, and theological arguments are always interwoven as far as the understanding of life is concerned. Genesis 1:26 may be selected as basis for a theological argument. The verse that is decisive for any theological anthropology reads: "Let us make men in our image, after our likeness. . . ." The Revised Standard Version, interestingly enough, reads along the lines of traditional theological anthropology: "Let us make man. . . ." The plural appears twice in verse 1:26. The first usage has been frequently examined and interpreted. The second, however, has found few commentators even though many noticed it and saw the decisive difference between the Elohist and the Jahwist text. In the Jahwist, when creation is finished, man stands alone and is only later joined by his wife. In the Elohist, on the other hand, there are many men at the beginning, humanity as such.

---

[28]K. O. Hondrich, *Theorie der Herrschaft* (Frankfurt: edition suhrkamp, No. 599, 1973) 30.

Theological anthropology is mainly based on the Jahwist text, and has suppressed the fact that the Bible speaks of many men and women at the beginning of time and creation. The correlation to the second Adam, of course, was another reason for this fact.

According to Genesis 1:26 the individual could not be considered unless the many were alive with him. Alive with him: the word according to the Old Testament means to stir up, to be in motion, to transcend the given toward the other.

The second point to be made concerns the "likeness of God." It also applies not to the single individual but to humanity as such. Humanity is created in his likeness, as God's partner. Hence, men live with each other as God lives with man; they behave to each other as God behaves to men. This correlation, then, includes that they *may* love and they *may* control and determine; they should love and they should determine, they must love and they must determine. It has to be done in this relation and in this correspondence. And yet, it has to be done in order that humanity is humanity in the likeness of God. It has to be done in fear and trembling just as it stands that God deals with his creatures in fear and trembling. The likeness of God is not added to life; it is essential to it. Where there is human life it is imbedded in the polarity of the ability to love and of the necessity to actualize the being of power, to exercise power, to control and determine other people's lives. In other words: Life is life always in the context of power and, if it goes well, in the context of love.

From the point of view of theology, however, another qualification must be added. Man controls and determines his fellowman and vice versa. But God tells him to let his behavior be qualified by love and not by death, to give him the "telos" love and not death. This is the real polarity that has come into the world through the incarnation. The word reveals that our controlling and determining power is a power that is directed at and shaped by love or death.

By this alternative we have corrected the earlier alternative between the controlling and loving. The word reveals that man under the condition of estrangement cannot but use his power as "power to death"; only under the condition of *grace* can he exercise the power that is directed at and is shaped by love.

FREEDOM, LOVE AND PERSONALITY.   The controlling power of men over men has taken on different forms in the history of mankind. There is a long history of successful and unsuccessful determination. Controlling power and authority based on divine degree, however, is not restricted to special institutions and special orders of creation. If there is any order of creation at all, then it is the pattern of controlling and determining each other's lives. Government as an expression of controlling and determining is in a certain sense democratized by the order of creation. We all, all men and women, stand under responsibility because we all control and determine other lives.

The process of controlling and determining has been institutionalized and has become subject to technical conditions. No longer does it only function from person to person directly but the process is accomplished by different means. This development has reinforced the tendency among men to give up the right to control and determine. Life seems to be simpler without the use of this special power. This unwillingness to exercise the power to control and to determine has reflected upon the concept of freedom and personality as well. This is a long story that for the sake of brevity we must compress into one sentence. We will not become persons by dissolving institutions which suppress us, but through our attempts to control them. Education to freedom, therefore, is education to the willingness to be a responsible person. Our humanness cannot be set against our basic vital constitution; it only can be its correlate.

The same principle also applies to love. To love means to deal with people in such a way that they gain the courage to determine and to control, while, at the same time, understanding that they have to be determined and controlled. Love is a dialectical movement that grows out of the interdependence of life; it follows life and anticipates it at the same time, so that the connection of mutual controlling and determining always gains a new quality. In one word, love is life with imagination.

It is because love follows upon life that power and love are related in such a close way. Love is a quality of the dynamics of power. Power that is directed at and shaped by love, however, wants more. It wants partnership that is more than partnership; it wants equality that is more than equality; it wants codetermination that is more than codetermination. There is coercion in love. But it is more than a coercion that solicits understanding, that accrues from the conviction that does not say: I must force you because I am right. It coerces because of the other's interest and because of the common future. The one can coerce the other under the conviction and in the hope that the other will likewise coerce, whenever it is necessary, for the common good. He who loves, says: I force you so that you may be strong. He who uses power to death says: I force you so that you will be weak.

The Right to Live and the Quality of Life

THE ONE AND THE OTHER.   The given definition of life has consequences for any system of ethics. There are three basic sentences—in the realm of middle principles—that can clarify these consequences.

To give to someone the right to live means, at the same time, to render to him/her the right to determine and to control other lives. Not one separated, individual life is at stake if we speak about life, but there are always many lives concerned. This fact can best be demonstrated with regard to the abortion issue. The value of the life of the fetus cannot be established separately from the life of the mother. Not only the mother determines the present life and the future fate of the child by the way she lives during pregnancy but also vice versa. The fetus also takes from the mother whatever it needs for its own development. As far as possible it defines the coexistence of mother and child in its own interest. Therefore as far as abortion is concerned, the right of the fetus to live cannot be the exclusive argument.

CHANGE OF THE QUALITY OF LIFE.   The right of one person to live necessarily influences the quality of life of the next. This consequence is basically valid because we are finite. However, it does not always apply because goods in the broadest sense of the word are not always scarce, even though scarcity in all areas of life increases rapidly.

The quality of life is a function of valuing in interpersonal relationships. In the process of controlling and determining, the quality of another life may be increased or diminished; both possibilities are given. In the process two factors or presuppositions become relevant. On the one hand, there is the possibility of personhood and our ability to differentiate our needs; on the other hand, there is the power which Tillich calls "Spiritual Presence."

The modification of the quality of life that depends on the existence of another person is related to one's ability to differentiate his/her needs. Quality of life in the form of the standard of living is without doubt a societal category. It cannot be dissociated from the common weal. But within this frame of reference there is a broad spectrum of possible evaluations of needs. Therefore, the very existence of another human being can be judged to increase the value of life even though the costs are high. For this valued relationship other needs can be abandoned. However, the value of the quality of life is a matter of personal evaluation. Over a longer period of time it may be difficult to stand by this personal evaluation against the societal evaluation of certain needs.

The positive modification depends, secondly, not only on the existence of another person but also upon the presence of the Spirit. One who destroys the connection of determining and controlling cannot be loved.

THE RIGHT TO LIVE AND THE SCARCITY OF MEANS. The third consequence, finally, includes the counter-thesis. Under the condition of human finitude and the scarcity of goods of life, one individual's right to life means a restriction of the quality of life of the others. For this consequence proofs can be found easily in and around any hospital of any country. Many of today's problems in medical ethics are related to this consequence. Whether or not a life is still worth living depends not only on the particular condition of the dying but also on the social context in the broadest sense. This context reaches from the personal relationship of a dying human being to the exploding costs of medical care that restrict the quality of life in other areas. But beyond that, there is an intimate connection between the preservation of life under any conditions in the hospitals of the societies with a high standard of living and the death by starvation of many people in other parts of the world.

The flux of our thoughts has returned to its beginning. We have returned to our basic propositions stated at the beginning of this essay. We cannot think about life as such without considering the quality of life. When the question of the "better life" is asked, then the floor is open for the discussion of the problem of what makes life worth living or not worth living. Americans may suppress this question (as it has been done in Germany for some time) and for good reason. But when the questioning has started, the problem can no longer be suppressed. Therefore I am sure we will discuss these problems for some time to come.

Concluding Remarks

We have already delineated the two basic maxims of Western culture, "human life is good" and "better life is better." These maxims were so unquestionably valid that only marginal groups reflected on the content of the "better life." Sometimes the oppressed sang: We shall overcome! Mostly they did not need to reflect on the quality of life because they knew what the better life is, namely, not to be sick, not to be hungry, and not to be deprived of human rights.

In a time when growth has become dangerous and when the right to live is claimed by all persons and for all persons, reflection upon life as such and its relationship to the quality of better life is the specific task of all those who are able to reflect critically. There is hard labor ahead of us, labor that requires the discipline of thinking, the knowledge of the thinking of the past, the openness for new ideas, the wide range of interest for all areas of life and finally sympathy for man in his predicament. I think we can learn all that from Paul Tillich.

And yet, we may be his students only if we read and study his writings critically. Therefore we may conclude with some very sketchy, critical remarks.

We tried in this paper to think through one specific line of argument out of Tillich's system. In doing so, perhaps, we dissolved a polarity that he tried to uphold, the polarity between individualization and participation. [29] Tillich attempted to deal with both poles. But despite the seriousness with which he speaks about the problems of participation, in the last analysis the polarity breaks down in favor of the self. Tillich has done more than most German philosophers and theologians in order to overcome the individualistic approach of German Idealism. And yet, perhaps due to the influence of C. G. Jung and psychotherapy, the self remains the center of the system. As Tillich grew older this tendency became stronger. In the course of this development his ethic also remained strongly individualistic. In *Morality and Beyond*, he writes: "the moral act is always a victory over disintegrating forces and . . . its aim is the actualization of man as a centered and therefore free person."[30] One could imagine that the aim of the moral act was defined as "the community of centered and therefore free persons." If this change would occur the entire system would look differ-

---

[29]In *The Courage To Be* (New Haven: Yale University Press, 1952) 86ff. Tillich most strongly emphasizes the polarity. There he also treats the concept of "participation." The treatment, however, remains curiously undialectic. He speaks almost exclusively of the subject, the Ego, who participates, but he loses out of sight completely the subject who is participated in himself.

[30]*Morality and Beyond*, 21.

ent. The way things stand now Tillich may not escape the reproach that in his system the "I" needs the "thou" because the "I" is estranged. The "I" uses the "Thou" in order to regain the centered self, in order to become a person. Due to this basic tendency even the concept of love, in spite of the clear distinctions and analyses related to it, somehow remains shallow. Tillich does not succeed in freeing love—so to speak—from the bondage of justice. [31] Finally, this may be the reason why Tillich does not come to terms with the concept of peace since the right understanding of love reflects itself in the concept of peace.

There are two lines of argument in Paul Tillich's system. One concentrates on individualization, the other on participation. In our paper we selected the one on participation for some reflections on anthropology and ethics. Did we neglect the other line? In the first volume of *Systematic Theology*, Tillich argues: "Ontologically the whole precedes the parts and gives them their character as parts of this special whole. It is possible to understand the determinacy of isolated parts in the light of the freedom of the whole . . . but the converse is not possible."[32] Hence, ontologically, participation takes priority to individualization. Then our line of argument may be justified even from the point of view of Paul Tillich.

---

[31]Cf. *Love, Power and Justice*, 72-90.

[32]*Systematic Theology*, I:184.

Part III
TILLICH'S
THEOLOGY OF CULTURE:
APPRAISALS OF
ITS STRENGTHS,
WEAKNESSES,
AND CONTEMPORARY
RELEVANCE

Philosophical Influences on Tillich's Development of a Theology of Culture

JOHN HEYWOOD THOMAS

One of the most revealing features of much recent Tillich study has been the appreciation of his solidarity with Barth and the other theologians who were concerned to offer a genuinely religious evaluation of culture. [1] Also this same analysis of Tillich has made clear the significance of the historical context of Tillich's early work, the importance of which for a reading of his later work has been evident to scholars for some time. Thus, as Professor Jean-Paul Petit points out[2] the sense of desolation which was the aftermath of World War I, the conviction that it had left "the whole house in ruins," was the decisive influence on all Tillich's reading and thinking for years to come. In a sense, then, the idea of a theology of culture was a response to this sense of desolation. That sense is that in which one can speak of all Tillich's work up to 1930 as the development of an understand-

---

[1] Cf. Jean-Paul Petit, *La Philosophie de Religion de Paul Tillich* (Montreal: Fides, 1974) 27.

[2] Op. cit., 23-24.

ing of religion in the total context of philosophy. The paper on the theology of culture is therefore to be viewed together with Tillich's first published article which appeared in the very same year, the article, "Der Sozialismus als Kirchenfrage." This pleads for a positive stance toward socialism on the basis of the theological critique of the bourgeois attitude of the Church which had joined forces with the exploiting powers. This alliance with socialism reveals the first current of thought which I wish to isolate as a philosophical influence; but it is not easy to identify the philosophy concerned.

We know from Tillich's own memoirs[3] that after the Russian Revolution of 1917 he and other thinkers met to discuss religion and socialism. Tillich does not identify these thinkers any more than he makes at all precise the definition of his role in the Religious Socialist Movement. Certainly he says that this was the first time he used the concept of kairos which he describes as "the hallmark of German religious socialism"[4] and that he edited and contributed to the two volumes of *Kairos (Zur Geisteslage und Geisteswendung*, 1926, and *Protestantismus als Kritik und Gestaltung*, 1929).[5] Further, he gladly and readily confesses his debt to Marx, saying that as early as 1905-1906 he had come under his influence as well as that of Kierkegaard's "aggressive dialectics."[6] Therefore it is all too easy for us to imagine that the current of thought with which we are here concerned is Marxism and that the theology of culture is some neo-Marxist weltanschauung. Thus it could be argued that what Tillich has done is to synthesise the Protestant critical attitude, "the Protestant principle," with the Marxist dialectic. This *could* be argued because it is clear that Tillich did seek a critique of idealism which was the ideology of the bourgeois society. This critique he saw adumbrated in the work of Schelling and Kierkegaard and his reference to this in the context of his being "on the boundary with Marxism" could likewise be seen as confirmation of the Marxist influence. Were we to take this view we would see his concern with concrete historical processes and events and his stress on the world of power and economics as typically Marxist motifs. This is to interpret the theology of

---

[3]Paul Tillich, *On the Boundary*, 78.

[4]Ibid.

[5]Ibid., 79.

[6]Ibid., 84.

culture as some kind of socialist pragmatism, and once again there are words of Tillich which would lend some credibility to the interpretation. Thus he says in *Protestant Era*:

> The situation of knowing is decisive for one's ability of inability to know. Only the "spiritual" man can judge everything, according to Paul, and only the man who participates in the struggle of the "elected group" against the class-society is able to understand the true character of being.
>
> Expressed in more concrete terms, the church or the fighting proletariat is the place where truth has the greatest chance to be accepted. In all the other spheres the general distortion of our historical existence makes it difficult, if not impossible, to find a true insight into the human situation and through it into being itself.[7]

It seems to me that, however plausible, this interpretation of the young Tillich as a Marxist is false. In the first place, it ignores the very clear definition[8] which Tillich gives of his debt to Marx. This was in three specific areas: first, the ideological interpretation of philosophy—i.e., the appreciation that all systems of thought have an ideological character; secondly, the unmasking effect of Marxism in which it resembles psychoanalysis; and finally, its prophetic passion. The important point to be noticed here is the *formal* nature of this indebtedness. If the theology of culture were in any significant way Marxist then the indebtedness would need to be concrete rather than formal. Secondly, the relation that Tillich saw between the theology of culture and traditional moral theology likewise distinguishes this theology from a Marxist programme. In the lecture on the theology of culture Tillich contended that it was no longer possible to do traditional moral theology; for in the extra-ecclesial situation that had been produced by the First World War it was essential to attack something more fundamental, namely, the cultural framework of modern life. "What was essentially intended in the theological system of ethics can only be realized by means of a theology of culture applying not only to ethics but to all functions of culture."[9] Secularisation thus demands not a different ethic or a different justification of ethics such as Marxism would provide but a different and more comprehensive theology. Finally, it could be said that the idea of a theology of culture was not only a theme that

---

[7]Paul Tillich, *The Protestant Era*, 280.

[8]*On the Boundary*, 85ff.

[9]Paul Tillich, *What is Religion?* (New York: Harper & Row, 1969) 160.

remained a primary concern of Tillich's throughout his life, but had ante-
dated his acquaintance with Marxism.

If the influence of Marxism is a tempting but false lead in the interpretation of Tillich's theology of culture, there can be no mistake about the
significance of his avowed opposition to nominalism. Time and again[10] Tillich expresses his distaste for and rejection of nominalism. However, it is
not at all clear whether this is the result of the argument in "On the idea
of a theology of culture" rather than its inspiration. In his vicious attack
on Tillich as a philosopher, A. M. Macleod has emphasised the difficulty
of distinguishing the philosophical influence at work in his development of
the metaphysics of his systematic theology.[11] Yet one thing is quite clear.
Tillich saw himself as standing in the firmly established line of philosophical
development from Plato onwards at least which is the tradition of ontology.
He often spoke of himself as a Platonist and as a conservative medievalist
by which I take it he meant to say that he was an Augustinian. The clearly
Platonic character of his thought meant that he regarded philosophy as ontology. It is of little consequence at the moment whether we regard this
ontology as essentialist or existentialist. What matters is that with such a
thoroughgoing ontological understanding of philosophy which insists[12] that
philosophy has an ontological purpose and that epistemology is based on
ontology and again that all philosophical analysis and interpretation is the
development of an ontology,[13] there will inevitably result a sharp opposition
to nominalism.

In this light then the comments on nominalism in the discussions of
theology of culture are seen as particular applications of the general principle. These are two points, the first made in the 1919 lecture and the second in that most remarkable piece of kulturwissenschaft, *The Courage to
Be*. In the latter, nominalism is criticised as resulting in heteronomy in religion and culture. This it does in two ways: by its typical dissolution of
universals and by the voluntarism which Occam introduced. First, the dissolution of universals results in an escape into authority inasmuch as the

---

[10]Paul Tillich, *History of Christian Thought*, 143ff, 198f; *Systematic Theology*, I: 196,
II: 144; *The Courage to Be*, 61, and 95; *Love, Power and Justice*, 4-11, 24f.

[11]Cf. Tillich, *An essay on the role of ontology in his philosophical theology* (London: Allen
& Unwin) 18-19.

[12]Cf. *Systematic Theology*, I: 18-21, 163-64.

[13]Cf. *Love, Power and Justice*.

individual can no longer have the courage to be as essential man. "Therefore the nominalists built the bridge to an ecclesiastical authoritarianism which surpassed everything in the early or late Middle Ages and produced modern Catholic collectivism."[14] Secondly, the Occamist doctrine of the priority of will to reason led to a voluntarism and an arbitrariness in individual life and an authoritarianism in politics.[15] In the paper on the idea of a theology of culture a central argument is the tendency of nominalism to empty culture of ultimate significance. It emphasises the purely utilitarian function of reason as technical reason and it reduces symbols to arbitrary signs, the results of human convention rather than the expressions of real ontological meaning.[16] Professor J. Luther Adams has pointed out the consequence of nominalism for a philosophy of art in particular as he mentions this theme in Tillich's early philosophy.[17]

There is a sense in which this last theme could be described as a subsidiary influence or even as the implication of an influence. For if we rightly read Tillich as applying a general principle of opposition to nominalism that general principle is the implication of his view of philosophy as ontology. Now the main influences at this point in his thinking, as I said several years ago, are Schelling and Hegel.[18] It is very easy for us to view the influence of Schelling in the light of Tillich's own claim that Schelling was the beginning of existentialism. This would lead us to interpret the connection with Schelling as ruling out in advance any connection with Hegel and we should then ignore the fact that in a very real sense the early agreement between Schelling and Hegel is a quest for a philosophy of spirit. It is very important also to remember that this agreement could with justice be called the genesis of Hegelian dialectical monism. I want to emphasise this because I am very conscious of two kinds of mistakes to which one is tempted in trying to interpret Tillich. On the one hand, the connection with Schelling is so startlingly obvious that one can overestimate Schelling's reference and read Tillich as some scholars do merely in the light of Schelling. On the other hand, one can all too easily fall into the trap of seeing the multiplicity

---

[14]*Courage to Be*, 130.

[15]Ibid., 61.

[16]*What is Religion?*, 155-83.

[17]*Paul Tillich's Philosophy of Culture*, Science and Religion, 91.

[18]Cf. *Paul Tillich—An Appraisal* (London, SCM Press).

of influences as signifying merely a philosophical confusion. What I want to ask is whether there is not a case for saying that Hegel's influence is almost as significant and certainly as pervasive as Schelling's.

Recently in a paper on the problem of defining a theology of culture[19] I have argued that Hegel is the main inspiration in the development of Tillich's theology of culture. Let me, then, take up two themes already mentioned—the unmasking effect of Marxism and the importance of the fact of secularisation—in order that I may fill out that particular argument. My contention was that Tillich found his problem foreshadowed in Hegel's thinking and that the revolutionary interest of the young Hegel gave Tillich reason to view with favour the Hegelian solution to the problem. It is very well known that the title "theological writings" is in some ways a misleading description of Hegel's early work. Yet as Peperzak has argued[20] there are two dangers in the interpretation of the young Hegel: on the one hand an interpretation can be too theological, but on the other it can equally be too political.

I am quite convinced by Peperzak's argument that if the young Hegel's thought is religious it is not so in any sense that separates religion from the rest of life. There can be no doubting his interpretation of the genesis of the Hegelian philosophy as a moral vision of the world which shows very clearly the influence of Kant's philosophy of Practical Reason. So just as the young Hegel had a moral vision which was religious, in the same way his religious thought cannot be isolated from his politics. At each step in its development the Hegelian religion carries within it a political significance. Further, if we consider the early thought of Hegel it will be agreed that the period 1790-1800 is of special interest and F. G. Nauen has characterised that period as the collaboration of Schelling and Hegel in some kind of revolutionary circle in Wittenberg.[21] They not only shared a cultural, intellectual and political outlook but their early thought of this period is regarded by Nauen as a unit. This helps us to understand how Tillich, whose fondness for Schelling goes back as far as his undergraduate period, could look to both Schelling and Hegel as guides in his attempt at a revo-

---

[19]*Creation, Christ and Culture, Studies in Honour of T. F. Torrance* (Edinburgh: T & T Clark) 276f.

[20]*Le jeune Hegel et la vision morale du monde* (Hague: Nijhoff, 1960).

[21]F. G. Nauen, *Revolution, Idealism and Human Freedom* (Hague: Nijhoff, 1971).

lutionary theology. Hegel's conclusion in the essay "The Spirit of Christianity"[22] seems very clearly the point of departure for Tillich's theology of culture. There is the same rejection of a one-sided pietism and of a one-sided secularism. Indeed the critique of the three options represented by Schleiermacher, Kant and Hegel himself seems to me very much in the spirit of Hegel. However, the two points I have mentioned now strike me as the most interesting, especially as the unmasking of false consciousness is the very meaning given to "secularisation" in Karl Löwith's *Meaning in History*.[23] His argument is that from Augustine to Hegel philosophers assumed that the Christian religion is the absolute truth.

> What distinguishes Hegel from Augustine in principle is that Hegel interprets the Christian religion in terms of speculative reason, and providence as "cunning of reason." . . . As the realization of the spirit of Christianity, the history of the world is the true theodicy, the justification of God in History.
>
> With this secularization of the Christian faith, or, as Hegel would say, with this realization of the Spirit, Hegel believed himself loyal to the genius of Christianity by realizing the Kingdom of God on earth. And, since he transposed the Christian expectation of a final consummation into the historical process as such, he saw the world's history as consummating itself. "The history of the world is the world's court of justice" (Die Weltgeschichte ist das Weltgericht) is a sentence which is as religious in its original motivation, where it means that the world's history is proceeding towards its judgment at the end of all history, as it is irreligious in its secular application, where it means that the judgment is contained in the historical process as such.[24]

It is Löwith's view that Hegel failed to grasp the "fateful ambiguity" at the heart of his own thinking and very tellingly Professor K. R. Dove, in his contribution to the Marquette Hegel symposium of 1970, spoke of Löwith's story of the result as a modern dress version of the Oedipus tragedy.[25] This view of Hegel had been, of course, stated with exceptional force and clarity in Löwith's earlier great book, *From Hegel to Nietzsche*, where he says:

> Whoever has really experienced a slice of world history . . . will have to come to the conclusion that Hegel's philosophy of history is a pseudo-theological secularization

---

[22]*Early Theological Writings*, 301.

[23]Cf. 2, 19, 49, 57-58, 200-202.

[24]*Meaning in History*, 57-58.

[25]*The Legacy of Hegel* (Hague: Nijhoff) 147.

of history arranged according to the idea of progress towards an eschatological fulfillment at the end of time.[26]

I have referred to Professor Dove's use of the Oedipus analogy. His estimate of Löwith is entirely negative and to his mind the unmasking which
this secularisation theme involves is a vulgar Marxist technique. Commenting on Professor Dove's paper, Professor Howard Kainz discusses
this view of Löwith's theory as a philosophical *Oedipus* and interestingly
turns to the Freudian use of the tragedy as an explanatory device. He
points out that in the case of an Oedipus complex the patient does not generally murder the father or marry the mother. Father and Mother are in-
ternalized. So he suggests that "perhaps Hegel has gone a bit further, or
the Secularization Hypothesis has gone further, than simply murdering
Christianity and forming an incestuous union with faith."[27] His view that
Hegel might have finally solved the controversy about the relationship and
the distinction between faith and reason seems to me a strangely sanguine
claim. Fortunately this has nothing to do with what he produces as good
evidence for saying that the secularisation theme to which Professor Dove
objects is authentically Hegelian.

I would like to note that Hegel himself offers a formulation which bears a striking
similarity to the Freudian metaphor. This formulation comes at the end of Hegel's
chapter on "Revealed Religion" in the *Phenomenology* after the advent of Christianity and the incarnation of Christ has solved the dichotomy between consciousness and self-consciousness. Around the last page in this chapter on "Revealed
Religion" Hegel makes a comparison between Christ and the Christian. He says
that, just as Christ had an explicit mother, a real mother, but only an implicit or implied father, the father being invisible and not directly accessible, so also the Christian has an explicit "father" (his own will and spontaneous action) and an implicit
"mother" (the sentiment or feeling of love, which has not yet become predominant
or explicated within Christianity). . . . The explication of the spirit of the Father of
Christ takes place (according to Hegel) when the historical, imaginative presentation of Christ as a past figure is done away with. No longer is he an historical figure,
but the historical figure is transcended. It is only when this takes place that the
Spirit of the Father becomes explicit, so that the father is no longer an unreal "beyond." Correspondingly, the implicit love of Christians becomes explicit, according
to Hegel, when the future expectation of salvation, of a Last Judgment (the eschatological expectations) is superseded, and is no longer an essential part of Chris-

[26]Löwith, *From Hegel to Nietzsche*, 219.

[27]*The Legacy of Hegel*, 158.

tianity; so that the Christian lives completely in the present, no longer in and for the future. [28]

What I have argued so far may seem a rather arbitrary historical connection, though I hope persuasive in its illustration of philosophical parallels. Therefore I want next to show what I believe to be the connecting link with Hegel as the main philosophical influence in the development of Tillich's theology of culture. My contention has been that Hegel's revolutionary philosophy had been a post-Kantian return to the traditions of theology which produced his distinctive interpretation of a Christian view of history. In such a view the contrast between "culture" as a value-word and the purely descriptive use of the term has no place. Hegel's historical method is therefore as valuational as it is descriptive and it is in a real sense the a priori technique of the biblical exegete. This historian was able to show how each art and culture exists in its own right and is yet a step forward in the unfolding of the divine spirit. Professor Gombrich has made the very telling point that a history of art becomes possible only in the light of such an interpretation as this. [29] Now it is not at all necessary for me to accept this contention of Gombrich and even if it were true it certainly does not follow that a theology of art is necessarily Hegelian. The real issue is whether Tillich's inspiration is this particular history of art with its distinctively Hegelian features and overtones. I can say at once that my case is a very generalised argument rather than the systematic analysis of historical evidence which alone can establish the case as a point to be made in the history of thought. If anyone says that therefore this is pointless exercise, I can only plead in excuse that useful theories are not always and only found among hypotheses built up painstakingly from evidence. This, then, is the historical connection I see between Tillich and Hegel—the cultural history of Jacob Burckhardt, for Burckhardt's great masterpiece, *Civilization of the Renaissance*, remained the focus of discussion about the Renaissance in the succeeding century.

Professor Momigliano has shown the links with Hegel, in particular those effected by the influence of one of Burckhardt's teachers, the classical scholar Boeckh, in whose writings the idea of a Volksgeist plays such

---

[28]Ibid., 159.

[29]*In Search of Cultural History*, 13.

an important part.[30] Professor Gombrich gives further evidence of Burck-hardt's building on Hegelian foundations in his description of the latter's *Cicerone* of 1855. It is, he says, "pervaded by the interpretation of Re-naissance art that had become commonplace by the middle of the nine-teenth century . . . the contract between the spirituality of the Age of Faith and the sensuality of the subsequent age. It was a polarity that had been . . . used, of course, by Hegel."[31] Commenting on Burckhardt's eloquent account of the "New Spirit" that came over sculpture and painting in the fifteenth century Professor Gombrich once again points out its Hegelian character.[32] Therefore, he argues, the lines of approach were staked out before Burckhardt began to write his book on the whole civilization of the Renaissance. What Professor Gombrich says of that book is most enlightening:

> In my youth that book was still a classic in German-speaking countries, and that meant that it was read by quite a large number of people as providing a passport to *Bilderung*, to "culture" in the Victorian sense of the term.[33]

Burckhardt had been at pains to make clear that his criteria of selection and arrangement were subjective; but, says Professor Gombrich, neither he nor indeed any of his subsequent commentators seem to have realized to what an extent his interpretation was informed by Hegel's theory of his-tory.[34] The reason for this is, he thinks, psychological: "One feels in good company in attacking Hegel; but to criticise the intellectual foundation of Burckhardt's work is a different matter. He is the father-figure of cultural history whose very tone of voice carries authority."[35] Nevertheless, he presses his point and illustrates the use of Hegelian categories and polar-ities by quoting what he describes as the heart of Burckhardt's book, the

---

[30]Arnaldo Momigliano, "Introduzione alla Greschische Kulturgeshichte di Jacob Burck-hardt," *Secondo Contributo all Storia degli Studi Classici* (Rome, 1960) 283-98.

[31]Op. cit., 17.

[32]Ibid.

[33]Op. cit., 18.

[34]Ibid., 19. This is a particularly important point when one is considering the claim that Burckhardt's stance throughout his work is essentially anti-Hegelian.

[35]Ibid.

contrast drawn between the mentality of the Renaissance and that of the Middle Ages:

In the Middle Ages both sides of human consciousness—that which faces the out-side world and that which is turned towards man's inner life—lay dreaming or only half-awake, as if they were covered by a common veil, a veil woven of faith, delusion and childish dependence. Seen across this veil reality and history appeared in the strangest colours while man was only aware of himself in universal categories such as race, nation, party, guild or family. It was in Italy that this veil was first blown away and that there awoke an objective attitude towards the state and towards all the things of this world while, on the other side, subjectivity emerged with full force so that man became a true individual mind and recognized himself as such.[36]

The Hegelian inspiration here is so obvious that it hardly needs to be indicated. The polarity of subjective and objective is one of the most pervasive contrasts in Hegel's philosophy and could with justice be said to be nowhere more important than in his philosophy of history.[37] Burckhardt's reference to Italy is peculiarly reminiscent of Hegel for two reasons. First, it echoes the contrast between the subjective and objective in which the subjective reaches its full flowering only in the objective.[38] However, besides this formal feature, there is the particular point about Italian history; for according to Hegel's trinitarian principle of historical development, the evolution from Persia to Rome is repeated in the history of the Christian period and that expression of the spirit in Rome which was the high point of ancient history and which corresponds to the Renaissance is due to a generalised subjectivity.[39] Nor is there lacking an acknowledgment from Burckhardt himself that his basic assumption was Hegelian as when he refers to zeitgeist in such a matter-of-fact way:

---

[36]Burckhardt, *Civilization of the Renaissance*, 95.

[37]Cf. Hegel, *Early Theological Writings*, 191, 206ff, 254f., and *Philosophy of History*, 40, 83, 250-60, 346f., 442.

[38]Cf. J. L. Navickas, *Consciousness and Reality: Hegel's philosophy of subjectivity* (The Hague: Nijhoff, 1976) and G. D. O'Brien, "Does Hegel Have a Philosophy of History?" *History and Theory*, X:295-317.

[39]*Philosophy of History*, 356-59, 456-61.

> Every cultural epoch which presents itself as a complete and articulate whole ex-
> presses itself not only in the life of the state, in religion, art and science, but also
> imparts its individual character to social life as such.[40]

Incidentally, it is significant too that Burckhardt borrowed the title of his opening chapter from Hegel whose phrase "The political work of art"[41] must be the source of Burckhardt's much-debated notion of "The state as a work of art."

If the general features and particular details of this most influential work are Hegelian then a fortiori the attitude of optimism which it expresses is even more so. An inevitable onward march of historical progress is what is clearly to be seen in history and that the Renaissance is part of this progress is the basic premise of Burckhardt's book:

> Freed from the countless barriers which elsewhere impeded progress, developed
> into a higher degree of individuality, and schooled by Classical Antiquity, the Italian
> spirit turned towards the discovery of the external world and its representation in
> language and art.[42]

This cosmological interpretation of the Renaissance leads Burckhardt to reject the conventional notion of the Renaissance as a return to the classics. He emphasises that it is one of the basic tenets of his book in which he insists that the Renaissance was not only the revival of Antiquity "but its close alliance with an independently existing Italian national spirit" and he speaks of the Renaissance as an "exalted world historical necessity."[43] Two things are here significant: first, that the process is world-historical and second, that it is a necessary one. It is precisely that combination of logical dialectic with a cosmological dimension which yields that Hegelian carelessness for the individual criticised so constantly by Kierkegaard. True to his Hegelian inspiration, Burckhardt bids us look at the race and not at the individual:

---

[40]Op. cit., 257.

[41]*Philosophy of History*, 280.

[42]Op. cit., 2.

[43]Ibid., 124.

It is certainly true that many a noble flower tends to perish in such a large process
. . . but one should not therefore wish that the great universal event had never
happened.[44]

The concluding pages of Burckhardt's great work show a certain reticence
and an impatience with Hegelian dogmatism but nevertheless amply reveal
Burckhardt's own acceptance of Hegel's restatement of the Christian doctrine of providence. Thus it is no coincidence that among his commentators
appears Löwith whose discussion of this theme in the history of ideas has
already been mentioned in this discussion.[45]

What seems to me the main interest of Professor Gombrich's argument is not so much the thesis that Burckhardt made the history of culture
as such possible as the claim that "the subsequent history of historiography of culture can perhaps best be interpreted as a succession of attempts
to salvage the Hegelian assumption without accepting the Hegelian metaphysics."[46] In particular I was particularly struck by his illustration of this
in the case of Marxism.

This was precisely what Marxism claimed it was doing. The Hegelian diagram was
more or less maintained, but the centre was occupied not by the spirit but by the
changing conditions of production. . . . Thus the task of the cultural historian remains very much the same. He must be able to show in every detail of the period
how it reflects its essential economic character.[47]

If there is any substance at all in the suggestion that Tillich was influenced
by Marxism, does it not become a particularly difficult matter to disentan-
gle the philosophical influences which were instrumental in shaping his theology of culture? If, on the other hand, my argument is right, then it has
the merit of being able to explain how the Marxist influence was in a very
real sense all of a piece with the rest. The same is true of the highly influential work of Dilthey, whom Professor Gombrich very aptly describes
as "the biographer and a very sophisticated critic of Hegel, who yet, I be-

---

[44]Ibid.

[45]K. Löwith, *Jacob Burckhardt, der Mensch inmitten der Geschichte* (Luzern, 1936).

[46]Op. cit., 25-26.

[47]Ibid., 26.

lieve, remained under his spell in the way he posed the problem of what he calls the 'structural unity of culture,' especially in his later fragments."[48]

In conclusion I should like to raise the question of the nature of a much-publicised influence on Tillich, the artistic movement called expressionism. I cannot hope to do more than ask the question, but ask it I must because I have suggested in what I have written on Tillich's theology of culture that this is both an influence and a tailor-made example for Tillich. In the first place, it needs to be said that expressionism was never a conscious grouping of artists on the basis of a common programme, loosely or indeed in any way defined. It is a concept used in the history of art retrospectively more than contemporaneously. As a movement it is difficult to define both in terms of avowed membership and as a matter of identifying individual artists as examples of it. Some of those whom one would naturally think of as members of the movement were the most anxious to reject the name. For example, Kurt Wolff, the principal publisher of the German Expressionists, not only violently disliked the term being used of himself, but argued that it gave those writers "a common stamp which they never in fact possessed."[49] Likewise, the painter who was generally considered the archetypal expressionist, Kirchner, told a critic in 1924 that he found it "more degrading than ever . . . to be identified with Munch and Expressionism."[50] Identifying some particular artists as expressionists rather than something else is extremely difficult also because they are as often called surrealist as expressionist, for example, Chagall. Thus it is not only a matter of how the artist sees his own work or what influences he is prepared to admit but a matter of style.

Difficult though it is thus to define, the term "expressionism" can be said to have a clear enough meaning as denoting a particular modern German movement in the period between 1910 and 1923. It absorbed all the "modern" movements of the period and gave them some common character. Thus it was that cubism in Germany is not a separate school of painters but an element, indeed a persistent element, in expressionism. Expressionism was a reaction to the special circumstances of this period and could be said to have been produced by the trauma of World War I. The

---

[48]Ibid.

[49]Willett, *Expressionism* (London, 1970) 7.

[50]Ibid.

intellectual climate was a welter of conflicting attitudes. Germany was tremendously nationalist and its nationalism spelled conservatism. Yet it was very much open to foreign influences and consequently the conservatism inevitably seemed oppressive. Expressionism captured this conflict of atmospheres and it lent the movement a quality of manic depression. Expressionism as a movement can be said to have begun in 1910; for by this time the new European artistic and literary influences had interacted with the German background in such a way that there were produced paintings which can properly be called expressionist. There was Munch whose works are startlingly expressive as is clear from the well-known lithograph, "The Cry," dating from 1895.

The term "expressionism" seems to have appeared on the German scene in 1910, but the evidence is somewhat uncertain. What is certain is that it was used in the following year in the catalogue of the Berlin Sezession to describe a room of French Fauve and early cubist paintings, then picked up by the critic of *Der Sturm* in the July issue. However, Willett quotes an anecdote which would suggest that it was in use in 1910.[51] It is said that at a sitting of the Sezession jury one member asked concerning a work by Pechstein "Is that Impressionismus?" and Paul Cassirer replied "No. Expressionismus." Apparently all the pictures submitted by Pechstein and Nolde were refused and the two artists organised their own show together with contributions from some others. This group, called the Neue Sezession, lasted until 1912 only, but was the first centre of expressionist art in Berlin.

Between 1910 and 1912 the typically angular, distorted, violently emotional style of the expressionists established itself. By 1911 the Negro influence asserted itself, probably as a result of the impact of Gauguin. Their palettes began to grow less brilliant and their forms became broken. If we take Heckel's 1912 woodcut, a typical piece of expressionism, as an example, it is clear that the themes are not only akin to the metropolitan literary interest of the time, but are evidence of their own reading of Dostoevsky. Munich as well as Berlin saw a regrouping of artists. Two younger artists, Franz Marc and August Macke, came into contact with Kandinsky and were to prove useful colleagues. They were joined by Le Fauconnier and Pierre Girieud, a follower of Gauguin. Kandinsky had been

---

[51]Ibid., 75.

working out some kind of visual mysticism and was now becoming an almost entirely abstract painter. By 1914 it was possible for the critic Paul Fechter to publish a study of the movement, *Der Expressionismus*. This was followed by two other studies, Hermann Bahr's *Expressionismus* and Walden's *Einblick in Kunst: Expressionismus, Futurismus, Kubismus*. From these studies one gains a view of expressionism as above all a reaction against impressionism and the materialist nineteenth century outlook which was its inspiration. The chief expressionist artists for Walden are Kandinsky, Chagall, Marc, Klee, and Campendouk with Kokoschka as a link between expressionism and impressionism. Their pictures are "expressions of a vision" with the painting treated strictly as "unity of a formally shaped surface." Both Fechter and Bahr regard expressionism as an anti-rational movement and also as an essentially German one. Its voluntarism was precisely what showed its German character: "It is the old Gothic soul which . . . despite all rationalism and materialism again and again raises its head," says Fechter. Bahr sees expressionism as the soul's struggle with the machine.

> Man is crying out for his soul, the whole period becomes a single urgent cry. And Art cries too into the deaf darkness, crying for help, crying for the spirit. That is Expressionism. [52]

Fechter too argued that the general movement was of more importance than the quality of any individual achievements and concluded with an appeal to a new religious sense.

What then is expressionism? German expressionism was a comprehensive movement. Despite the fact that it was something of a ragbag of styles it possessed a remarkably coherent spirit and it was associated with a particular generation inasmuch as its impact on German artists was the most profound in the period 1910-1920. Many of its concerns were the common concerns of modern men: industrialisation, the utopian hopes for urbanisation, and also the sense of individual isolation. What characterised the expressionists was the sense of dynamism and vitality they showed in their determination to express these feelings as strong emotions. It could then be said that the hallmark of expressionism is this primacy of active, restless emotion as a feature not only of the subject matter but also of the

---

[52]Quoted in ibid., 100.

form. This emotional character is what produces the distortion. The expressionists made use of the discoveries of the cubists and the futurists, exploiting their angularity and sense of movement and disintegration to produce in their representational art a deliberate distortion, while in their non-representational work, where clearly there can be no distortion as such, there was a very characteristic force of attack on the materials themselves. Finally, I should like to say that perhaps in a typically wrongheaded way Lukács's argument that it was "mandatory" that any wholehearted expressionist should go over to Hitler suggests the political interest of the movement. It is easy enough probably to show that this judgment is as wrong as is his similar estimate of Kierkegaard.[53] What matters perhaps is that there were thinkers in the 1930s for whom expressionism symbolised the tragedy of Nazism—the rotten form in which an ideal of German socialism was now to be found.

It seems to me therefore that I was right to show extreme caution in my estimate of the influence exerted on Tillich by the artistic movement of expressionism and to describe it as being as much of a tailor-made example as an influence. For tailor-made example it is. There can be no better example of the contrast between form and content which also displays the interrelation of the two. The very essence of expressionism was not mere distortion, but distortion that expressed the way in which emotional force informed subject-matter. Furthermore, expressionism as an art-style is a good example of that triad which was the elements of the formula Tillich employed for his theory of a theology of culture: form, substance, and content. What I said about non-representational art illustrates the way in which an element of distortion can be seen in the very material of the painting. If we generalise the significance of expressionism into something like Herbert Read's "fundamentally necessary word like 'idealism' and 'realism'," then I believe that this confirms the fundamentally Hegelian influence which I have tried to show in the development of Tillich's theology of culture.

Perhaps in conclusion I should say that I am not concerned to denigrate Tillich's achievement. All I have done is to suggest what seems to me to be the main influence at work in the development of this still neglected theology. There are several questions which need to be raised which are

---

[53]Vide *Der junge Hegel.*

partly biographical and partly philosophical. I am content if I have made us pause before saying blithely that, of course, when he was developing his theology of culture, Tillich had moved far away from any Hegelian world of thought. For whether right or wrong in this matter of the Hegelian influence, I am sure that Tillich's theology of culture owes more, much more, to the tradition of metaphysics in Germany than it does to either the politics of the postwar period or to the exciting movements in the world of art.

Hegel, Tillich, and the Theology of Culture: A Response to Prof. Thomas

ROBERT R. N. ROSS

Prof. Thomas' thesis, as I understand it, is the claim that Hegel is the main philosophical influence in the development of Tillich's theology of culture. A secondary claim is that the "connecting link" between Hegel and Tillich is the cultural historian, Jacob Burckhardt, about whom Prof. Thomas accepts Gombrich's thesis that Burckhardt's historiography of culture (in particular of the Renaissance) is fundamentally Hegelian (the Renaissance as a "world-historical" process and "a necessary one").

A third claim of Prof. Thomas' is really an assumption implicit in the first two. It is suggested by his acceptance of Gombrich's remark that the history of historiography of culture subsequent to Burckhardt was "a succession of attempts to salvage the Hegelian assumption [whatever that was] without accepting the Hegelian metaphysics." Marxism is seen as just such an attempt. Prof. Thomas' assumption therefore comes to this: his analysis assumes that any theology of culture—not just Tillich's— would have to build on an essentially Hegelian foundation. Hence, any possible influence by Marx on Tillich would also have to fit within the sphere of Hegel's influence. In this way, Prof. Thomas can rather comfortably (too comfortably, I think) argue that Tillich's debt to Marx is quite secondary to his debt to Hegel. But that is only because the possibility of establishing *directly* what was or was not the influence of Marx is ruled out in advance.

My first remarks will grant Prof. Thomas his thesis, and then suggest that if one does so, certain problems about the internal coherence of Tillich's theology of culture arise. My second remarks will suggest that there perhaps may be some reasons *not* to grant Prof. Thomas his thesis.

I

If Tillich's idea of a theology of culture was, as Prof. Thomas suggests, a response to a particular historical event (namely, WWI), one of the more important expressions of this theology is Tillich's concept of *Kairos*, a concept which signifies the uniqueness of a historical event. Tillich distinguished (although perhaps arbitrarily, with respect to NT usage) the notion of *Kairos* from that of *Chronos* in order to indicate that certain times have a *unique* and specific qualitative nature; that there are times in history which constitute "turning points," demanding our *decision*, our *response* in some special way, because they are times in which the Unconditioned is uniquely related to the present.

What this suggests, first of all, is the fundamentally prophetic character of Tillich's theology of culture. If Prof. Thomas can call Tillich's "prophetic passion" merely a *formal* indebtedness to Marx, this may only mean that Tillich obviously can draw his prophetic passion from a tradition independent of Marx. Far more important, however, is the fact that to interpret Tillich's theology of culture as fundamentally influenced by Hegel's dialectical interpretation of history and historical change—one in which history is seen as displaying a process wherein change is understood to occur as a matter of logical necessity—means that the *methodology* of Tillich's theology of culture would have to stand in considerable tension with his *purpose* for it.

To see historical events in Hegelian terms is to see them, Prof. Thomas says, as (a) occurring as a part of a world historical process—in a "cosmological" dimension, and (b) as occurring *necessarily*. Now clearly Tillich is quite comfortable in using what perhaps may be a version of Hegelian dialectic as a part of his ontological analysis of culture—an analysis, contra nominalism, which treats universals and the *categories* of analysis as real. Indeed, Tillich may be less interested in "salvaging the Hegelian assumption" than in *replacing* Hegelian metaphysics with one of his own (i.e., Tillich certainly does not reject metaphysics).

But if Tillich's theology of history were fundamentally Hegelian, this would mean his concept of *Kairos* would have to be under considerable strain. Why?

The concept of *Kairos* is designed to display the meaning of the *uniqueness* of certain historical events: i.e., to point to their meaning which is a *result* of their idiosyncratic and unique character, and to the sense in which this uniqueness forces *us* into a *personal* relation with that event because we are forced to come to a *decision* based on it, make a response to it. This, I take it, is the purpose of prophecy: namely, that a historical event and its interpretation puts *us* under a judgment to which we must respond and then, ourselves, try to *change* history. But understood in terms of a Hegelian view of history, what is unique now becomes "necessary" and our response to such an event becomes *irrelevant*. One might push Hegel's view of history "theologically," as it were, and then read this into Tillich so that for Tillich the unique event would not have the "necessity" of some logical (i.e., theoretical) process of evolution but what one could only call, I suppose, *divine* necessity. Of course, I don't know whether one would be any better off, for all that. For with this move, while the "necessary" Kairotic event is not "theologized"—i.e., connected more strongly with *divine* purpose—at the same time it raises far more seriously the problem of theodicy. If I say WWI is the Kairotic event of God's judgment of human history—and if the Kairotic event is given the character of Hegel's "necessity," albeit in religious terms—then the event of WWI surely looks as if it should be the occasion for *disbelief* in any such thing as a "divine purpose." At the same time, one must acknowledge there is always a double-edged character to any prophetic interpretation of historical events—i.e., it cuts *both* ways. For if WWI is interpreted as a divine judgment of human history, then it is also, and equally, the occasion for the human judgment of divine history.

Now a voluntaristic interpretation of divine acts in human history removes the "necessary" character of historical events, perhaps—although at the expense of raising the question of the *intelligibility* of historical events. That is, what is *utterly* arbitrary, by will alone, does not look to have an *order*, does not look rational, looks "psychotic." And Tillich, to some extent, does reject a *purely* voluntaristic understanding of historical events as a part of his critique of the "nominalist dissolution of universals."

As Prof. Thomas points out, Tillich thought this resulted in a heteronomy, an escape into authority in which both the events in individual life—and the Divine Life—look arbitrary, empty of any ultimate significance.

On the other hand, I don't think Tillich gave up voluntarism entirely, but I will return to this in the second part of my remarks when I suggest Tillich may not be so Hegelian as Prof. Thomas thinks. What I am arguing here is that *granting* Prof. Thomas' claim that Tillich is fundamentally Hegelian, Tillich's concept of *Kairos* would have to be inconsistent with a Hegelian view of history.

II

The concept of *Kairos* certainly is inconsistent with *Tillich's* assessment of Hegel's view of history, which leads me to my second point: namely, that Tillich is not fundamentally Hegelian as Prof. Thomas suggests—i.e., at least in the *way* Prof. Thomas suggests.

In his "Kairos" essay in *The Protestant Era*, Tillich indicates that Hegel's philosophy of history falls under the category he calls the "dialectical type" of the "relative form" (vs. "absolute," e.g., Barth) of philosophy of history. Within this category there are three sub-forms: "theological," "logical," and "sociological." To the "theological" belongs Joachim de Floris' three eras of the Father, Son and Holy Spirit; to the "sociological" belongs Marx; to the "logical" belongs Hegel.

Now while Tillich sees his philosophy of the *Kairos* as *related* to the dialectical interpretations of history (i.e., there is a *formal* relation in that Tillich understands theonomy, autonomy, and heteronomy as themselves dialectically related to one another, since each of these concepts "drives beyond itself"), Tillich also sees there being some important *differences*.

(1) First, there is in Tillich's doctrine of *Kairos* no final stage in which dialectics (per contradiction) ceases to operate. For Hegel, Tillich suggests this occurs with the advent of the Germanic nations, in which the Absolute Spirit actualizes itself for the "last time."

(2) Second, there is in Tillich's doctrine of the *Kairos* not only the horizontal dialectic of the historical process, but also the *vertical* dialectic operating between the Unconditioned and the conditioned. However one reads Hegel, Tillich saw this vertical dimension as *absent* in Hegel's philosophy of history.

(3) Finally, there is in Tillich's doctrine of *Kairos no logical necessity* in the historical process. Rather, it moves through "that unity of freedom and fate which distinguishes history from nature."

Hence, I conclude that Tillich's own analysis of his concept of *Kairos establishes* that his position is not Hegelian—at least that he saw himself as doing things significantly different from those which would be entailed by a Hegelian view of history. What kinds of things were they?

James Luther Adams suggests that Tillich sought to overcome the loss of the dynamic in Hegel's logical rationalism by a method he called "meta-logical"—a method whose purpose was to achieve the dynamic quality appropriate for a *living* universe which requires *living* import, meaning. While for Hegel the *idea* is basic, for Tillich the dynamic, form-creating meaning is basic. In "The Philosophy of Religion" Tillich says:

> The living dialectic of the elements of meaning (i.e., of form and import) which penetrates the whole of reality, should be grasped. Metalogical intuition of essences is not directed toward particular things and qualities: it does not remain attached to the individual form, but rather it perceives the tensions and polarities that seem to it to constitute the really essential element in the essence. The intuition (*Schau*) of the inner *dynamic* in the structure of the meaning-reality is the goal of metalogic.

It is just because the metalogical method knows the infinite tension between form and import that it cannot consider even trying to apprehend objects of meaning in the manner of the Hegelian dialectic. "The awareness of the infinite of everything real makes such an intention impossible."

Prof. Adams goes on to say that Tillich uses the tradition of Boehme, Schelling, Nietzsche and Fichte and a dynamic, voluntaristic conception of reality plus certain elements of Neoplatonic thought in his criticism of the "relentlessness" which characterizes Hegel's view of history. From Schelling, Tillich draws on the theory of potencies; he utilizes Nietzsche's "creative spirit" and the Neoplatonic idea of the unspeakable Darkness, the abysmal One—all held together in a kind of unity, which, through Tillich's metalogical method, apprehends the Unconditioned content within the conditioned forms. It is, as Prof. Adams indicates, a method of *coincidentia oppositorum*—a philosophy of paradox which affirms the paradoxical immanence of the transcendent.

Why is Tillich so *hesitant* to acknowledge his "debt" to Hegel, particularly if, as Prof. Thomas contends, "Hegel's revolutionary philosophy was a post-Kantian return to the traditions of theology which produced his distinctive interpretation of a Christian view of history"? My intuition is that it is because Tillich saw himself as attempting to do something substantially different from Hegel.

In his essay "On the Idea of a Theology of Culture," Tillich says that religion is not attributable to any particular psychic function, and this is given as the reason why the theory of Hegel, who assigned religion to the *theoretical* sphere of the mind, has not survived. That is, religion is not *one* psychic aspect of culture, but an attitude of the spirit in which *all* psychic elements are united to form a *complex whole*.

Prof. Thomas says that he accepts Peperzak's argument that if the young Hegel's thought is religious it is not so in any sense that separates religion from the rest of life. Now perhaps Prof. Thomas is meaning that Tillich is misreading Hegel at this point. But the fact remains that Tillich himself evidently saw Hegel as separating religion to the theoretic sphere.

Prof. Thomas says the critique of the three options represented by Schleiermacher, Kant and Hegel is itself in the spirit of Hegel. First, I think that remark needs to be *shown*. But second, it is also interesting that Tillich says of the three that Schleiermacher's theory (religion as feeling) "is the one nearest the truth."

This is not to say that I don't find Prof. Thomas' thesis quite tempting, however. Yet the claim Prof. Thomas makes about Tillich's indebtedness to Marx—that it was a *formal* one—might just as easily be made about Tillich's debt to Hegel. Namely, while Tillich appropriated certain *formal elements* from Hegel's philosophy, he was doing something, on the one hand, far more within the realm of traditional theology in his theology of culture (I have suggested prophetic theology), and, on the other hand, Tillich was doing (or trying) a good deal more than that, too.

What it boils down to is who really knows whom Tillich was "really" influenced by. I am inclined to think it is a specious question. In the course of an article on Tillich's views about the existence of God I came to the realization that Tillich was probably just as influenced, at times, by Aquinas as he was by Augustine, even though sometimes it is hard to see. Unfortunately, such little "realizations" by themselves don't tell you much about the validity of *Tillich's* arguments. Moreover, Tillich stands out as almost a special case of the fruitlessness of this worry, since, at one time or another, Tillich seems to have shown the influence of just about everyone (and that should not be taken as a remark of criticism).

I would like to conclude by expressing some concern about Prof. Thomas' account of Gombrich's interpretation of Burchkhardt as a Hegelian. At least one should be aware of the possibility of arguing the other way. Burckhardt was very hostile toward "systems" which understood the process of historical development as capable of being reduced to the process of some rational and ordered plan. I think he would have shared Tillich's views about the "relentlessness" or "inevitability" of Hegel's history of the world spirit. Finally, Burchkhardt placed a great deal of emphasis on the belief that historians should study *human* history and not abstractions masquerading as history. History understood as the working out of pre-determined logical relations was simply blind to the importance of individual originality and creativity in history—a view which had influence on Croce, for example. I don't claim to know how to settle that debate any more than the one over the primacy of a Hegelian or Marxist influence on Tillich's theology of culture. I would only urge that whatever philosophical influences on Tillich seem useful to determine, they should be allowed to stand (or fall) directly on their own.

Theonomy and Technology: A Study in Tillich's Theology of Culture

RAYMOND F. BULMAN

The last three or four years have marked a quiet but significant revival of scholarly interest in the work of Paul Tillich. During this time, the American Academy of Religion issued an invitation for membership in the newly formed North American Paul Tillich Society, a permanent section of the mother organization. The enthusiastic response with which this call was met bears witness to the persisting relevance of Tillich's thought and the current renewal of vitality in Tillich studies.

There is no doubt that the publication of three notable biographies[1] within this same short period of time has lent impetus as well as a certain popular interest to this resurgence of Tillich research. Apart from the popular and admittedly interesting discussions concerning the relative merits of these frequently conflicting biographical sketches, the more technical work on Tillich's theological writings has achieved important, though undramatic momentum. The major emphasis of this more subdued research is on the political, ethical and social implications of Tillich's contributions.

---

[1]Rollo May, *Paulus* (New York: Harper and Row, 1973); Hannah Tillich, *From Time to Time* (New York: Stein and Day, 1973); and Wilhelm and Marion Pauck, *Paul Tillich: His Life and Thought* (New York: Harper and Row, 1976) vol. I.

Unquestionably, the academic leadership of Prof. James Luther Adams—the undisputed patriarch of Tillich scholars—accounts to a great extent for the interest in this particular direction. More basically, however, I believe that the national and cultural mood of today in the wake of Watergate and Vietnam—with all its skepticism and disillusionment about our myths and certainties of the past—is sufficient explanation for the current concern over political and social ethics, which finds its way into Tillich studies, as it does into so many areas of today's academic reflection.

While scholarly work on Tillich's thought in the Sixties concentrated heavily on the *magnum opus, Systematic Theology*, today's Tillich scholar seems more inclined to investigate the entire corpus and to take greater note of the central role played by political and social concerns in the earliest formulation of some of Tillich's key theological categories. This new emphasis in no way undermines or replaces interest in *Systematic Theology* and the other well-known works of the American period. But it does see them in greater continuity with the earlier works of the German period (1919-1933) and, as a result, views them from a decidedly different perspective.

There are two aspects of this new avenue of research which encourage me to believe that it will continue to thrive and prove fruitful in the future. First, the Tillich scholar of the Seventies cannot help but find striking parallels between the political, social and religious turbulence of our own time and that of the Weimar period in which Tillich's theology of culture first found its inspiration and expression. Secondly, he will find a source of confidence in the realization that Tillich's theoretical apparatus and outlook arose from the context of his deep personal and active participation in the struggles of that cultural situation.

One significant effect of the renewal of scholarly interest in Tillich's early work is the growing conviction that, despite the obvious diversity of subject matter, these early works reveal a highly organized structural unity. A careful analysis reveals a tightly woven architectonic structure which proves to be identical with Tillich's "theology of culture"—a complex of principles, methods and goals already formulated in his earliest scholarly efforts. While *Systematic Theology* appears to contain its own unique method and organization, I believe it can readily be shown that this represents a later development of the same fundamental structure proposed in the theology of culture.

Accordingly, I believe it is most suitable and consonant with Tillich's own thought to investigate and interpret his theological reflections on various aspects of culture, politics and society precisely from the vantage point of his theology of culture. The theology of culture provides us not only with a method and principles, but also with an overriding goal and concern. The special thrust and aim which pervade all of Tillich's theological work—and especially that of the early period—was the critical interpretation of our technological civilization, for he was convinced that, despite all its ambiguities and problems, technical culture was dominant in our time and was not likely to decrease in influence. For this reason he insisted that a correct understanding of both its assets and liabilities was absolutely essential for any viable (answering) theology as well as for any effective plan of social or political reform.

In this paper I will attempt to explore Tillich's specific reflections on the theological implications of technological culture—its values, weaknesses, dangers and hopes. If my previous contentions are correct, such an investigation should logically begin with a review of the principles of the theology of culture.

The Principles

I have already alluded to the powerful influence of Tillich's personal involvement in the political situation of post-World War I Germany on the development of his theological views. Not only his experience in the trenches of France, but his subsequent involvement in the struggle between the conservative element in the Church and the challenge of Marxist Socialism made him painfully aware of the tremendous gap which separated the preaching of the Church from the secular culture, and particularly from the needs and aspirations of the working classes. He entered the ranks of the Religious Socialist Movement and became one of its leading theoreticians in an attempt to bridge this gap and to reconcile the positive element in Christianity and Socialism.

The tensions entailed in these mediating efforts are vividly apparent in his 1919 address "Über die Idee einer Theologie der Kultur,"[2] which was primarily directed at countering the secularizing trends of the principal (Marxist) socialist movement. In this work he explained his understanding

---

[2]Paul Tillich, "On the Idea of a Theology of Culture," in *What is Religion?*, 155-81.

of the role of religion in culture and of theology among the academic disciplines. In so doing, he was laying the groundwork for his future theology of culture.

It would be a mistake to think that the theology of culture is restricted only to those works which are specifically directed to an interpretation of the cultural situation in politics, social justice, art, science, education and the like. Tillich's entire theological enterprise is essentially a theology of culture, so that even the famous method of correlation which dominates *Systematic Theology* was developed precisely in order to mediate between religious awareness and the ongoing secular culture. Tillich tells us as much in his 1959 foreword to *Theology of Culture*:

> In spite of the fact that during most of my adult life I have been a teacher of Systematic Theology, the problem of religion and culture has always been in the center of my interest. Most of my writings—including the two volumes of *Systematic Theology*—try to define the way in which Christianity is related to secular culture.[3]

A careful exploration of these writings from the policy statement of 1919 to his last public address consistently reveals the following principles as essentially operative in the theology of culture. I will comment on them only briefly, insofar as they are, no doubt, very familiar to any serious student of Tillich's thought.

(1) *Religion is the substance of culture and culture is the form of religion.* This is the most fundamental statement about the relationship of religion to culture and, as Tillich pointed out, "the most precise statement of theonomy."[4] He related this position not only to a philosophical perspective, but also to his Lutheran tradition—the *intra-Lutheranum*: that the finite is capable of the infinite.[5] By this he understood that all finite reality can be revelatory of the divine and every created object can become a symbol of ultimate reality. The task of the theologian of culture is to discern this religious depth in all creative human activities, no matter how secular and profane. Only when a culture is united to its own religious depth can

---

[3]Paul Tillich, *Theology of Culture*, ed. Robert C. Kimball (New York: Oxford University Press, 1964) v.

[4]Paul Tillich, *The Protestant Era* (Chicago: University of Chicago Press, 1948) 57.

[5]Paul Tillich, "Autobiographical Reflections," in *The Theology of Paul Tillich*, ed. Charles W. Kegley and Robert W. Bretall (New York: The Macmillan Co., 1964) 5.

it achieve a real sense of meaning and direction. Such a situation is theonomous.

(2) *Theonomy is the symbol of a complete religious humanism.* Precisely at that point where a culture achieves unity with its religious depth, there it attains its fullest human realization. Theonomy is not opposed to autonomy, for that would make it anti-humanistic. It consists rather in the transparency of all autonomous, human creative acts to their own religious depth.

The biblical religious symbol for theonomy is the "Kingdom of God." Like its religious correlate, theonomy cannot be brought about by human resources or effort. Man can only remain open to its reception and there can be no perfect theonomy under the conditions of estrangement. Through this openness, however, theonomy can be achieved in a real though fragmentary way.

Historically, an ongoing dialectical tension marks the struggle for theonomy in human culture. In our times mere autonomy (shallow secularism) has achieved a complete victory. But this kind of autonomy cannot stand alone. While it represents a valid protest against religious (and political) heteronomy or authoritarianism, it lacks depth, and therefore does not produce a complete humanism. It has lost an essential human dimension.

Full human realization is only possible when human dignity and independence are united to their essential religious substance in a theonomous situation. Otherwise a shallow autonomy leaves the door open to new secular forms of "quasi-religious" heteronomy, such as fascism, nationalism, scientism, or Communism.[6]

(3) *Theonomy reveals itself in the historical process through special, decisive moments called "kairoi" which constitute a breakthrough of the Eternal into human history.* In his early writings, which strongly reflect his political and social involvement, Tillich used the notion of "belief-ful realism" in response to the Marxist concern for historical consciousness. In this respect Tillich found Marx's dialectic not only to be true to the empirical realities, but also to be more in line with "the classical Christian doctrine of man."[7] "Belief-ful realism" signified an interpretation of history

---

[6]Paul Tillich, *Christianity and the Encounter of the World Religions* (New York: Columbia University Press, 1953) 12ff.

[7]Tillich, *The Protestant Era*, xv.

which was grounded in historical process and yet open to the transcendent meaning beneath the surface of political and social movements.

Within the framework of belief-ful realism or "self-transcending" realism,[8] Tillich began to use the New Testament term "kairos" to signify a special, historical, revelatory moment. Since, as was the case with Schelling, Tillich understood the struggle for humanity as taking place in human consciousness, "kairos" meant not only an historical moment, but also a kind of *thinking*.[9] "Kairos" is not only belief-ful and realistic; it is also *involved*. It is a knowledge which comes from faith within the risk, decision and hope of participation in history. Without active involvement and urgent response, the "Kairos" moment is not perceived.

The "Kairos" is therefore the moment in faith when the Religious Depth reveals itself within the ambiguity of the historical process. It is an extension of the notion of theonomy to the historical realm.

Before leaving the discussion of principles, I would like to point to an important fact which must not go unnoticed. The concept of "theonomy" is not just one of several important Tillichian principles. *Theonomy is the key concept of the theology of culture*. It appears in many contexts throughout Tillich's work; there is autonomous reason, theonomous culture, theonomous morality, theonomous depth, etc. The notion of theonomy permeates Tillich's entire theological inquiry. It symbolizes Tillich's religio-philosophical vision of reality which grounds the notion of the religious substance of culture, preserves the inner tension between religion and humanism and clarifies the ideal and direction toward which the humanization of culture should aim. Tillich expressly proclaimed that it was "under the banner of theonomy"[10] that he launched his theology of culture.

Now that we have considered the foundations and principles, I would like to turn my attention to the application of these principles to the cultural situation which faces us today. I have chosen an issue which seriously concerns us all in a wide variety of ways, and which, I feel, is decisive for our

---

[8]"Belief-ful realism" is Tillich's earlier term, used in his 1927 essay, "Gläubiger Realismus," found in the collection *Religiöse Verwirklichung* (Berlin: Furche-Verlag, 1929). When Tillich revised and lengthened this essay for *The Protestant Era* in 1948, he used the term "self-transcending realism."

[9]See Paul Tillich, *The Interpretations of History* (New York: Charles Scribner's Sons, 1936).

[10]"The Idea of a Theology of Culture," 180.

present historical concerns—the value and future of our technological culture.

Fortunately, Tillich has offered us a great deal of profound reflection on the topic. I will proceed by presenting and evaluating his view vis-à-vis alternative theological viewpoints. Finally, I will attempt to go beyond Tillich's own writings in an effort to adapt his analysis to a changed situation, and to modify, if necessary, aspects of his interpretation.

The Meaning and Future of
Technological Culture

THE THEOLOGICAL CONCERN ABOUT TECHNOLOGY. Technological civilization in all its diverse forms—from systems analysis and computerized data to jet travel and mass production—completely inundates our environment. Technology entails far more than the use of machines and sophisticated tools. It is an extremely complex organization of means for attaining predetermined results. Technology radically changes not only our way of life, but also our way of thinking. Enhanced transportation and communication tend to enlarge the urban complex—creating the megalopolis. At the same time the resulting increased concentrations of people become more and more dependent on the technological systems that draw them together. Technology forces us to put greater importance on rational decision and the acquisition of knowledge, especially on the accumulation and organization of data. It inevitably creates a knowledge- or reason-oriented society. The pervasive influence of technology on society is not just a question of new hardware. It effectively makes "our contemporary situation . . . qualitatively different from that of past societies."[11]

If Paul Tillich's theology of culture has anything significant to tell us about the human meaning of technology, it is on these grounds alone worthy of our most serious consideration. Since the end of the 1960s our technological culture has become more and more subject to very serious criticism. Theological criticism of the technocracy has come a long way since Harvey Cox wrote *The Secular City*. Professor Cox's own more recent writings clearly illustrate a decisive turn of direction from a glorifi-

---

[11]Emmanuel G. Mesthene, *Technological Change: Its Impact on Man and Society* (New York: New American Library, Inc., 1970) 25.

cation of technological culture to a recognition of its destructive powers.[12] While Cox still maintains an optimistic hope for the future of technical society, one clearly senses a growing anti-technical, anti-scientific attitude among many contemporary interpreters of culture. We need not go to Theodore Roszak, Carlos Castaneda and the proponents of the counter-culture to discover this rising pessimism about technology. Environmentalists, humanistic psychologists and evangelical theologians, such as Jacques Ellul, prophetically lament the dehumanizing effects of technocratic society. As a result of careful studies carried on by a variety of experts at the Harvard University Program on Technology and Society, Emmanuel Mesthene, the non-polemical and highly objective director of the program, made the following general evaluation:

> New technology creates new opportunities for men and societies, and it also generates new problems for them. It has both positive and negative effects, and it usually has the two *at the same time and in virtue of each other.*[13]

This objective appraisal seems valid enough and interdisciplinary teams such as Mesthene's will doubtlessly help us a great deal to understand both the complexities and the possibilities of our technological culture. I believe, however, that the role of theological reflection and evaluation in this most important and far-reaching contemporary issue is not only helpful but absolutely necessary.

While science and technology can provide us with means and with practical results, they are motive-free and can of themselves give us neither direction nor hope.[14] The need for hope is always crucial, but it is especially so during a period of rapid social and cultural change. The late British scientist C. A. Coulson was convinced that the essential Christian doctrines of Creation, Incarnation and Redemption provide the only real basis for our hope in the future of technological society and that the prin-

---

[12]This is very clear in *The Seduction of the Spirit* (New York: Simon and Schuster, 1973).

[13]Mesthene, *Technological Change*, 26.

[14]This point has been forcefully presented by physicist, Werner Heisenberg, in a recent article on the diverse functions of science and religion: "Science and Faith," *Cross Currents* (Winter 1975) 464-73.

cipal gift that the Christian can give to the world today is the sense of this hope. [15]

Whether or not we can share Coulson's enthusiasm about the Christian basis of hope, we might more readily accept Teilhard's bio-psychological argument that motivation and hope are necessary ingredients for the human "zest for life." The observable laws of energetics alone convince us that only the continuing rise of authentic hope will guarantee the activation to their maximum of the forces of self-evolution. [16]

Theologians by profession necessarily search for hope, motivation and values, so that whatever our own religious or philosophical views may be, the urgency of the present cultural crisis does not permit us to overlook their analysis and appraisal of the challenge of modern technology. This is all the more the case when the theologian in point is of the universal intellectual stature of a Paul Tillich.

Nevertheless, the secular mind (in which term I include us all) is understandably wary of theology. We rightly fear that the theologian, with his concern for the transcendent, might too easily present us with a kind of *Lebensferne philosophie*—a perspective far remote from the realities of everyday existence. Certainly, we must demand that any theological analysis of technology recognize in full the negative effects of its structures, such as depersonalization, loss of values, overcrowding, environmental pollution, false economic hopes and the threat of nuclear holocaust. At the same time, we can require that it recognize the liberating power and positive potential which we all likewise experience, and that it point out to us the avenues of hope for activating these potentials. I will try to show that Tillich's theological interpretation of technological culture admirably fulfills these requirements.

ELLUL AND THE THEOLOGICAL REJECTION OF TECHNOLOGY. It will prove helpful to compare Tillich's interpretation with that of Jacques Ellul, no doubt the sharpest theological critic of modern technology. Ellul correctly understands technology (*technique*) in its broadest context and implications, as suggested by the Harvard Program Studies. Like Mesthene he emphasizes that technique is much more of a process with its own au-

---

[15]C. A. Coulson, *Faith and Technology* (Nashville: The Upper Room, 1971) 29-30.

[16]Pierre Teilhard de Chardin, *Christianity and Evolution*, ed. and trans. by Rene Hague (New York: Harcourt, Brace, Jovanovich, Inc., 1969) 223-25.

tonomous logic and goals than it is a conglomeration of machines. The technological process acts almost as an independent agent, imposing its goals on man and forcing him to submit to the function of forever changing ends into means. "Technique transforms everything it touches into a machine."[17]

Machines themselves and even science have become an instrument of technique. Technique forces itself on all spheres of life, including the moral, the psychic and the spiritual. There is absolutely no possibility of a technical humanism. Christianity always has been and should continue to be opposed to the relentless, dehumanizing process of technique.[18] The technological city—the technopolis—is not only a product of technique; it is the very symbol of the sinful, demonic structures of our technological culture. There is, accordingly, no hope for the cities. Rather, a definitive break must occur between the earthly Jerusalem and the heavenly City of God.

> Man is not to be counted on to transform the problem of the city. He is no more capable of transforming the environment chosen for him and built for him by the Devil, than he is of changing his own nature. Only God's decisive act is sufficient.[19]

I doubt very much that Tillich himself was personally acquainted with or even aware of the work of Jacques Ellul. The work of the French theologian has only recently become popular in this country. Whether he knew him or not, what is clear to me is that Tillich knew very well where to locate Ellul's brand of theological interpretation. In a very perceptive address on religion and society delivered in New York toward the end of World War II, Tillich distinguished three types of religious thought which affect our social outlook.[20] These were basically the following:

> (1) That which emphasizes man's essential goodness and neglects the essential distortion of his nature. (Here Tillich located especially the theology of Ritschl and of the Social Gospel.)

---

[17]Jacques Ellul, *The Technological Society*, trans. by John Wilkinson (New York: Alfred A. Knopf, 1965) 4.

[18]Ibid., 32-38.

[19]Jacques Ellul, *The Meaning of the City*, trans. by Dennis Pardee (Grand Rapids: William B. Eerdmans Publishing Co., 1970) 170.

[20]Paul Tillich, "Trends in Religious Thought That Affect Social Outlook," in *Religion and World Order*, ed. F. Ernest Johnson (New York: Institute for Religious Studies, 1944) 19.

(2) That which emphasizes the existential distortion at the expense of man's existential goodness.

(3) That which emphasizes the tension between man's essential goodness and his existential distortion.

Characteristically, Tillich identifies his own thought with the dialectical outlook expressed in the third category. Under the second position he includes what he calls both naturalistic and supernaturalistic pessimism. Although in this essay he does not specifically identify his naturalists, this terminology is used in some of his other works[21] in reference to European nihilism, radical existentialism, to Schopenhauer, Feuerbach, Marx, Freud, and Sartre. The supernaturalistic pessimist he identifies specifically in the address as Kierkegaard and Karl Barth. The relationship of Ellul's thought to that of Barth is particularly obvious. For all such supernaturalists man has *lost* his essential nature and it can be restored only in the Christian event. We might even suspect that Tillich had Ellul specifically in mind as he further describes this theological outlook:

> No historical integrity or progress toward integrity can be imagined. The fulfillment is transcendent. The Kingdom of God has nothing to do with history. History is left to man in his existential distortion and to the demonic powers controlling him.[22]

Interestingly enough, Tillich points to the "tower of Babel" story as a symbol very dear to the heart of this second category of theologians. It represents for them "the tragic impossibility that mankind ever will reach political and cultural unity."[23] By this Tillich no doubt means the rejection of the historical realization of theonomy, even in a partial way. In Ellul's recent work, *The Meaning of the City*, he puts great stress on King Nimrod and the Babel story as the symbol of man's arrogant desire to glorify himself, "to make a name for himself." From this pride and hubris proceed man's inability to communicate and live in harmony: "In and because of the city, men can no longer understand each other and get along."[24]

---

[21]See, for example, *The Courage To Be* (New Haven: Yale University Press, 1952) 116-31.

[22]Tillich, "Trends in Religious Thought," 24.

[23]Ibid.

[24]Ellul, *The Meaning of the City*, 19.

It is not difficult to forecast the direction (or the lack of direction) toward which such a theological interpretation will lead. Should we have any doubt about it, Ellul makes it very clear that the modern Christian must dwell in the city, but make no effort to change it. I believe that Harvey Cox's analysis of Ellul is quite correct when he states that while the French theologian recognizes the existence of *corporate sin*, he fails to do justice to the import of *corporate grace*, whereby even the structures of evil can be redeemed. In Cox's view this is a distorted form of Calvinism, based on a "curiously thin doctrine of creation."[25]

TILLICH'S DIALECTICAL APPRAISAL OF TECHNOLOGY. The principles of Tillich's theology of culture protect him fully from the theological pessimism of the Ellulian type. Religion is the substance of culture: There is no purely secular realm. The presence of the infinite in the depth of all human creations—however distorted on the surface—is guaranteed. This was the significance for Tillich of the *infra Lutheranum*—that the finite is capable of the infinite (*finitum capax infiniti*).

It is significant that Ellul attributes the evil structures that constitute technique to the work of the devil. Tillich distinguishes between the "demonic" and the "satanic." The demonic is the distortion of something positive and good, a consequence of man's religious estrangement, whereas the satanic signifies the "absolutely negative" force of destruction. The unredeemableness of technological culture in Ellul's analysis would signify a satanic rather than a demonic presence in Tillich's terminology. When Tillich identifies industrial civilization and technical society with the "spirit of self-sufficient finitude"[26] and insists that our struggle is against the "powers and principalities," i.e. the evil forces in man and society, he seems strikingly close to the theological pessimism of Ellul. But in his letter to Eduard Heimann, Tillich reminds us that they "never spoke of the satanic but only of the demonic structures."[27] In every concrete reality the negative is carried along by the positive. The demonic has reality only as

---

[25]Cox, *The Seduction of the Spirit*, 74.

[26]Paul Tillich, *The Religious Situation*, trans. by H. Richard Niebuhr (New York: The World Publishing Co., 1932) 48.

[27]Paul Tillich, "Ein Brief zu Eduard Heimanns siebzigstem Geburtstag: Karios—Theonomie—Das Dämonische," in *Hamburger Jahrbuch für Wirtschafts—und Gesellschafts-politik* (1959) 4:14 (henceforward to be cited as "Ein Brief").

a distortion of the positive element, and in the power of the infinite the distortion can be removed as the positive is brought to the fore. However hopeless the situation, the hope for a new theonomy is necessarily an essential feature of Tillich's ontologically based theology of culture.

This radical difference between Ellul's and Tillich's analysis of technological culture should not create the false impression that Tillich was mild in his criticism of technology. He identified technological reason with the shallow autonomy of secular culture. Like autonomy, technology itself is a form of protest—a protest against the heteronomous demeaning of human intelligence and creativity. As a protest, however, it has no positive content; it cannot stand on its own, despite its ultimately humanistic and religious merit. (Ellul, by way of contrast, maintains that technology is the product, pure and simple, of man's stubborn pride and rebellious disorder—the creation of Satan.) While technology has a definite positive element for Tillich, it is nonetheless true that he saw this element as depraved by demonic distortion.

The essence of this distortion is the total victory of technical reason in our time. Only ontological reason is qualitative and open to depth. Technical reason separated from reason in the broad sense is detached, calculating and quantitative. With the triumph of technical reason an essential human dimension has been lost as the "noncognitive sides of reason have been consigned to the irrelevance of pure subjectivity."[28] The resulting loss of depth has created a sense of meaninglessness and loss of direction. In short, technical society has proved dehumanizing and profoundly alienating for modern man. Tillich is in full accord with Ellul that the greatest threat of technology is its power to "thing-a-fy" the person, to make him a thing among other things.[29] At the opposite end of the theological spectrum from Ellul we can find writers who present us with the simplistic model of technology as a purely neutral force the beneficial potential of which has been marred by purely accidental personal selfishness and sin.[30]

---

[28]ST I:73.

[29]ST III:74: "In transforming objects into things, he destroys their natural structures and relations. But something also happens to man when he does this, as it happens to the objects which he transforms. He himself becomes a thing among things."

[30]See, for example, Jean de la Croix Kaelin, O.P., "Faith and Technology," in *Christians in a Technological Era*, ed. Hugh C. White, Jr. (New York: The Seabury Press, 1964) 109-25.

Such a view is superficial and fails to recognize the corporate nature of sin. It naively draws our attention to the liberating features of technology, failing to see, as Tillich did, that the liberator must itself first be liberated from its own evil structures.[31]

Unlike Ellul, however, Tillich did believe that technology could be liberated and redeemed. Its demonic distortion conceals its positive element. Technology is rooted in nature itself. It is the product of the human spirit which is made in God's image. Its inner *telos* is moral and humanistic:

> Victorious technology was originally an agency for the emancipation of man from the demonic powers in all natural things. It was a revelation of the powers of spirit over matter. It was and it remains for innumerable people a means of deliverance from a stupid, beastlike existence. To a large extent it is the fulfillment of that which the Utopias of Renaissance philosophers dreamed of as a kingdom of reason and of the control of nature.[32]

It must not pass unnoticed, however, that the above passage originally appeared in Tillich's German work, *Die Religiöse Lage der Gegenwart,* in 1926. This was the Tillich of the Religious Socialist period who attributed the distortion of technology primarily to corruption of a capitalist, profit-oriented economic system (he essentially retained this view later on), and who at that time enthusiastically expected and worked toward a reformed social and political order. The belief that he was living in a time of *kairos* and on the verge of a new theonomous period certainly influenced his optimistic statements about the transformation of technology.

FROM ENTHUSIASTIC ROMANTICISM TO WAITING ON THE "SACRED VOID." In the dynamic period of political involvement following World War I the enthusiastic and confident Paul Tillich did not hesitate to draw attention to the innate goodness of technology and to make a plea for its future transformation in the true service of humanity.

> Art and technology can be united through the inner beauty of technical construction.

---

[31]Tillich, "Ein Brief," 15.

[32]Tillich, *The Religious Situation,* 49.

. . . A piece of technical beauty is holy in speaking out against all the falsehood that today permeates the market place. [33]

In a way that might surprise the student who is primarily familiar with the works of the American period, the early Tillich discussed with detailed concreteness many specific positive as well as negative features of technological civilization. In 1927 he wrote about the technological city: its meaning and promise; contradictions and threats. Long before Ellul he saw the technopolis as a symbol of our age. He reminds us of the importance for earlier man of the house and the village to defend himself from "the inhospitableness of endless space." [34] The technological city, far from symbolizing man's arrogance and depravity, represents a great leap in human development, in which the earth is appropriated, controlled and made hospitable for man. The modern home is also structured in a way that symbolizes the outlook of technological culture. It is open, with large windows and foundations high above the soil, for modern man is fearlessly open to explore and control nature (endless space) and anxious only when hemmed in by tradition (the narrowness of the cave) from searching for new ideas and possibilities. [35]

Characteristically, even in this early work, written from a standpoint of greater hope and expectation, Tillich did not fail to indicate the bleaker features of technological culture. While technology banishes the original strangeness of things, it still fails to make them familiar to us. The Technical City, with its world of things created for man's service, tends to draw everything, including ourselves, into the emptiness of its own process— making us the slaves of our own technical creations. [36] The Technological City is the symbol of pure autonomy; its structures are strictly rational and highly organized but are lacking spiritual depth. The Technological City must be negated and yet preserved through the creation of a theonomous unity of form and meaning.

While the very structure of Tillich's theology of culture insured that he would not lose sight of the "demonic" distortions of technology, his work

---

[33]Paul Tillich, "Logos und Mythos der Technik" in *Gesammelte Werke* (Stuttgart: Evangelisches Verlagswerk, 1972) IX:302-303 (henceforward to be cited as GW).

[34]Paul Tillich, "Die Technische Stadt als Symbols," in GW IX:308.

[35]Ibid.

[36]Ibid., 310-11.

prior to the Nazi takeover reveals, nevertheless, a more lively hope for this imminent theonomous transformation of our culture. Following the defeat of Religious Socialism and his banishment from his homeland, Tillich could no longer foresee a new kairos on the horizon. Rather, he now spoke of a "spiritual vacuum" and an "inner void."[37]

But even this more somber outlook did not indicate a loss of hope, for the present cultural situation is not to be understood only in terms of predominant victorious movement (i.e., technological reason), but also in terms of "an increasingly powerful protest against the movement."[38] To this movement Tillich gave the general name "existential protest" by which he understood an entire cultural reaction against the depersonalizing forces of technical society.[39] The protest was expressed in art, literature, philosophy and depth psychology and bore witness to the surviving power of the spirit and consciousness of theonomy. The protest changed the spiritual vacuum to a "sacred void"—a time of waiting and preparation. He adds, furthermore, that "this preparation was done in the depth of industrialized civilization, sometimes by people who represented its most antireligious implications."[40] The outlook of a chastened and disheartened Tillich is still a far cry from the supernatural pessimism of Jacques Ellul.

As the end of World War II and the impending defeat of Nazism came more clearly into view a spark of his earlier enthusiasm was cautiously rekindled for a short time. The spirit of his religious socialist days thoroughly permeates his participation in American religious discussions on "War Aims."[41] But these new hopes were also soon to be shattered as the demonic, authoritarian powers of Communism crushed the humanizing elements of the proletarian ideal and the "kairos" goal of a world state was strangled by the revived forces of nationalism.[42]

---

[37]Tillich, *The Protestant Era*, 60.

[38]Tillich, *Theology of Culture*, 43.

[39]Paul Tillich, "The Person in a Technical Society," in *Christian Faith and Social Action* (New York: Charles Scribner's Sons, 1953) 138.

[40]Tillich, *Theology of Culture*, 45.

[41]Paul Tillich, *War Aims* (New York: The Protestant, 1941). This is a brochure containing three articles on the topic written for *The Protestant* in 1941.

[42]Tillich, "Ein Brief," 14.

But despite this new defeat for the realization of concrete theonomous goals, Tillich refused to abandon the vision of a theonomous, unified culture. Furthermore, it was this vision that he considered decisive:

> It is a fact that the kairos events occur and have historically structured power, even when its hopes are not immediately fulfilled. This is true of the prophets and of the men of the New Testament, including Jesus.[43]

The prophets had, after all, failed for the most part in their attempts to influence the Israelite leaders, and the kingdom of righteousness preached by Jesus had ended in the defeat of the cross. But the spirit of prophetic protest against the hubris of national power remains a powerful force in Jewish consciousness and the ideals of Jesus Christ persist in the churches and in Western civilization—even in its more secularized forms. The kairos is "in preparation long before and it continues to work long after."[44]

The intellectual grounds on which Tillich was able to find continued hope within so many setbacks are to be found in the second principle of the theology of culture. Authentic human fulfillment and religious realization are identical. Accordingly, any stirring of protest in the name of humanity, any positive step, however limited, in the direction of humanizing our society, reveals the persistent presence of a Sacred Power within the depth of profanized culture. The disintegration produced by the victory of autonomous technology need only be a stage in the dialectics of history. This stage can yet be overcome by the breakthrough of the power of the New Being.

The myth of the New Being, like the Spiritual Presence and the Kingdom of God, is a religious, symbolic expression of the notion of theonomy. Faithful to biblical doctrine, Tillich insisted that theonomy is achieved only fragmentarily under the conditions of existence. With Ellul he would oppose the neo-Pelagian view that the Heavenly Jerusalem can be brought about by human effort. But even the fragmentary, partial or hidden presence of the Kingdom is very real. Under the power of this presence we can not only wait, but we must help prepare for a new theonomy. The Kingdom of God has not only a supra-historical aspect, as stressed by Ellul. It also

---

[43]Ibid., 12.

[44]Ibid.

has an inner-historical side which is experienced in special moments of kairos. Through the kairos the kingdom is operative in advance within the here and now. The kairos is not the *eschaton*. It is not enough to sit and wait.[45]

In his critique of technological culture Tillich tries to keep things in perspective by reminding us that man is never at home in his world, even when no special threats or inhospitableness confront him.[46] This is part of the human condition—the universal tragic estrangement of our existence. This inevitability of human estrangement does not diminish the impact of Tillich's critique of technology but it helps remind us that all human creations are marked with the ambiguity of distortion and alienation. But where there is existential estrangement and alienation there is also the basis of essential, unambiguous being. There is always hope for the religious union with the healing substance of culture. This reunion and conquest of separation (essentialization) is possible through the power of the Spiritual Presence which is operative even when the theonomous situation is hidden.

THE CONCEPT OF A HIDDEN THEONOMY.   In his 1949 article, "Beyond Religious Socialism," Tillich draws a somber picture of the world situation following World War II and resigns himself to the realization that there is no realistic hope for a new theonomy:

> The expectation we had cherished after the First World War that a "kairos," a fulfillment of time, was at hand, has been twice shaken, first by the victory of fascism and then by the situation after its military defeat.[47]

In the place of a creative kairos, Tillich saw spiritual emptiness, a vacuum. But even this vacuum could "be made creative . . . if it is accepted and endured and, rejecting all kinds of premature solutions, is transformed into a deepening 'sacred void' of waiting."[48] The "waiting" in a sacred void is different from that of a spiritual vacuum. It is *hopeful* waiting, in spite of

---

[45]Paul Tillich, *The Eternal Now* (New York: Charles Scribner's Sons, 1956) 123; and ST III:396.

[46]Tillich, "Die Technische Stadt als Symbol," 307.

[47]Paul Tillich, "Beyond Religious Socialism" in *The Christian Century Reader*, ed. Harold Fey and Margaret Frakes (New York: Association Press, 1962) 125.

[48]Tillich, *The Protestant Era*, 60.

the apparent lack of hope. Nor is Tillich content to proclaim this paradox-ical hope. He tried to identify the grounds of this hope within the very con-crete context of the political and cultural situation, just as he had done after the victory of Nazism. His 1958 letter to Eduard Heimann, a colleague in the days of Religious Socialism, gave us a clear picture of these grounds.

In the letter he defends the ongoing validity of the key Religious So-cialist concepts of "kairos," "theonomy," and the "demonic." In his discus-sion of "theonomy," he admits to Heimann that we have now witnessed the complete victory of a relentlessly overpowering technological culture, which has provoked in its turn an equally dangerous heteronomous reac-tion, both religious and political. Both movements, however, would be im-possible, for they would destroy each other, without the presence of a *hidden theonomy*.[49] Fortunately, Tillich does not leave us with the haziness of a mystifying, poetic metaphor, but goes on to describe the workings of this "hidden theonomy" in our culture:

> In the extreme form of autonomy, i.e., in scientific analysis and technical ex-periment, there is a growing awareness of the ultimate meaning of these activities. At the same time the authoritative forms in religion and politics are striving to jus-tify themselves by appealing to an autonomous criterion of truth. Without the hidden theonomous unity the autonomous side of culture would sink into complete mean-inglessness and the heteronomous side into sheer willfulness.[50]

Returning to his earlier theme of the importance of protest and con-sciousness he also describes this hidden theonomy as a theonomy of "question" rather than of "answer." Accordingly, he assures Heimann that despite the appearances, theonomy survives as a useful concept and that it is substantially the same theonomy for which they had hoped and strug-gled in the days of religious socialism.[51] It is characteristic of the paradox-ical and dialectic structure of Tillich's theology of culture and it is likewise distinctive of the personal courage of the man, Paul Tillich, that he was consistently able to discover victory in defeat.

---

[49]Tillich, "Ein Brief," 13: "Meine Antwort ist, dass keine der beiden Seiten möglich wäre ohne die Gegenwart einer verborgenen Theonomie."

[50]Ibid., 14.

[51]Ibid.

Conclusion

In short, we can say that Tillich's appraisal of technological culture constitutes a kind of historical realism which tried to discover its ultimate meaning within the concreteness and uniqueness of the political and social situation. At the same time it was a "belief-ful" realism—in the biblical sense of belief, which implies daring, involvement and action.[52] His activities and reflections of the Religious Socialist period illustrate this kind of knowledge derived from involvement and participation. While his early works abound in reflections on the liberating and humanizing potential of technology,[53] this early enthusiasm was deeply shaken by the historical events surrounding the two World Wars.

But despite these setbacks and disappointments, Tillich never resigned himself to an Ellulian-type pessimism and withdrawal from the struggle. The vision of theonomy, which is the core of Tillich's theology of culture, refuses to accept any culture as so secular, autonomous or profane that it ceases to be rooted in the infinite and divine reality. Even within secularized, technological culture man can be justified and discover the religious depth of meaning for which that culture seems to have no place. The only hope for a new theonomy, he insisted, lies "in the depth of industrialized civilization."[54] Even when the "kairos" moment is judged to be exceedingly remote, "kairos" *thinking* must prevail. "Kairos" thinking is the way to a belief-ful realism which can unite the eternal viewpoint to the world of time. Tillich believed that the concrete situation following World War II was a sacred void that demanded waiting. But unlike Ellul's inactive waiting, "kairos" thinking entails a waiting with involvement and decision in the actual situation.

The negativity of the later Tillich must be evaluated within the total framework of the theology of culture. Throughout his work we can recognize a clear and consistent pattern: The ecstasy of faith begins with desolation, courage is found within the depths of despair, victory is discovered

---

[52]ST III:371.

[53]Cf. for example: "Logos und Mythos der Technik" (1927), "Die technische Stadt als Symbol" (1928), and "Das Wohen, Der Raum und die Zeit" (1933) in GW IX; also *The Religious Situation* (1932).

[54]Tillich, *Theology of Culture*, 45.

in defeat. Similarly, when he expresses little hope for a new "kairos," he also reminds us that "the new in history comes when people least believe it."[55] The absence of an actual theonomy is counterbalanced by the presence of a hidden theonomy, and this is why for Tillich "waiting is not despair. It is acceptance of our not having, in the power of that which we already have."[56]

Within the current confusion and controversy over the value and future of technological culture I believe that Tillich's theology of culture provides us with a coherent methodology and a well-balanced perspective suggesting a direction which "unites in a special way theological optimism and pessimism and overcomes the alternative."[57]

Since the time of Tillich's death, furthermore, we find ourselves in what I believe is a substantially different cultural situation. Vietnam, Watergate and the growing economic, political and social crises of today reveal more powerfully than ever the demonic structures of technological society. At the risk of appearing melodramatic and presumptuous I will venture to suggest that if Paul Tillich were still with us today, he might well discern within the depths of our anxiety and desolation the dawn of a new "Kairos." He might perhaps repeat to us today his prophetic words of long ago: "We live in such a moment; such a moment is our situation."[58]

---

[55]Paul Tillich, *The Shaking of the Foundations* (New York: Charles Scribner's Sons, 1948) 182.

[56]Ibid., 152.

[57]Tillich, "Trends in Religious Thought," 28.

[58]Tillich, *The Shaking of the Foundations*, 183.

Theonomy and Paradox: A Response to Raymond Bulman

JOHN R. STUMME

I appreciate very much the paper of Prof. Bulman. He has given us a concise analysis of Tillich's dialectical attitude toward technological culture, a helpful comparison of Tillich and Ellul, and a creative attempt to view our own situation with the insights of Paul Tillich. It is interesting for me to see one well versed in Tillich's thought taking on the difficult task of addressing the present dilemmas of society.

Prof. Bulman has done us a valuable service in reminding us of Tillich's profound interpretation of the modern era, so sensitive as it was to the demonic distortions and creative possibilities of our time. A few years ago, when the limits-to-growth people first sounded their warnings, I was surprised to discover that already in 1923 Tillich had attacked autonomous, bourgeois society for its "infinite desire for domination," its willingness to sacrifice all to "infinite activity," its "limitless rational will to power in industry," and its "limitless economy."[1] Over a half-century ago, Tillich, on the basis of his theonomous vision, criticized the notion of unlimited

---

[1]"Basic Principles of Religious Socialism," *Political Expectation*, ed. by James Luther Adams (New York: Harper & Row, 1971) 74, 75, 76, 77.

growth and perceived what might well be important ontological roots of our ecological crisis. Tillich's theology of culture *is* worth taking seriously, as Prof. Bulman has argued.

Prof. Bulman has, I believe, presented a largely accurate outline of Tillich's basic theological perspective on culture. If I differ with him at this point—and it may be only a terminological difference—it would be that I place greater stress on the concept of paradox. The paradoxical immanence of the Transcendent, the "breakthrough" of grace into concrete reality, in other words, the doctrine of justification, shapes Tillich's theology of culture at its most basic level. Prof. Bulman has stated that "Theonomy is the key concept of the theology of culture." I am uncomfortable with most attempts that say this is *the* key, including this one. Tillich's theology is too integrated to make one concept the key. Moreover, paradox is more fundamental than theonomy; theonomy is one way of expressing the paradox.

Utilizing the typology of H. Richard Niebuhr's *Christ and Culture*,[2] I understand Tillich as a theologian of paradox who saw "Christ as the Transformer of Culture." Because of his dialectical attitude toward culture, Tillich could not accept the sharp opposition of "Christ against Culture" (as in Ellul) nor the easy accommodation of "Christ of Culture" (as in Cox of *The Secular City*). Although he spoke of synthesis, he opposed the layered view of reality of "Christ Above Culture" and envisioned synthesis only in paradox. Tillich was a paradoxical thinker, but he challenged the dualism and conservatism of "Christ and Culture in Paradox." The thrust of his theology was the conversion of the present in light of the breaking in of Transcendence. It does not help to create a new type such as "Christ the Depth of Culture" (as Carl Armbruster suggests),[3] for depth is simply another way of speaking of paradox. In light of his Lutheran background and in light of his efforts to change culture, Tillich is, I think, most adequately described as one standing on the boundary between Niebuhr's "Christ and Culture in Paradox" and "Christ the Transformer of Culture." I surmise that Prof. Bulman might possibly be in substantial agreement with this analysis. And I agree with him that this perspective,

---

[2]*Christ and Culture* (New York: Harper Torchbooks, 1951).
[3]*The Vision of Paul Tillich* (New York: Sheed and Ward, 1967) 282-304.

though it is not without problems of its own, is a valid and fruitful one for the theologian in interpreting culture.

Prof. Bulman's paper has touched upon many complex and controversial issues. There is much in it worth further discussion. For example, is Mesthene really "highly objective" in his study of technology (what does "objective" mean in appraising technology?) and is his analysis really "valid"? There is, of course, the interesting methodological question: How does the theologian decide if Mesthene's views are valid or invalid? What for Prof. Bulman is the relationship between Tillich and Mesthene? Is Prof. Bulman attracted to Mesthene because he finds that Mesthene's views have a certain affinity with Tillich's? Or is he attracted to Tillich because he accepts Mesthene's views? Or is it a little of both? What should be the way of relating theological and empirical study?

Or, again, is it actually so, as Prof. Bulman claims, that "science and technology . . . are motive-free and can of themselves give us neither direction nor hope"? This seems to be another way of stating that technology is neutral. But is not this the very position that Ellul has so effectively criticized when he shows technique to be an autonomous process with its own goals and directions? Perhaps Ellul is correct in his analysis at this point in spite of his faulty theological presuppositions. And how does Prof. Bulman's claim square with Robert Heilbroner's contention that technology has its own "imperatives," its own built-in values, such as efficiency, control of the environment and the priority of production?[4] If Heilbroner is right, then technological society does have a self-propelling direction.

These are difficult issues which are vital to any discussion of technology, but upon which I have no new light to shed. I wish, therefore, to focus the rest of my remarks directly on Tillich and Bulman's interpretation of him. My many agreements with Prof. Bulman I will bypass in order to highlight some differences and to raise some further questions about Tillich's view of theonomy and technology.

Prof. Bulman has emphasized the continuity between the early and the late Tillich, and certainly the consistency and coherence of his fundamental structure of thought is amazing. But when it comes to his concrete analysis and critical interpretation of society, I am as impressed by the *discon-*

---

[4]*An Inquiry Into the Human Prospect* (New York: W. W. Norton & Co., Inc., 1974) 77-78.

tinuity of his thought as its continuity. By this I do not simply mean the difference between the optimism of his early period (which cannot simply be dismissed in toto as romantic) and the pessimism of his later period. The more decisive difference is that in Germany Tillich was a socialist and in America after 1945 (or before) he was not. In his early work his major theological concepts were also socialist concepts. The kairos was "the socialist hour,"[5] the principle demonic structure of the present was capitalism, and the theonomous society was a socialist society. Later, however, the concrete reference of these terms is lost, and they hang suspended in the air, largely unconnected with historical realities. In his later period, Tillich's criticism of society is, for the most part, much more domesticated. He no longer takes his starting point for theological reflection from the strivings of the oppressed but from the anxieties of the overclass. He no longer calls for "the socialist decision" but rather speaks of "the lost dimension." He analyzes and supports the space program without the tough, critical class analysis which was present when he analyzed the Technical City.[6] The guardian of the void was hardly the "dangerous man" for the interests of society that the proclaimer of the socialist *kairos* had been, who was dismissed from his chair at Frankfurt.

Perhaps these contrasts are overdrawn, but I make them sharp so that the significant differences between the socialist and the non-socialist Tillich will not be slighted. Prof. Bulman suggests in a parenthesis that Tillich "essentially retained" his earlier views on capitalism. If he did, he kept it a well-hidden secret. To say that he did undercuts the diversity in Tillich's thinking. In drawing upon Tillich's notion of theonomy, we have to make clear whether we are speaking of a socialist or a non-socialist hope for the future.

A further question troubles me, and that concerns the viability of utilizing Tillich's concept of theonomy in our present context. Prof. Bulman has suggested that for Tillich "theonomy can be achieved in a real but fragmentary way." The question I pose is, "What *is* the reality of theonomy?" What makes it real? What would have to happen to make it occur? The theonomous society is a public symbol and therefore it involves not only a

---

[5]"Die Theologie des Kairos und die Gegenwaertige geistige Lage. Offener Brief an Emauel Hirsch," *Theologische Blaetter* XIII:II (November 1934) 319.

[6]"The Effects of Space Exploration on Man's Condition and Stature," *The Future of Religions*, ed. by Jerald C. Brauer (New York: Harper & Row, 1966) 39-51.

subjective change, a change of consciousness alone, but also changes in the structures of society. What are these changes? How would openness to Transcendence alter technological society? Are there moral preconditions or moral consequences to theonomy? In what way is the theonomous society also the just and the good society? What is the content of the theonomous hope?

Prof. Bulman's paper illustrates the dilemma. At one point he states that Tillich believed "that technology could be liberated and redeemed." He supports his statement by quoting the young Tillich (the quote speaks of technology as "liberating," not "liberated," and in the context of autonomy, not theonomy), and then he qualifies his interpretation by suggesting that the remark was shaped by Tillich's early enthusiasm. Thus, we are left in uncertainty about the meaning of a liberated and redeemed technology. Is it so that Tillich, when he envisions theonomy, is either romantic, longing back to the High Middle Ages or to his own idyllic past, or vague, offering little help for shaping historical realities? I think not, although both dangers are present. The more important point to make here, however, is that we who want to apply Tillich's insights to our situation must avoid romanticism and undue vagueness.

Tillich insisted that theonomy was a symbolic, not an empirical, concept. He resisted making theonomy into a utopia, and he did not think it possible to create a blueprint for the future. This we can accept. And yet the question remains: What is the historical reality and significance of this symbol?

Prof. Bulman finds value in the concept of "the hidden theonomy." He believes it is characteristic of Tillich's dialectical and paradoxical thinking and a sign of his courage that was able to find victory in defeat. Perhaps so. But I think it could just as accurately be seen as a neat way out of a tough spot. Any theonomy is a hidden one, but this one is a hidden, hidden theonomy. Tillich sees hope in an "existential protest" against the dehumanizing tendencies of technological society. Prof. Bulman sees significant difference between this position and Ellul's. I wonder. Prehaps there is a touch of irony that at this point, Tillich and Ellul, in spite of their different theologies, both believe that writing and saying "no" is the decisive task of the present. And both believe this is possible because of grace in spite of the emptiness and demonic distortions of autonomous society.

The concept of the hidden theonomy is a concept of consolation, a word of comfort in a time of despair. The concept of theonomy, on the other hand, is an enticing and invigorating vision, offering new possibilities and tasks. The theonomy concept does seek to give hope and direction, as Prof. Bulman argues. In these bewildering times it does in principle offer what is needed: a norm to judge the present and a vision to direct our actions. Yet theonomy, at least as it has been presented here, does not tell us what this direction is. It is not enough to call for a new sense of Transcendence; we must identify the groups that bear this Transcendence. It is not enough to call for theonomy; we must spell out its historical and structural implications. One of Tillich's significant contributions, especially in his early writings, is that he took on the risk of doing these things. He dared to be concrete. Unless we do this, unless we clarify the direction that theonomy leads us, it is premature, if not presumptuous, to proclaim the coming of a new kairos.

I make these comments with gratitude for Prof. Bulman's helpful paper.

Aesthetic Elements in Tillich's Theory of Symbol

DONALD R. WEISBAKER

I

Among scholars devoted to the study of theology, even in very wide and open contexts, the title of this piece may prove puzzling. For while it is true that theologians must attend to branches of philosophy like metaphysics, epistemology, and logic to do responsible work, only a limited attention is paid the realm of values known as the aesthetic. However, it may be argued that more attention to aesthetic modes of thought is necessary for the most honest expository and critical work in Tillich since even a casual reading of his works reveals that a good deal of reflection on his part was devoted to art, especially but not exclusively, in relation to religion. His reflections in this area gave rise to a number of addresses and essays, some published, some unpublished, on the subject. He was a critic, analyst, and in a technical and philosophical sense, an aesthetician, that is, a theoretician of art.[1] His reflections upon art often melded with, influenced, and

---

[1] See Charles W. Kegley, "Paul Tillich on the Philosophy of Art," *Journal of Aesthetics and Art Criticism* 19 (Winter 1960) 175-84.

were influenced by his reflections upon theology. At times the two modes of reflection are difficult to separate, but attention to the aesthetic dimension of his thought can be a useful tool for getting at some of the theological meanings of this difficult and occasionally evasive thinker.

One way to begin this task is to become sensitive to Tillich's own claims concerning the influence of art upon his philosophical and theological reflection. These statements should be taken quite seriously. For while it is true that many in the world of theological scholarship are familiar with those statements, in no approaches to his work has this biographical detail been appreciated fully. Biographically it can be claimed that it was experience with aesthetic objects that really awakened Tillich to those things which his theology sought to talk about and which provided him with a clue to the chief means of talking about them. It was experience in the aesthetic realm which fully opened Tillich's eyes to a depth element in human experience—which is what his theology is about—and which provided him with the clue that this could only be spoken about in and through symbols. Another way of putting this point is to say that for Paul Tillich aesthetic experience had a biographical priority and it provided potent analogues for his talking about religious experience. More than that, it provided him with a central concept of his theological work, namely the concept of symbol. This he claimed as "the center of [his] theological doctrine of knowledge."[2] It is also the case that aesthetic experience and modes of aesthetic reflection provided categories, relationships, and insights for aspects of his theological work other than symbol theory.

In order to give credibility to claims about the influence of the aesthetic in the life and thought of Paul Tillich, one can turn briefly to some elements of his biography. There are several sources of information about Tillich's life story.[3] The earliest of them, an introduction to his *The Interpretation of History*, makes the following point about his experience of art:

> Upon experience (of art) followed reflection and philosophic and theologic interpretation, which led me to the fundamental categories of my philosophy of religion and

---

[2]Charles W. Kegley and Robert W. Bretall, eds., *The Theology of Paul Tillich* (New York: Macmillan Co., 1964) 333.

[3]Introductions to *The Protestant Era* (Chicago: University of Chicago Press, 1948) and *The Interpretation of History* (New York: Charles Scribner's Sons, 1936). "Autobiographical Reflections" in Kegley-Bretall. *On the Boundary, An Autobiographical Sketch* (New York: Charles Scribner's Sons, 1966).

culture, namely form and content. . . . The concept of the "breakthrough," dominant in my theory of revelation, was one in connection with it.[4]

In an address entitled "Human Nature and Art," delivered at the Minneapolis Institute of Arts in November of 1952, Tillich makes the point about
the cruciality of art even more sharply. He tells that while on furlough in
Berlin from his duties as a chaplain in World War I he saw a picture "by
Botticelli and had an experience for which I do not know a better name than
revelatory ecstasy. The level of reality was opened to me which had been
covered up to this moment, although I had some feeling before of its existence."[5] This affirmation on his part that art opened him to new dimensions of reality is confirmed, then, in a final biographical statement, which
was among the last things he did in 1964-1965. In that he says:

> The discovery of painting was a crucial experience for me. . . . I recall most vividly
> my first encounter—almost a revelation—with a Botticelli painting in Berlin during
> my last furlough of the war. Out of the philosophical and theological reflection that
> followed these experiences I developed some fundamental categories of philosophy
> of religion and culture, viz., form and substance. It was the expressionist style
> emerging in Germany during the first decade of this century . . . that opened my
> eyes to how the substance of a work of art could destroy form and to the creative
> ecstasy implied in the process. The concept of the "breakthrough," which domi-
> nates my theory of revelation, is an example of the use of this insight.[6]

It is obvious that the language varies somewhat in each of these statements, but they are sufficiently united to allow some general observations

---

[4]Trans. N. A. Rosetzski and Elsie L. Talmey (New York: Charles Scribner's Sons,
1936) 15-16.

[5]Paul Tillich, "Human Nature and Art," one of three lectures under the general title,
"Art and Society," delivered for the faculty, students, and friends of the Minneapolis School
of Art at the Minneapolis Institute of Arts, November 5-7, 1952. Now in the Tillich Archive,
Harvard University, p. 2. This statement by Tillich is more pointed and specific than his
1936 statement and less qualified than the one cited next from *On the Boundary*.

[6]Paul Tillich, *On the Boundary, An Autobiographical Sketch*, 27-28. While there is a
redundancy in citing several sources to document the relationship between art and religious
awareness in Tillich, the virtue in citing all three of them lies in showing the consistency of
his interpretation of his experience. Beyond this, citation from this third source has a
higher degree of authenticity in that, although it is essentially the same work as that which
appeared in Part I of *The Interpretation of History*, Tillich was in position to affirm the English text of *On the Boundary*. *The Interpretation of History*, on the other hand, appeared
while Tillich was still very unknowledgeable about English; it is also widely considered a
poor translation of his German original.

to be made. First, it appears that experience with art initially made Tillich fully conscious that human awareness can be directed toward a dimension of which surface forms are only the expression. Again, it is obvious that aesthetic experience led rather directly into reflection upon religious matters. Finally, there is what appears as the most significant element of all in these biographical details, that in these experiences there was contained the germinal elements of Tillich's notion and theory of symbol. This is expressed in the idea that "the substance of a work of art could destroy form." What he seems to mean at this point is that an artist, in order to get at deeper meanings, distorts the normal forms of things in the world. The artist "breaks" them or "destroys" them so that they may become symbolic of that which he wishes to convey—a depth beyond the normal, surface reality of everyday life. This could be said in another way which is perhaps more adequate: What Tillich perceived in art was a transformation process which produced *expressions* of the human awareness of deeper levels of meaning. In short, he saw in art the prime example of the symbolic process, that is, the transformation of elements from the real world into expressions of a profound element in human awareness. We may call this process of which Tillich became most deeply cognizant in relation to art "symbolic transformation." Once it became established for him he never let go and this notion of "the symbol" became exceedingly fruitful for him. Out of aesthetic experience came a key element of much of his future work. If we are to understand him aright, we ourselves must gain further understanding of the way this early insight took on new dimensions and grew to the point of being a very important element of his major work, *Systematic Theology*. The basic thrust of this paper, then, will be devoted to shedding some further light on the Tillichian concept of symbol through systematic attention to the relation of that concept to the aesthetic.

II

Tillich's development of his notion of symbol was devoted mainly to the idea of religious symbol for a long period of his writing after the experience we have cited. Finally, however, he returned to direct reflection upon aesthetic symbols, especially in relation to religious ones, during the 1950s and early 1960s. It is on material deriving from those ten to twelve years that it is useful to concentrate, for in this period Tillich produced work both published and unpublished on the subject. Both kinds of material are of use

in understanding his ideas, for although the unpublished materials intro-
duce no seminal ideas not found in the published work, they yet fill out his
theory of artistic symbols. In this way, they are helpful in obtaining a further grasp of the elusive and sometimes ill-fated subject of the symbol in
general.

One may begin with his 1952 lectures to the Minneapolis Institute of
Arts in which Tillich sought to answer the question, "what is the nature
of a being that is able to produce art?"[7] His answer was in terms of the
now familiar definition of man as "finite freedom." Each part of this understanding of man has a bearing upon art, as finite man yet belongs to an
infinity from which he is excluded. And there arises in man an urge to express the infinity from which man is excluded. From this there arise symbols both artistic and religious. Tillich says, "Men create the gods as
symbols of that which has created him [sic], the infinite from which he is
separated and to which he is longing to return."[8] Man's finitude does not
exclude him only from the infinite within existence, however; it excludes
him also from other finite things. As the most centered being, man is the
most excluded being. This exclusion drives to a desire to participate. Cognition appears to Tillich as an expression of this desire, but it is finally unsatisfactory because we never participate in "what the things mean for
themselves."[9] This latter phrase is obviously a rather arcane one; but it is
essential to hear because he contrasts the artistic endeavor with cognitive
endeavor and suggests that art is able to get beyond the cognitive stricture
because "the arts penetrate into the depths of things which is beyond the
reach of cognition."[10] He also says, "intuitive participation in works of art
liberates us from the loneliness of our separated existence in a much more
radical way than the cognitive participation can. In knowledge the distance
remains decisive. In art the union, the uniting love, dominates."[11] In this
way Tillich spells out the role of man's finitude in artistic production. When
he turns to the role of freedom in this respect, he is more brief in his statements, but he does say things that clearly echo his World War I experience

---

[7]Paul Tillich, "Human Nature and Art," 4.

[8]Ibid., 5.

[9]Ibid.

[10]Ibid., 6.

[11]Ibid.

with art. He admits that human freedom is a philosophically debatable idea, but he claims that whatever else may be true of freedom, art is a witness to man's transcending the merely given through freedom. By means of the arts man introduces "the discovered into the realm of the given in forms which transcend the given."[12] Art is, in other words, a transforming activity. It breaks ordinary forms for the sake of expressing an awareness of deeper dimensions of reality. The end product of art is effective symbolization of participation by man in realms that transcend the finite and the given.

At this point a knowledgeable reader is probably aware of a rather close analogue between this description of the dynamics of artistic symbol formation and the dynamics of religious symbol formation as Tillich spells that out in his theology. The question may very well be raised, then: Is there any distinction between artistic and religious symbols and the experience which underlies the creation of each? In a group of lectures at Wheaton College, Massachusetts, delivered in 1961, Tillich addressed this problem rather directly and provided a further basis for our understanding of the whole process of symbol creation in art and religion. The general title of these lectures was "Expression in the Life of Religion." It is the second of these presentations which provides distinguishing clues about religious and artistic symbols, for the question seems to have arisen in relation to this lecture. In a question-and-answer session afterward, which is at least partially recorded as a part of his presentation, Tillich makes an effort at making the distinction. He tells us: "The symbolized in the artistic creation is a meaning embodied in an encountered reality encountered [*sic*] for the encountering artist and for those who participate in his experience."[13] Again, he makes the point this way: "That which is symbolized, that towards which all art points, every artistic creation points, is a meaning which is embodied in an encountered reality, in the subject matter which the artist chooses."[14] In an attempt to say what that meaning is, Tillich talks of the power of twentieth-century existentialist art to express the human situation very profoundly and hints that in so doing art is getting back

---

[12]Ibid., 9.

[13]Paul Tillich, "Through Literature and Art," second of three lectures under the general title "Expression in the Life of Religion" delivered as the Marjorie Otis Memorial Lectures at Wheaton College, Norton, Massachusetts, on February 23-24, 1961. Now in the Tillich Archive, Harvard University, p. 10.

[14]Ibid.

to its roots, that is, to the deeper dimensions of reality. In an earlier context he had spoken of a style that is "religious" without religious content and named three paintings as representative of this: Van Gogh's "Starry Night," Picasso's "Guernica," and "River Without Edges" by Chagall.[15] To be religious without having religious content, for Tillich, means that this art is expressing not any affirmations, but rather the negativity, meaninglessness, and despair of the human situation. Such art possesses what one can only call the preliminary religiosity of being concerned, but being without any answer. One might say that it is implicitly, but not explicitly, religious. From these things one gathers that the unique power of artistic creations is the expression of an awareness of separation, brokenness, and estrangement. Artistic symbols possess, in the first place, a "preliminary" awareness in that they mediate an awareness of the questions of human existence for which assumedly religious symbols are the answer. But one must be very careful at this point, for the distinction between artistic and religious symbols, which seems to be made with some neatness here, quickly breaks down upon a moment's reflection. Tillich knew that no simple dichotomy in which artistic symbols make man aware of questions and religious symbols provide answers would do. Any of us can see that religious symbols involve artistic effort (as in the building of a cathedral) and that the two value realms combine in other ways which a question-and-answer dichotomy vastly oversimplifies.

In the body of this second lecture, then, Tillich makes plain that religious and artistic symbols may effectively combine in religious art, which apparently then would be at least partially expressive of an awareness of the answer to the human predicament. In this sense religious art would function somewhat like theology functions in relation to philosophy. In this latter relation Tillich tells us that philosophical concepts "are conceptually transformed mythological symbols, and that therefore all ontology combines a mythological substance with a philosophical form."[16] What theology does or should do, as far as Tillich is concerned, is to keep alive this re-

---

[15]Paul Tillich, "Religion and the Visual Arts," a lecture delivered at Connecticut College in November 1955. Now in the Tillich Archive, Harvard University.

[16]Paul Tillich, "Through Symbols and Concepts," first of three lectures under the general title "Expression in the Life of Religion," delivered as the Marjorie Otis Memorial Lectures, 1961. Now in the Tillich Archive, Harvard University, p. 12. Tillich's statements in this unpublished lecture echo a position about which he had a lifelong consistency, namely that philosophy and theology have a common point in their concern about the ultimate or unconditioned. (See his *What is Religion?* and the introduction to *Systematic Theology.*)

lationship between symbols and concepts. That is, theology must prevent one or the other from becoming totally dominant in the life of the individual or of the religious community, for the domination of symbols too easily leads to a tendency to literalize and an emphasis upon concepts appeals to the mind, but not to the total human person which religion is to grasp. Analogously, in art religious symbols can be transformed, apparently by human aesthetic prowess, into purely artistic symbols. This process Tillich tends to think of as an aestheticism; for him it is a danger as great as the tendency to literalize religious symbols. And as theology is to mediate between symbols and concepts, so religious art is to mediate between religious and artistic symbols, allowing neither to dominate the other if true religious art is to exist. Tillich becomes very specific about this function of religious art when he says, "And religious art is the analogon to theology."[17]

III

Now we should be in position to step back and reflect in a general way upon what has been said so far. The general claim herein made has been that attention to the aesthetic dimension of Tillich's thought can be a useful tool for opening his sometimes hazy and confusing thought. More specifically, it is our thesis that attention to the aesthetic element in Tillich's experience and thought can give us useful clues to the meaning of one of his key conceptions which is so central to his theology—the idea of the symbol.

From what has been said up to this point it should be obvious that a symbol for Tillich is the result of a transformation process in which some concrete aspect of reality—and he is clear that anything in reality subjects itself to this process—becomes expressive of an awareness had by him for whom the symbol is effective. The thing selected from the phenomenal field does not retain its usual natural or historical appearance, however. He talks of the artist as breaking ordinary forms for the purpose of expressing an essential element beneath the surface. Analogously, he argues that to mistake the historical personage of Jesus as what Christianity is about is to fall into idolatry. The ordinary historical form, Jesus of Nazareth, is "broken" by the New Testament writers who are creating a symbolic

---

[17]Paul Tillich, "Through Literature and Art," 9.

expression. It is only as the Christ that he functions effectively. That is, Jesus *as the* Christ, as a transformed reality, as having become a symbol, is alone the key to the faith of the West.

Let us raise some questions, however, concerning the mechanism of this transforming process. First, what enables it? The answer which emerges from a general consideration of Tillich's statements about both artistic and religious symbols is that their creation is enabled or empowered by participation. We know the Tillichian formula to the effect that symbols participate in the reality to which they point. This language on his part has been the cause of much confusion of meaning. Its initial assertion would seem to be that there is a mysterious but real ontological relationship between a symbol and the reality symbolized. If this were Tillich's meaning, then he would be caught in all the dilemmas of Plato as Plato sought to use the metaphor of "participation" for the relationship between essences and their imperfect realizations in existence. Tillich's theory may have its dilemmas, but they are not due, in our judgment, to a purely Platonic understanding of the participation of symbols. This is not to say, however, that no form of idealism underlies Tillich's theory, but initially his own notion appears much more phenomenological, perhaps Husserlian. That which participates in the symbolized reality is, in the first place, the consciousness of him for whom the symbol functions. To put it another way, the key to symbol theory in Tillich appears as participation, but it is the secondary or indirect participation. The first element to engage in the participatory process by which symbols come into being is the consciousness of the artist or the genuinely religious man; that consciousness exists in a particular way vis-à-vis the depth dimension. The mode of that consciousness is the mode of "awareness of participation in." In what? Religiously Tillich is quite specific that the awareness is of the divine and of one's being related to it or participating in it.[18] Aesthetically Tillich talks of participation in a special realm of meaning. And he is willing to define beauty as "the power of mediating a special realm of meaning by transforming reality."[19]

---

[18] See Paul Tillich, *Systematic Theology* (Chicago: University of Chicago Press, 1951) I: 109.

[19] Paul Tillich, "Human Nature and Art," 12. See also *Systematic Theology* (Chicago: University of Chicago Press, 1963) III:64.

This participation by consciousness itself in depth leads to the symbolic transformation of the surface phenomena of nature and history. Symbols are produced to express the depth awareness of human consciousness. But we must be careful. In Tillich the symbols exist and function only for him for whom participation is real. For others what appears is the ordinary surface reality of everyday life. If that reality is broken or distorted, as for instance in a Picasso painting, it appears that way—broken or distorted and without symbolic power. What this means is that when symbols are effective, the real *locus* of them is in the consciousness which participates. To borrow a phrase from Husserl, symbols are "transcendentally located." They appear as symbols only in and through the prior participation of consciousness which are united with depth.

This priority of participation by consciousness—we can even say, the priority of a peculiar cognitive content of consciousness—has an importance in the theology of Tillich which is quite fundamental. For him the consciousness which participates and thus possesses awareness of depth is the essence of religion. It is this consciousness which has produced the symbols of religion out of the materials of nature and especially of history. We might say that the informed consciousness has sought a way to express its awareness. And by the imaginative transformation of elements from the real world it has found that way. This taking of elements from the real world for the sake of imaginatively transforming them into symbols expressive of depth awarenesses in religion Tillich calls an *analogia imaginis*.[20] He contrasts this with the classical *analogia entis*, which was purportedly a way of knowing God. The *analogia imaginis* is, by contrast, "a way (actually the only way) of speaking of God."[21] Another way of putting this point would be to say that the *analogia imaginis* supplies the all-important concrete element in the Divine-human relation. All relations between man and God must have this concrete element to make "God-talk" possible, for otherwise there would be only the mystical, awesome, and ineffable awareness of the Divine.

A second question, perhaps even more important, concerning the process by which natural and historical materials are transformed into sym-

---

[20]Paul Tillich, *Systematic Theology* (Chicago: University of Chicago Press, 1957) II: 115.
[21]Ibid.

bols centers in the fact that Tillich has apparently collapsed authentic religion and art into an undifferentiated mass. Both art and religion seem to root in an experience of a "transcendent" reality which each seeks to symbolize and which symbolization sometimes becomes combined as "religious art." One cannot escape a sense of this melding of art and religion if one pays attention to the experience which is said to underlie each at its most intense authenticity. Art is based upon "a meaning" found in an encountered reality. The arts penetrate the depths of things. Most specifically, in speaking about the relationship between religion and art Tillich has said, "that every artistic expression is in itself an expression of Ultimate Reality."[22] And when writing of the revelatory experience which is the foundation of religion, Tillich asserts that two things are experienced concerning the mystery that is God—his reality and one's own relation to that reality.[23] The common point in both religion and art here is that the symbol systems of each mediate something that transcends the ordinary. The one central question, then, which should focus many concerns, is the deceptively simple one: Are the symbols of art and the symbols of religion rooted in an experience of the same transcending reality?

It is this most central question which Charles Kegley also took up with respect to Tillich's outlook.[24] Quoting a 1959 address by Tillich, Kegley portrays him as denying that the "ultimate reality" expressed by the authentic artist is God:

> The term "ultimate reality" is not another name for God in the religious sense of the words. But the God of religion would not be God if he was not first of all ultimate reality. On the one hand, the God of religion is more than ultimate reality. Yet religion can speak of the divinity of the divine only if God is ultimate reality. If he were anything less, namely, a being—even the highest—he would be on the level of all other things. He would cease to be God. If the idea of God includes ultimate reality, everything that expresses ultimate reality expresses God whether it intends to do so or not.[25]

---

[22]Paul Tillich, from the cover of the program for "An Exhibition of Contemporary Religious Art and Architecture," Union Theological Seminary, New York, December 1-16, 1952.

[23]*Systematic Theology*, I:109.

[24]Charles W. Kegley, "Paul Tillich on the Philosophy of Art."

[25]Ibid., 179. The material cited by Kegley is also available in *Criterion*, a publication of the Divinity School of the University of Chicago, III (Summer, 1964).

Having cited this, Kegley goes on in a sympathetic vein to suggest that what Tillich is striving to do is to unite the ontological category of being or ultimate reality and the axiological category of ultimate value, namely, God, thus making God most real and most valuable. But Kegley denies for Tillich that the artist is "always and necessarily encountering God when he encounters ultimate reality."[26]

Now, it would not be perceptive to disagree with Mr. Kegley that Tillich is striving to unite ontological and axiological categories in his paradoxical claim that God both is and is not ultimate reality. But what does appear clear also is that since, for Tillich, nothing other than God ever is "ultimate reality," at times when the artist encounters ultimate reality and symbolizes this in his work, he is encountering God and symbolizing that. What Kegley is trying to protect Tillich from—and one must be very sympathetic with Charles Kegley here—is the complete identification of artistic and religious symbols which would be implied by asserting that every encounter with ultimate reality is an encounter with God. How encounters with ultimate reality are not always and necessarily encounters with God, as Kegley wants to maintain, is precisely a central problem for Tillich's outlook, however. And one cannot establish that these encounters are not synonymous and that artistic and religious symbols are not identical by a mere assertion.

At this point, then, the question may be raised again as to whether art and religion rest in an experience of the same transcendent reality so that the symbol systems of each express the same thing ultimately. It would appear fair to say that a sensitive reading of the corpus of Tillich's work reveals that he did *not intend* such an identification. Both religion and art for Tillich have cognitive elements in them; he is clear that both of these aspects of human culture, when they are authentic, root in their cognition of a reality beyond the phenomenal, and it would appear that he occasionally sees this transphenomenal reality as the same for each. That he did not intend a complete identity of religious and artistic symbols may be brought out best by the simple observation, however, that no claim of healing power is ever related to an artistic symbol. To put it another way, religion aims beyond the cognitive toward the totally salvatory. Religion aims at healing

---

[26]Ibid.

the estrangement not only between man's reason and the objects of knowledge—an estrangement which art can apparently help to overcome—but also it aims at man in his total being and not only at his reason. It bids him, by an act of the will and not merely by an act of cognition, to accept the acceptance which is there and to affirm his being in relation to the ultimate ground of all being, the "God above God." There is, in other words, a final appeal to the will in religion, a voluntarism, if you please, which apparently does not exist within art and its symbols. It is for this reason that Jesus as the Christ is an ultimate symbol, a final revelation not to be exceeded. The Christ is final in symbolic power, not because it is aesthetically supreme, but because the symbol commends itself to all that man is.

This is the way, as we perceive it, that Tillich's intention goes. Art and religion, with their respective symbols, are not to be finally identified. But the sympathetic elicitation of an intention is not the same thing as the uncovering of adequate criteria for differentiating artistic and religious symbols. Indeed, that we have to postulate an unrealized intention on Tillich's part is at the same time the admission of a certain failure in his systematic outlook. To judge this as a serious failure on Tillich's part at this point would be too hasty in relation to the evidence so far presented. But one thing must be made clear. When Tillich makes use of analogies from artistic symbols to present the religious symbols of Christian faith, the confusion we have sought to demonstrate enters in. This is true with respect to the central symbol of faith, Jesus as the Christ. And it may be a confusion of symbolic modes that underlies the weakness or incompleteness which some have sensed in Tillich's christology, where even a brief exploration will bring out some sense of the problems.

IV

To see how there is a very complete similarity between the creation of an artistic image and the emergence of the religious symbol, Jesus as the Christ, one needs only pay attention to that little-noticed but really important phrase which Tillich introduces into Volume II of *Systematic Theology* and which we have briefly discussed before. Tillich is talking about the relation between the historical Jesus and the biblical testimony about him and these statements are made:

> The power which has created and preserved the community of the New Being is not an abstract statement about its appearance; it is the picture of him in whom it

has appeared. No special trait of this picture can be verified with certainty. But it can be definitely asserted that through this picture the New Being has power to transform those who are transformed by it. This implies that there is an *analogia imaginis*, namely, an analogy between the picture and the actual personal life from which it has arisen. It was this reality, when encountered by the disciples, which created the picture. And it was, and still is, this picture which mediates the transforming power of the New Being.[27]

There is here a complete and deliberate identity between the symbolic processes which create the images of a painter and those which produce the symbols of faith. As the painter has his subject matter or object in the real world, so the biblical writer has in the concrete life of Jesus of Nazareth. As the painter transforms his subject matter to express what he cognized through it, so the biblical writers transform the actual personal life of Jesus into the biblical picture of the New Being. With an artist, one may hardly recognize the subject matter when he is finished. As Tillich so often asserts, an artist breaks the form of the thing to bring out or express a new reality. The subject matter is trans-formed into an aesthetic object. The biblical writers also do this kind of thing with Jesus so that no special trait of the picture they paint can be verified with certainty. That is, there may be very little correspondence between their picture of him and the actual life of Jesus. There is an analogy between their picture and the actual personal life, but not a correspondence. An analogy implies likeness, yes, but even more so it implies difference. It gives one a way of talking about something, but one must be aware that the difference between the literal meaning of one's talk and the symbolic meaning is vast. It is the symbolic meaning which has the power to mediate the transforming power of the New Being. And "the picture has this creative power, because the power of the New Being is expressed in and through it."[28]

So close is the likeness between the emergence of the New Testament picture of Jesus as the Christ and the creation of a painting that Tillich is able to go on to compare the New Testament picture with an expressionist painting and to discuss several elements within the New Testament which are used to "express" what the writers experienced in relation to Jesus. What they experienced, of course, was New Being or the Christ, and Tillich can even give a name to the symbol which the New Testament picture of Jesus is; the symbol is named "Jesus as the Christ." And just as every

---

[27]*Systematic Theology*, II: 114-15.

[28]Ibid., 115.

symbol, aesthetic or religious, points away from itself, so also does this symbol. Where does it point? Again, we can answer by analogy with the aesthetic. A painting does not point back to its original subject matter by way of pointing beyond itself; it points rather to a meaning cognized or an encounter known in relation to that original subject matter. The original subject matter was a piece of finite reality which became transparent to a reality beyond it and it is that reality to which the painting points. Likewise, the New Testament does not point back to Jesus, its original subject matter. The idolization of Jesus is clearly eschewed by Tillich. The New Testament points beyond the finite individuality of Jesus of Nazareth to a universal reality to whom (which?) he was transparent. There is in Tillich this insistent refusal to identify Jesus with the reality to which religion, at its authentic best, is meant to relate men. What is this reality? In the second volume of *Systematic Theology* it receives the name "New Being." New Being, then, is no longer a symbolic thing; it is a state of human being made possible by man's being grasped by that which is beyond all finite reality and which has "grasped" men in all times and in all places. In other words, man is to see in the symbol a new possibility for his own life, a possibility whose actualization depends upon union with the same thing which transformed Jesus, namely, the Christ. Jesus (functioning) as the Christ points to a reality (New Being) possible for man by virtue of a special union.[29]

---

[29]We have separated the reality of New Being from the symbol—Jesus as the Christ—which points to it. The reader may wonder if this is justified since New Being and Jesus as the Christ are often identified. This is an attempt to clear up some confusion created by Tillich's occasional tendency to identify New Being and the Christ. He does this, for example, when using St. Paul's notion of being "in Christ" to express being related to the New Being. The truth seems to be that Tillich works with three terms: "New Being," "the Christ" and "Jesus as the Christ." And these must be distinguished. New Being is brought by the Christ. (See *Systematic Theology*, II:150, 177). That is, the Christ is a universally operative healing reality which brings New Being as a reality in its turn. When the reality of the Christ unites with the human reality of Jesus of Nazareth a new "double-reality"—Jesus as the Christ—exists which has the power to transform those who experience it directly in history and who receive it as what it is. Then they produce the symbol—the New Testament picture of Jesus as the Christ—by means of which others can know of this transforming "double-reality." In other words, Jesus as the Christ, as an historical reality known by the early disciples, was an embodiment of New Being. Put in ontological terms, New Being was *actual* in history and the symbolic picture of Jesus as the Christ in the New Testament points to that actuality. It would appear to be this idea-structure which allows Tillich to refer to Jesus as the Christ as *M*an, that is, as the archetype of humanity transformed into New Being by the power of the Christ. Tillich puts it thus: "In his being, the New Being is real, and the New Being is the reestablished unity between God and man. We replace the inadequate concept 'divine nature' by the concepts 'eternal God-man-unity' or 'Eternal God-Manhood.'" (*Systematic Theology*, II:148.).

With this much said, however, a potent caveat must be raised. For the logic of our exposition gives the impression that "the Christ" is a final and non-symbolic naming of God. Whatever God is, he is not to be named in this or any other fashion. Put most boldly, Tillich's symbols point beyond themselves, first to the human reality of New Being, but also to an ultimate Christ, an evanescent, indefinite, mystical something about whose character and reality many exponents of Tillich's symbol-theory have despaired. One further section, then, may bring us closer to the root of this despair. What we must finally ask is, is there any insight to be gained into Tillich's theory by stepping back to view this whole process of symbolization in a larger philosophical landscape where we can find clues to the aesthetics which clearly inform what he is saying theologically?

V

That a system of symbols is needed to express an otherwise ineffable awareness of participation by consciousness in a transcending reality is the clue to the philosophical context or landscape that will shed further light on Tillich's meanings. What he appears really to be involved in is the old philosophical concern with the relation of the infinite and the finite. Indeed Tillich makes plain that finite man belongs to an infinity from which he is estranged.

This question of the relation of the finite and the infinite can be expressed in another way, a way that was favored by Schelling, whose influence on Tillich with respect to this question is marked. Schelling tended to think of the question in terms of why there is anything at all. What sense can be made of a universe of finite things which do not seem to be self-explanatory? Tillich expresses this Schellingian concern in terms of the "ontological shock"—why is there something and not nothing?—which can raise the question of God for man. Schelling's own answer to this puzzle was posed partly in opposition to Spinoza and to Fichte. Spinoza dissolves the finite (subject and object) in an infinite object or substance. For him man and all there is are only modifications of the one infinite. Fichte, on the other hand, made the phenomenal world (human subjects and the realm of objects) a product of an infinite or absolute ego, which was not identical with any particular empirical ego or collection of them. To these proposals Schelling objected because they not only seemed to remove individuality—and in the case of Spinoza, freedom—from man, but also undercut the necessary conditions of conscious life. What he proposed instead was a philosophy of identity. In this outlook an absolute, variously named also as Reason and the infinite, transcended the distinction of finite subject and finite object. Both finite subject and finite object find themselves grounded in this absolute which is neither subject nor object, but subject and object in identity. For him what this meant was that, since that which is absolute is neither subject nor object, man and the world of objects (the finite) can be said to relate to a transcending reality which does not dissolve either finite subject or finite object. The absolute manifests itself in the finite subject and the finite object, but cannot be called either Subject or Object. Although Schelling does not hesitate to provide some "names" for this final reality, it is not hard to see the root of Tillich's resistance to naming God, even as the "ultimate reality" expressed in authentic art. Tillich's reservations seem to rest in the desire to avoid making God into any kind of Object, even the healing object (reality) of the Christ, for he was aware of the philosophical danger which Schelling was trying to avoid, of turning the phenomenal world into a phantasm grounded pantheistically in an impersonal reality. There is real perceptiveness in Kegley's suggestion that the word "God" is for Tillich an axiological word and that, as such, it cannot quickly be identified with any particular sort of thing.

It is the philosophy of art built by Schelling upon this philosophy of identity that is most instructive for present purposes, however. The main outlines of this are not hard to grasp in the context of Schelling's idealism. Since finite subject and object are both grounded in an absolute which is neither, as an artist creates, the same reality is working through his consciousness as is working in nature. Nature is a kind of unconscious "poetry" or expression of this absolute spirit. In and through the artistic human consciousness, however, a different kind of object is produced than is found in the world of nature. Using our modern technical language, this is the "aesthetic object." What makes this object in the world different is the fact that something of what the artist is subjectively is mirrored in it. The art object contains an objectification of the self to the self. In it there is a melding of subject and object. Put in the Tillichian language, the subject-object split has been overcome. Schelling himself speaks of the work of art as manifesting an identity of unconscious object and conscious subject. In a sense, object has become subject and vice versa. The real and the ideal have united. This identity of subject and object in the work of art is the concrete image of what is ontologically true. What is infinite "enters into the finite and is intuited *in concreto*."[30] Schelling does not mean to tell us, any more than Tillich would, that the artist is necessarily aware of this "symbolic" function of his art. What is more accurate is to say that the intuition of one who views the work of art may find the infinite expressed in this finite product of human intelligence. In the words used earlier, particular consciousness may find symbolized in art a reality in which they have a "prior" participation ontologically.

Now, the parallels between Tillich's own statements about art and those of this essentially Romanticist theory of Schelling are so close that any attempt to point them out would be a redundant working of the obvious. But two things do need to be said. The first is that Tillich does what Schelling does not do, at least directly. Paul Tillich makes a transfer from the aesthetic into the religious realm. His theory of the functioning of the aesthetic symbol is essentially the same as his theory of the functioning of a religious symbol with the exception that he does not wish to collapse one of these value realms into the other. This is an intention at which he has not fully succeeded. But given the essentially "religious" functioning of the artistic symbol in Schelling, it is not to be wondered that Tillich, in his dependency, could not finally separate the two.

The second observation to be made concerns the question of the meaning of that mysterious Tillichian notion that a symbol participates in the reality to which it points. In the context of the romantic aesthetic theory that informs Tillich's theory of the religious symbol the final meaning of the participation of a symbol must be that it participates in the reality of the subjective consciousnesses which create it. In the case of the New Testament picture of Jesus as the Christ, which Tillich regards as a supremely symbolic creation, the consciousnesses were those of the writers. Any religious symbol, however, participates first in that subjective reality. The symbol participates in subjective reality as the objectification or mirroring of what the self (selves) is (are). Self and objective image cohere and cannot finally be separated. In turn, then, both participate in an absolute reality—God, in Tillich's terms—which transcends subject and religious symbol and in which they find an identity. This ontological union of all finite things in a transcending reality Tillich unabashedly ex-

---

[30]Schelling, *Works*, vol. III, ed. Schroeter. Cited by Frederick Copleston, *A History of Philosophy* vol. VII, part I (Garden City NY: Image Books, 1965) 152.

presses in *Systematic Theology* when, in speaking of God, he says: "He is not a separated self-sufficient entity. . . . For the external dimension of what happens in the universe is the Divine Life itself. . . . A world which is only external to God and not also internal to Him, in the last consideration, is a divine play of no essential concern for God."[31] This final reality Tillich refuses to name with other than the religious word "God," and he will not identify the Divine even with His self-alteration as the world. God is not ultimate reality, the Absolute, the Infinite, the Christ, or even Being-itself. Perhaps only by refusing to name God literally can Tillich affirm that He is known. For to name God literally rather than symbolically is to perpetuate a distinction between naming subject and named object, thereby implying that the subject-object gap is not overcome and that no knowledge of God is really had. In the long run, Tillich is more than an idealistic philosopher a la Schelling; he is a religious mystic also. Union with the Divine is an epistemological and ontological fact, but can never be communicated directly.

---

[31]Paul Tillich, *Systematic Theology* (Chicago: University of Chicago Press, 1963) III:422.

An Evaluation of the Christological Dimensions of Tillich's Theology of Culture

ROBERT H. BRYANT

Tillich states that the Spiritual Presence or the divine Spirit, which elevates humans "through faith and love to transcendent unity of unambiguous life, creates the New Being above the gap between essence and existence and consequently above the ambiguities of life" (*Systematic Theology*, III:107, 138f.).[1] "The quest for the New Being," he holds, "is universal because the human predicament and its ambiguous conquest are universal" (ST, II:86ff.). While acknowledging that this quest in each religion and cultural context is prone toward profanization and demonization, he accepts the Christian witness that the decisive and the normative revelation of the New Being is the Christ-event (ST, II:118ff.).

This central paradox of the Christian message can be summed up in the affirmation: "in one personal life essential manhood has appeared under the conditions of existence without being conquered by them" (ST, II:94). Or, alternatively, the paradox can be expressed as the disclosure of "essential God-manhood" in the personal life of Jesus as the Christ. But

---

[1]*Systematic Theology*, 3 vols. (Chicago: University of Chicago Press, 1951-1963).

Tillich preferred the less redundant wording "essential manhood" to "the essential God-manhood" (loc. cit.).

Fr. Georges Tavard has argued, however, that either expression—"the essential man" or "the essential God-manhood"—refers to a universal. Thus the consequence is that Tillich's christological formulation is unable to overcome the dichotomy between such an abstract allusion to universals and concrete human existence. As long as the normative revelation of God is conceived of as a universal, it can never fully and exclusively be identified with any particular event, even the historical life of Jesus of Nazareth (*Paul Tillich and the Christian Message*, 172).[2]

In an earlier critique Charles Hartshorne identified the root of this dichotomy in ambiguities in Tillich's statements about God. Hartshorne showed that, while Tillich often referred to God as "absolute," "the unconditioned," "the eternal," and as "being-itself," he insisted that every ascription of finite-human conditions or qualities in a literal or non-symbolic way must be rejected. Therefore, one should not speak of God as ever conceivably being a finite historical self. According to Hartshorne, Tillich failed to recognize that "finite" is only a different category than "infinite" and so does not necessarily imply greater limits or inferiority. Some of the main difficulties in Tillich's discourse about God could be overcome, Hartshorne thinks, if Tillich had been willing to refer to God in consistently dipolar terms as "infinite-finite" and "eternal-temporal." Unwillingness to use such dipolar terms or categories results in such an abstract view of God that to try to worship this "God" could be subtly idolatrous (C. Hartshorne, "Tillich's Doctrine of God," in C. W. Kegley and R. W. Bretall, eds., *The Theology of Paul Tillich*, 165ff.).[3]

David Griffin has more recently argued that Tillich's christology is self-contradictory: Tillich's assertions that Jesus of Nazareth was completely open to or "transparent to" and was inseparably united with God require "a doctrine according to which God is an individual being as well as in some sense being-itself. Only on such a basis could one make intelligible the kind of activity between God and the creatures that Christian faith requires, the foundation of values in a reality transcending the tem-

---

[2](New York: Scribner, 1962).

[3](New York: The Macmillan Co., 1961).

poral flux, and something determinate in God that something in a finite being might especially reveal" (D. Griffin, *A Process Christology*, 48f.).[4]

Tillich's christological formulations show that, although he wished to, he did not succeed in developing a conceptuality that could overcome the dichotomy between universal Being and particular existence. Much, if not all, of his theological interpretation of culture suffers from this basic deficiency.

The consequences which follow from this deficiency become evident as Tillich attempts to specify the content and deal with the social-cultural application of his concepts. With two representative examples, I shall attempt to show that Tillich's concepts, because of their very generality or abstractness, make it difficult for him to relate them to particular contexts of human decision-making. Furthermore, I shall indicate that Tillich, perhaps conscious of this difficulty, at times chooses to avoid dealing with the "practical problems" which arise in such contexts.

For the first example, I turn to Tillich's discussion of "the moral imperative" in his *Theology of Culture*.[5] In chapter 10, entitled "Moralisms and Morality: Theonomous Ethics," he defends the term and the experience of the "unconditional" in opposition to various relativists who have reacted to "demonic" absolutizing references to it.

He acknowledges that those who criticize Kant's interpretation of the categorical imperative as establishing "a system of ethical forms without ethical contents" are justified but insists that Kant's "greatness" lay in making "as sharp as possible the distinction between morality which is unconditional, and moralisms [specific systems of ethical ideals or norms] which are valid only conditionally and within limits" (TC, 135).

But does Tillich in his discussion of the "moral imperative" overcome the weakness above for which he recognizes Kant has been appropriately criticized? He evidently does not. He defines this imperative as "not a strange law, imposed on us, but it is the law of our being. In the moral imperative we ourselves, in our essential being, are put against ourselves, in our actual being." He states furthermore that "the moral command is unconditional because it is we ourselves commanding ourselves" (ibid., 136). Since, however, he has only a few lines earlier endorsed the conten-

---

[4](Philadelphia: The Westminster Press, 1973).

[5](New York: Oxford University Press, 1964).

tion of Kant and of social scientists that individuals and cultures differ end-lessly regarding the content of moral ideals or imperatives, how can Tillich himself escape the dilemma of ethical relativism (skepticism) or absolut-ism which he holds has afflicted many others?

He tries to avoid the absolutizing possibilities latent in his definition of the moral imperative by asserting that "a self-affirmation has no uncondi-tional character. . . . But morality as the self-affirmation of *one's essential being* is unconditional" (ibid., 137; italics mine). In his *Systematic Theol-ogy*, especially vol. II, Tillich devotes considerable attention to character-izing essential human being or authentic human existence as the union between who persons actually are and who they potentially can be. More-over, he both discusses in detail and affirms the Christian message that only in the historical person of Jesus as the Christ has this union between potential being and actual human existence really occurred. In references to "one's essential being" here in connection with the moral imperative, Tillich assumes that he has already given that concept adequate specific content elsewhere in his treatment of christology. In fact, though, Tillich is simply arguing in circles, defining one abstract generality ("one's essen-tial being") by others ("the essential manhood" or "the essential God-manhood").

He wants to escape the relativizing and skeptical possibilities lurking in his definition of moral imperative by averring that "the contents . . . of the moral self-affirmation are conditioned, relative, dependent on the so-cial and psychological constellation." To state this is not, according to Til-lich, to align one's self with self-contradictory relativisms of any sort, but, like any sensitive apologist, to grant the important insight they affirm, namely that humans are finite or spatially and temporarily contingent (TC, 137).

To grant this insight is worthwhile, but to establish an alternative pos-ition to such relativisms, Tillich needs to show *how* one can self-critically employ the unconditional moral imperative, which he claims that he and most other humans are conscious of, in making particular moral decisions. This, as far as I can see, he fails to do in this chapter or otherwise in Part Two ("Concrete Applications") of the *Theology of Culture*. To illustrate, he raises hopes that he might do this when he refers to the issue of birth con-trol. He makes this reference, however, only incidentally, in criticizing Ro-man Catholic views of natural law as having "definite contents" which the Church can authoritatively state. In contrast to these Catholic interpretations of natural law, Tillich states the "Protestant principle" as offering a better possibility of "a dynamic concept of natural law" (TC, 137f.). One looks in vain, though, for any suggestions regarding *specific ethical criteria* which the Protestant principle or "the unconditional moral imperative," in whatever formulation, would generate in relation to birth control.

For a second example, I choose Tillich's discussion of the ways churches relate themselves to other social groups (ST, III:212ff.). He states that "the churches, in paradoxical unity with their Spiritual essence, are sociological realities, showing all the ambiguities of the social self-creation of life. Therefore they have continuous encounters with other sociological groups, acting upon them and receiving from them" (ST, 212). Given this statement and Tillich's own involvement in the conflict between some of the churches and the Nazi government in the 1930s, one might expect that, in the context of this topic, he would try to show how his more general theological concepts and principles could be applied to making decisions regarding specific problems.[6] On the contrary, he immediately cautions: "Systematic theology cannot deal with the practical problems following from these relations, but it must try to formulate the ways and principles by which the churches as churches relate themselves to other social groups" (loc. cit.).

Tillich is evidently assuming here that one can and should distinguish sharply between systematic theology, concerned with formulating general doctrinal concepts, and Christian ethics or various sub-areas of Practical Theology, devoted to applying such concepts. Some, but not all, systematicians of European background wish to make this sharp distinction; but Karl Barth, for instance, treats ethical issues extensively within his

---

[6]In his *The Religious Situation*, published in Germany in 1929 and translated with this English title by H. Richard Niebuhr (New York: Henry Holt, 1932) as well as in other addresses and essays which he prepared in the 1920s through the 1940s, Tillich shows that he was very much aware of the problem of the relations between churches and civil governments as well as concerned about how Christians together with other sensitive persons should respond to the important social-cultural and political problems of the time. One cannot fault the extent of his thoughtful concern with these issues and the degree to which he took personal risks in expressing himself regarding them, particularly in Germany during the early 1930s. However, I still contend that his main tendency in his published speeches and writings between 1920 and 1940 was to develop the broader philosophical-theological principles and categories for interpreting the situations of that time rather than formulating specific criteria for decision-making. Cf. P. Tillich, *Political Expectation* (New York: Harper and Row, 1971); *The Protestant Era* (Chicago: University of Chicago Press, 1948).

Church Dogmatics. While space considerations would have undoubtedly prompted Tillich to feel he could not deal in detail with many ethical issues within his three-volume work, he might have decided to give more particular attention to at least a few such issues for illustrative purposes. This issue of the relations between churches and governments would seem to be one which his personal experience would have especially equipped him to discuss in this manner. Unfortunately, he decides against this for the methodological reason mentioned above.

He should be credited, however, for the brief but thought-provoking fashion in which he delineates three ways the churches and social groups have and do relate: by "silent interpenetration," "critical judgment," and "political establishment" (loc cit.).

In connection with the way of critical judgment, he observes: "A society which rejects or persecutes the bearers of the prophetic criticism against itself does not remain the same as before. It may be weakened or it may be hardened in its demonic and profane traits. . . . Therefore the churches should not only fight for the preservation and strengthening of their priestly influence (for example, in the realm of education), but they should encourage prophetic criticism of the negativities in their society up to the point of martyrdom and in spite of their awareness that the result of a prophetic criticism of society is not the Spiritual Community but, perhaps, a state of society which approaches theonomy—the relatedness of all cultural forms to the ultimate" (ibid., 213f.). Within this same paragraph Tillich tersely mentions the early church's criticism of imperial Roman society's "pagan" patterns of behavior and thought.

Such an observation provokes a number of questions: How and when is one to decide to "fight" for a greater "priestly influence" as compared with more "prophetic criticism"? Who is to make such decisions within a particular church: the "top" official?, the majority of clergy?, the laity? By which procedures? How are church people in such different situations of church-government conflict as South Korea, the Soviet Union, Italy, Chile, and South Africa to derive any helpful particular guidance from such broad generalizations as those of Tillich? Anyone who has lived long in one of those situations feels all the more frustrated by such "profound" abstractions uttered by prominent theologians, because s/he has frequently experienced the bitter disagreements which arise among church "leaders" who interpret and apply these generalities in widely opposing ways.

In commenting upon the third way—"political establishment"—whereby the churches exercise their inevitable "royal" function in relation to other social groups, Tillich sees "only one limit" to this way (in which churches compromise with the State and other prevailing institutions). This limit is that "the character of the church as expression of the Spiritual Community must remain manifest." This is gravely endangered if "the royal office of the Christ, and through him of the church, is understood as a theocratic-political system of totalitarian control"; or, if, at the opposite extreme, the State forces the Church to act as only one subservient department among many within a larger governmental bureaucracy, thereby depriving the Church almost entirely of its "royal office" (ibid., 215).

But, once again, one painfully notes that Tillich has not provided any specific criteria to enable anyone to decide how or when either extreme is reached; or, even more important, he has not indicated which intervening signs to look for that a church is approaching either extreme. A theologian employing a more inductive, contextually oriented method (e.g., H. Richard Niebuhr) would painstakingly try to provide such criteria.

I have carefully selected the two examples above from many other available ones in Tillich's writings to demonstrate that his theology of culture is seriously weakened by the over-generality or abstractness of his concepts and that this basic deficiency is frustratingly evidenced time and again in his conscious methodological refusal and/or self-conscious unpreparedness to formulate particular criteria or otherwise to deal selectively and even at moderate length with germane "practical problems." Usually, when facing the need to elaborate such specific criteria, he moves away from the issue at hand and proceeds to set forth more generalizations on another topic.

I have argued furthermore that this deficiency illustrates his failure to develop a conceptuality that could overcome the dichotomy between universal Being and particular existence. My contention, moreover, has been that this weakness in conceptuality is centrally evident in Tillich's christological formulation. In his key christological statement, namely that the normative revelation of God is that of "essential manhood" in Jesus as the Christ, Tillich fails to argue convincingly how such an abstract concept could or did constitute a particular historical revelation of God, or how it did unite with a particular person, Jesus of Nazareth.

Which conceptuality would have been most likely to enable Tillich to overcome the dichotomy which so gravely weakens his christology and consequently his entire theology of culture? I would contend that the *dipolar* interpretation of reality (including God), based upon Whitehead's organismic philosophy, but elaborated more fully by Charles Hartshorne, is best equipped to do that. Unfortunately, Tillich, in reply to Hartshorne's essay referred to earlier, while granting some minor points in Hartshorne's critique of his doctrine of God, rejects Hartshorne's major concept of dipolarity, namely that God be characterized as "finite" as well as "infinite" ("universal," "unconditional," "eternal," etc.). He objects to Hartshorne's ascription of literal finitude to God on the grounds that this would assume that the deity is "structurally" dependent upon contingent or creaturely being and therefore would undermine the classical religious affirmation of divine majesty (*Theology of Paul Tillich*, ed. Kegley and Bretall, 179f., 339f.).

Tillich failed to grasp that Hartshorne, by affirming the literal finitude of God, far from intending that God should be regarded as deficient in any way, actually was arguing that God's being and experience are not only completely inclusive but God is uniquely capable of relating to (perceiving) *definitely* each and every other entity in ways most appropriate to the latter's own particular context. This means that God is *the* one truly concrete, individual person who "feels" with full intensity and has the inexhaustible resources to identify with the life experiences of each human other being (ibid., 179f.).

There is not space here to develop more fully the truly helpful implications of Hartshorne's dipolar metaphysics for christology and theology of culture. This has been and is being ably done by such authors as David Griffin (op. cit., esp. chs. 7-10), John Cobb and Peter Hamilton.[7]

The central emphasis of Hartshorne and others of Whiteheadian persuasion just mentioned upon concrete, particular, as well as universal, dimensions of experience or reality and upon the interrelatedness of all entities, is closely congenial in some significant respects to the inductive, contextualist orientation of the theology and ethics of H. Richard Niebuhr. I stated above that this orientation and method of Niebuhr, had Tillich been cognizant of it and willing to use it at least occasionally, would have enabled

---

[7]See John Cobb, *Christ In a Pluralistic Age* (Philadelphia: Westminster Press, 1975); Cobb, *The Structure of Christian Existence* (Philadelphia: Westminster Press, 1967); Peter Hamilton, *The Living God and the Modern World* (Philadelphia: United Church Press, 1968).

him to develop the specific criteria for making ethical decisions which he lacked. I have in mind especially the guiding questions which Niebuhr recommended that one ask in regard to each social-cultural context: (1) What *is* happening here? (Note the emphasis upon the indicative rather than the imperative.) (2) How is *the One God* present and acting here among the many other beings? (3) What are *most appropriate* (responsible) *responses* to the actions of this One God foremostly but also to those of the many?[8]

---

[8]H. Richard Niebuhr, *Radical Monotheism and Western Culture* (New York: Harper and Row, 1960); *The Responsible Self* (New York: Harper and Row, 1963).

Liberation Theology of Culture: A Tillichian Perspective

H. FREDERICK REISZ, JR.

The Apparent Impasse

Can a Tillichian approach to the theology of culture be illuminating in the current discussions of Liberation Theology? The answer to that question is far from evident. On the one hand, Latin American liberation theologians have specifically called into question the utility of discussion with representatives of European theology. We need but recall Hugo Assmann's widely reported renunciation of any dialogue with European theologians because they are Europeans and thus steeped in imperialism.[1] On the other hand, Tillich's propensity for asserting the importance, indeed necessity, of ontological questions and theological formulations as the context of theological ethics fights against Liberation Theology's insistence upon the primacy of *praxis*. There appears to be an impasse in discussions between Third World "liberation" theologians and the established contemporary theologians of the West.

---

[1]Archie Le Moyne, "Report on a Symposium: When Traditional Theology Meets Black and Liberation Theology," in *Christianity and Crisis* 33:15 (September 17, 1973): 177-78.

In this essay I wish to call that impasse into question. I want to suggest how a Tillichian might begin to bring helpful content into the ongoing process of the formulation of a Theology of Liberation. Such an interest does not evolve out of fear for the extinction of Tillichian theology but rather out of the desire to use Tillich's powerful theological insights in a new situation and a new time. This essay is only suggestive of possible insights which might advance conversations across the continents should the "kairos" arise for such communication.

Liberation Theology

Liberation Theology has been a publicist's creation in that no centralized school of theology exists. Indeed the current assault upon Latin American theologians of liberation by theologians from other Third World countries illustrates this point. However, Liberation Theology also is an emerging theological stance, if not a full-blown theology. As such it stands as a challenge to the contemporary tradition of Western theology. There are clear differences between it and European political theology as represented by the work of Moltmann and Metz.[2] It is powerful in its insistence that for the poor and oppressed all reality constricts to the immediacy of their oppression. There is no life-meaning and power apart from that reality and its reversal. Any theologian, indeed more precisely, any human, who does not take that oppression seriously as the primary reality and listen to the ciphers of the "real" that arise from it is ethically invalidated. Theology must arise out of the experience of the wretched of the earth as they seize the real through their liberation. Meaning is discovered in this process. Theology must emerge out of the process of liberation through the commitment of the theologian to the *praxis* of the social group of the oppressed gaining power and meaning, that is life.

Liberation Theology is not now a new theology but a new "way" of doing theology. As Inquiñiz has put it:

---

[2]For a clarification of these differences consult: Jürgen Moltmann, "On Latin American Liberation Theology: An Open Letter to José Miguez Bonino," in *Christianity and Crisis* 36:15 (March 1976): 57-63.

I would say that this theology emerges from a particular process of liberation. Any liberation process is relevant inasmuch as it questions Christians about their theology, their understanding of their faith, their interpretation of the Bible.[3]

The Theology of Liberation challenges our more established Western orientations to the meaning of reality on the basis of oppression which exists in our midst and as a result of our history. Our theologies have been constitutive elements of that history. The route to insight can only be through the route of participation in the *praxis* of liberation.

Rather than speaking of the being, essence or nature of God, liberation theologians first concentrate upon those testimonies to the action of God which have most attracted the oppressed in their quest for liberation. Thus theology becomes testimony to the liberating action of God primarily in the biblical testimony to the Exodus, Jesus' associations with the poor and oppressed of his society and the Resurrection. These event-testimonies are the *kerygma* of Liberation Theology. This *kerygma* is the sufficient and nonimperialistic testimony to God. Further assertions concerning God may only grow out of the *praxis* of liberation when meaning will be freed to arise. Reflection upon the nature of God unrelated to the specific liberation *praxis* of the oppressed community is simply a form of escapism or a distraction which serves the counterrevolutionary strategies of imperialism. On this basis, Tillichian theology is virtually rejected out of hand.

I want to raise the possibility that such a rejection might be too quickly done. In fact, a Tillichian understanding of God as Spirit might be extremely helpful in the *praxis* of creating a liberating culture.

Beyond the Gulf

While the discussion needs to be carried further beyond the present gulf between theologians in the Americas and Europe, I do not wish to do so at the cost of the vital life-affirming and life-risking commitment of Christians to the primacy of justice and full life-power and life-in-meanings for the oppressed. What I say here is thus suggestion rather than assertion, more for the purposes of interest arousal than for present dialogue.

---

[3]Dow Kirkpatrick, "Liberation Theologians and Third World Demands: A Dialogue with Gustavo Gutierrez and Javier Iguiñiz," in *The Christian Century* 93:17 (May 12, 1976): 457.

Liberation Theology as it exists in its many localities and expressions is a cry to be heard, a demand for justice that cannot be neglected—a prophetic demand. The theology that will emerge from the *praxis* will be important testimony to God. However, now we have only a nascent theology of liberation, not a *theo*-logy. The writings of these theologians are not systematic formulations of the meanings of religious symbols, most especially those concerning God, that is yet to come. Liberation theologians are forming a prologue to a possible theology. In this sense, Liberation Theology might be more adequately termed a theology of culture—an oppressive culture—and a commitment to revolutionizing *praxis*. "Liberation" theologians define "theology" in its most general sense as the reflections of believers.

Several problems concerning the current state of liberation theologies need to be mentioned. Writings from theologians in the context of an emerging *praxis* of liberation have not been particularly illuminating concerning the power and meaning of the symbol "God" except as an authenticator of liberation. Is it not possible that reflection on the meaning of God as practiced by Christians through the centuries has an enlarged content which could be illuminative for the oppressed? Indeed, I suspect that such content exists already among the religious poor and is suppressed at the peril of liberation. Even if subliminally, has not the religion of the oppressed usually defied that of the oppressor? The question now to be asked is whether the oppressed persons have or had a view of God adequate to the task of liberation. Liberation theologians have said, "No!" because of the cultural dominance of the oppressors' image of God. Thus we highlight certain "acts" of God, i.e., the Exodus, the Resurrection, as testimony to what is possible and God's sanction of liberation. I want to suggest that Tillichian theology can articulate a view of God as Spirit which can ground liberation *praxis*. Hence it need not be assumed that *theo*-logy, a doctrine of God, will be the opiate of the people.

Liberation theology is forthright in refusing to compromise the potential for revolutionary action designed to free the oppressed. Any adequate doctrine of God must be an expression of the possibilities for a liberated humanity as the temple of God. Any theological quest for the knowledge of God is suspect as a diversion from the task of the establishment of justice. Thus, as Gutierrez puts it: "To know God is to do justice." In fact, the doing of justice is the route to the revelation of the presence of God. These two themes merge in Gutierrez's work:

To know Yahweh, which in Biblical language is equivalent to saying to love Yahweh, *is* to establish just relationships among men, it *is* to recognize the rights of the poor. The God of Biblical revelation is known through interhuman justice. When justice does not exist, God is not known; he is absent.[4]

It is apparent that theological reflection outside the struggles for the oppressed and with them is not merely deficient but more seriously unable to "know" God. On this basis, much of past European theologians, including Tillich, have been dismissed from consideration.

Tillich and the European Exiles

Many of the liberation theologians have rejected an association with European and North American theologians for reasons outlined above. Where individual theologians have completely developed a speculative theology apart from all experiential roots and engagement in *praxis*, such a rejection might be necessary. However, it is evident that the Latin American liberation thinkers are steeped in their European roots, if only through Kant, Hegel, Marx, Feuerbach, Freud, Gogarten, Bonhoeffer, and Metz.[5] Even with these forefathers, Latin American liberation theologians rarely mention Tillich. Contemporary theologians from the "oppressor" powers are rejected because of the assumed imperialistic influences in their thought. Perhaps it is merely a breaking with the "Fathers," but theologically, it is claimed that their doctrines of God are crucially inadequate because they do not flow from a commitment to *praxis*. The *theo*-logy does not arise out of the struggle of the oppressed.

This banishment is harder to understand in relation to Tillich's early work. Perhaps the over-concentration in Tillich research and criticism upon *Systematic Theology I* is to blame. In any case, I am convinced that this needs to be corrected.

Clearly as the political writings of Tillich emerge into republication and are given increased attention, his works will at least join the arena of debate. The writings of religious socialism and the interpretation of history are of importance precisely because they are theological reflections that

---

[4]Gustavo Gutierrez, *A Theology of Liberation*, trans. by Sister Caridad Inda and John Eagleson (Maryknoll NY: Orbis Books, 1971) 193.

[5]Moltmann, "On Latin American Liberation Theology," 57, 59.

arose out of commitment to the *praxis* of the 1920s and early 1930s. These need to be made accessible in multiple languages by Tillich scholars. The mounting interest in Tillich's political-ethical writings in North America is evident. Speaking of Tillich's "The Socialist Decision," Franklin Sherman has provided an interesting summary of six problems or perspectives to be observed in building a new socialist society.[6] From the standpoint of an ethicist these provide remarkable content for reflection by persons in the praxis-context of liberation. Since Tillich himself spoke of religious social-ism as the "living out of the roots of human being," a phrasing very similiar to Gutierrez's emphasis upon the human temple of God, one would hope that Liberation Theology would turn to a consideration of Tillich's works as they have reflected upon Marx and other "Europeans."

Beyond the interest in Tillich's ethical works on religious socialism, I believe that his doctrine of God can provide a basis for a theology of lib-erating culture. It is in this area of theology that Liberation Theology has seemed most vulnerable. Besides the spotlighting of certain actions of God, liberation theologians have not articulated a *theo*-logy, an illumination of the more encompassing meanings of the religious symbol, "God." They are convinced that such meaning will emerge out of the *praxis* of liberation. God will be "known" in acts of human love liberated. However, I believe that an articulate doctrine of God arising out of the religious depths of common human experience can illuminate what is "liberating" and provide the context for the *praxis* of revolution and liberation. Tillich's doctrine of God as Spirit has such potentialities.

Tillich's Doctrine of God as Spirit
and a Theology of Liberating Culture

I am convinced that liberation theologians are not aware of the experi-ential base and content of Tillich's writings on religious socialism and the interpretation of history. Obviously, his notion of "kairos" has received some attention. However, this has not been tied sufficiently to these ear-lier works in the minds of the general theological community. As further scholarship is published on these aspects of Tillich's thought they will con-tribute to the thinking of "liberation" theologians.

---

[6]Franklin Sherman, "Tillich's Social Thought: New Perspectives," in *The Christian Century* 93:6 (February 25, 1976): 171.

I want to suggest that Tillich's doctrine of God actually can be helpful to the intentions of liberation theology if not to its actual growing content. In *Tillich Studies: 1975*, John B. Lounibos wrote a probing article opening up this discussion.[7] While he wrote specifically concerning structures of liberation derivable from Tillich's ontology, I wish to continue that discussion on the basis of Tillich's doctrine of God. We have noted that Liberation Theology in its various manifestations has not developed a *theo*-logy— an articulated doctrine of God. Certainly the liberating actions of God have been preached. However, a theology of God does not appear to shape the *praxis* of liberation nor has it illuminated probable forms for the liberated society or culture. In some forms, Liberation Theology is primarily a religious accompaniment to the more central performance of a local revolution on behalf of the oppressed. In other cases, Liberation Theology is a more highly articulated ideology of the revolutionized culture. In still other cases, it is an emphasis upon an embryonic theology of culture or world orders whose faith expressions recall the liberating acts of God but cannot yet proclaim symbols speaking of dimensions of the divine Life itself. The reality of God is affirmed but the content of *theo*-logy is avoided for fear of a *praxis*-vitiating transcendence.

I am convinced that Tillich's doctrine of God as Spirit can provide that development of symbolism of the divine Life which will not destroy the demand for the integrity of "all people that on earth do dwell." The following explication of a Tillichian conception of God as Spirit should be fruitful in founding a true *theo*-logy of liberating culture.

In an essay in *Tillich Studies: 1975*, I undertook a brief exposition of a Tillichian doctrine of God as Spirit built upon a serious consideration of *Systematic Theology III*. God as Spirit is "the union of Life-power and Life-in-meanings." Using this definition of God by Tillich, I proposed an interpretation which combined Tillich's expressions of the functions of processes of life with those determining the New Being as process. These terms when used in the context of a theology of God as Spirit present a Tillichian orientation to God who is in process. I defined God as Spirit as follows:

---

[7]John B. Lounibos, "Paul Tillich's Structures of Liberation," in *Tillich Studies: 1975*, ed. by John J. Carey (Tallahassee: Florida State University, The North American Paul Tillich Society, 1975) 63-75.

Life-power can be cogently interpreted by means of the three functions or processes of Life: self-integration, self-alteration (or creativity), and self-transcendence. In God as Spirit, Life-power is an element symbolizing God's *integrity*. God is his own power as immediate presence. However, the power of God is not just his self-integration but also the power of *creativity*. Spirit goes out from himself to ground existence. God as Spirit is originating, sustaining, directing and fulfilling creativity. Life-power is both the depth and fulfillment of the power of actualization.
. . .

God as Spirit is not just Life-power, the dynamic pole, but also Life-in-meanings, the formal pole. *Life-in-meanings* can be interpreted adequately in terms of the principles determining the New Being as process: awareness, freedom, relatedness, and transcendence. God as Spirit grounds and unites these in his own being and fulfills them to a preeminent degree. Spirit takes up and transforms in a creative synthesis through the Divine Life the meaning of actualities. Spirit is God alive in perfect fulfillment of meaning at each moment. Thus Spirit is total *awareness* of and total *relatedness* to all actualized meanings. The *freedom* of God is his destiny. The *self-transcendence* of God as Spirit is his ability to ground and fulfill all meaning—any actual meaning—while maintaining his centered integrity through change.[8]

This definition of God as Spirit as it is further developed in that article moves toward a *theo*-logy, a view of God, which could found a theology of liberating culture. Insofar as Liberation Theology is suspicious of a transcendent "Being" who would leave the world behind, this doctrine of God as Spirit encompasses the processes of Life. Insofar as Liberation Theology intends a fuller actualization of humanity or fulfilled Life for the oppressed, this definition of God as Spirit points toward those principles which enable and constitute the New Being in any age. It is obvious that God viewed as Spirit expresses dimensions of Life. Tillich's insistence upon the multidimensional unity of Life enables one to correlate our human experiences of liberated fulfillment with the symbols generated by our religious experience. From this perspective, the definition of God as Spirit is not an abstraction washing out from actuality the elements of concreteness, but rather this definition is an expression of that revealed in the depths of our common human experience as the ultimate dimensions of Life. For this reason, I feel that an approach through the definition of God as Spirit is more likely to communicate to liberation theologians than one correlating the symbol "God" with the philosophical concept-symbol "Being-itself," although I would not want to deny the latter.

---

[8]H. Frederick Reisz, Jr., "Ambiguities in the Use of the Theological Symbol 'Spirit' in Paul Tillich's Theology," in *Tillich Studies: 1975*, 97-98.

If we accept the above definition of God as Spirit as the basic insight into the structures, processes and meanings of Life-fulfillment, then certain ethical dimensions of personal-social-political development or liberation can be sensed. Thus we can ground intentions for the *praxis* of liberation upon a *theo*-logy—a basic apprehension of revelation which has grasped us at the religious depths of our common human experience.

The processes of Life (self-integration, self-alteration or creativity, and self-transcendence) and the four principles determining the New Being as process when coordinated reveal that in each of the processes of Life a pairing of two of the principles determining New Being tends to dominate. This dominance takes the following form:

Process of Life	*Predominant Principles*
1. Self-integration	Awareness and Freedom
2. Self-alteration	Freedom and Relatedness
3. Self-transcendence	Relatedness and Transcendence

Several things need to be noted in this suggestive schema. First, in each of the processes of Life all four of the principles determining the New Being would be actualized, but the indicated pairs of principles would be primary for the process. Second, you will note that a progression develops. The final term in the pairings of "principles" is the first term in the subsequent pairing. This suggests a developmental schema in which the processes of Life cluster together because of the linkage of the principles. Thus the triad of processes fulfills Life—an individual, group, society, etc. The principles, by asserting themselves to constitute actuality, move this process inevitably onward. The divine Life itself is the supreme actuality of these processes. Third, for an individual or a group, any liberating process would be a fulfillment of Life and the establishment of new being. Thus a theology of liberation should reflect upon these elements. I will now pursue that reflection.

A Theology of Liberating Culture

Given the elements articulated above grounded in a theology of God as Spirit, what can be said to give content to a theology of liberating culture? This Tillichian schema begins to illumine the deficiencies of truncated modes of the processes of Life. If any culture or sub-culture life-community lives under these truncated modes of Life, they are oppressed in not being able to actualize the fulfilled unity of life-power and life-in-meanings.

Self-integration is necessary for self-identity. As blacks have shown us in America, this "pride" is a necessity for the revolution of the oppressed. However, self-integration with only *awareness* of the self leads to a narrowed subjective parochialism or a stereotyped ego-group image. Self-integration with only elements of *awareness* and *freedom* leads to a revolutionary anarchism or a chaotic fractionalism which is counterrevolutionary. Self-integration which only includes the elements of *awareness, freedom,* and *relatedness* potentially can eventuate in being co-opted by the environing elements of society which oppress. Finally, the self-integration of a culture or subgroup which involves only the elements of awareness, freedom, and transcendence may become a type of ideological abstraction incapable of effective actualization in a liberated culture. Liberation requires identity and self-integration so that there is a centered cohesion of power and meaning. This cohesion involves awareness, freedom, relatedness and transcendence even though the actualization of such integration depends most centrally upon the principles of awareness and freedom. Liberation movements have to awaken the oppressed to awareness of their condition and their potentialities and convince them of their freedom to act, to revolt, to resist.

Self-alteration or creativity is necessary for growth and change, for the irruption of the new liberated being of a person or group. Liberation movements have variously manifested this creativity in the forms of their intended societies as well as in the manner of educative-liberating processes and revolutions that seek those "ends." Self-alteration which is just *freedom* is chaotic, undisciplined and incapable of the formation of centered order which is needed for survival and identity. Self-alteration which is only *freedom* and *relatedness* risks becoming a creative liberal ideology without the impetus and awareness for *praxis,* for action. Finally, self-alteration only as *freedom, relatedness,* and *awareness* is often not able to envision the "newness" possible in a revolutionizing "kairos." Thus the liberation movement can become satisfied with less than true liberation transcending the present oppressions. Liberation requires creative alteration of the entire *theoria* and *praxis* of society so that systemic oppression can be exorcised. Such creative alteration requires freedom, relatedness, awareness and transcendence even though the actualization of such creativity depends most centrally upon the innovative power of freedom and the power of relatedness to generate form and content. Thus a liberation movement must create the environment in which freedom is a possibility without isolating the group from its relation to the actualities of all dimensions of life.

Self-transcendence is necessary for vision and continuing liberation. Liberation movements must look beyond the *praxis* of the moment if they actually are to liberate. Because systems of oppression are so pervasive, the power of such transcendence can grasp a movement allowing it to persist and evolve sustaining as well as innovative alternative forms of social-life. Self-transcendence merely as *relatedness* and *transcendence* can become rootless, forgetting its grounding in the past of the group and the depth of their life experiences. Ivan Illich has pointed to this danger in our systems of liberal education. Self-transcendence which is just *relatedness*, *transcendence* and *freedom* can become a euphoric escapism as so prevalently seen in some appropriations of mystical religion in our time. Finally, self-transcendence as *relatedness*, *transcendence*, and *awareness* leads to the frustration of rising expectations without the freedom for fulfilling *praxis*. Liberation requires a transcending of the present self-conceptions of the individual and group as well as a transcending of present oppressions. Such liberation will not lose self-affirmation, integrity and pride, if it includes all the principles of relatedness, transcendence, freedom, and awareness, even though relatedness and transcendence are those principles which must primarily enable this transcendence. A liberation effort must build into its *theoria* and *praxis* the transcendence which enables critical assessment and innovative projections of new intentions.

Besides the possibility of a truncated manifestation of the three processes of Life in a culture or liberation movement, there is also the possibility of the dominance of the secondary (but necessary) pair of principles in each of these processes. Such aberrations would also fight against actual liberation. If in the case of *self-integration*, a person or group lets this process be dominated by the secondary principles of *relatedness* and *transcendence*, then one faces the problem of co-optation. This inverted process leads to a return to colonialism or a variant of "Uncle-Tomism." The self or the group becomes centered in an identity not their own. They become "integrated" into another group in the worst manner, losing their own identity and integrity. Thus, the danger of liberalism which emphasizes the primacy of "universal transcending principles" relates to all of humanity and becomes threatening to the pride and self-integration or centeredness of liberation movements. Similarly, it is possible for the principles of *awareness* and *transcendence* to dominate the processes of self-alteration. In those instances, the liberation movement stands at the brink of a utopianism without the possibility of actualizing *praxis*. This misconceived process of creativity can also become ideological fanaticism in which the self-identity of the group and the adherence to a transcending ideological corpus destroys the possibility of actualizing *praxis*. To counteract this possibility, Liberation Theology stresses the concrete participation with the oppressed in the societal situation of oppression and expresses a suspicion of any theory or ideology or theology which does not arise out of the common human experience of a rational matrix. A creative movement which builds the self-awareness of oppression and then merely preaches an ideology becomes schizophrenic. Finally, *self-transcendence* is not a liberating process of Life if the secondary principles of *awareness* and *freedom* dominate that process. Such a balance of principles leads to ideological fanaticism in which a self-centered ideology is given free rein to dominate all *praxis* such that effective *praxis* is diminished and the creative and critical capacities are abolished. Liberation under these conditions often seeks to actualize intentions derived from self-centered awareness by means which in essence repeat the means used by the current mode of oppression. In such situations, the oppressed are often led into a new form of oppression.

In this short essay, we have argued that a Tillichian theology can be illuminative for Liberation Theology. Further we have indicated a doctrine of God as Spirit which can ground such a theology and out of which a theology of liberating culture can be constituted. We hope that these suggestions might lead toward the furtherance of a dialogue that has been thought to be impossible.

Notes on Contributors

Eberhard Amelung (Ph.D., Harvard) is Professor of Ethics at the German Federal Military Academy in Munich. He has published *Die Gestalt der Liebe: Paul Tillichs Theologie der Kultur* (Gütersloh, 1972).

Robert H. Bryant (Ph.D., Yale) is Professor of Theology at the United Theological Seminary of the Twin Cities, New Brighton, Minnesota. He has published *The Bible's Authority Today* (Augsburg, 1968).

Raymond F. Bulman (Ph.D., Columbia) is Professor of Theology at St. John's University in Jamaica, New York, and has published *A Blueprint for Humanity: Paul Tillich's Theology of Culture* (Bucknell University Press, 1981).

John J. Carey (Ph.D., Duke) is Professor and Director of Graduate Studies in Religion at Florida State University in Tallahassee. A past president of the North American Paul Tillich Society, he edited *Tillich Studies: 1975* for the Society.

John Powell Clayton (Ph.D., Cambridge) is Lecturer in Religious and Atheistic Thought at the University of Lancaster in England. He has edited *Ernst Troeltsch and the Future of Theology* (Cambridge University Press, 1976) and, with S. W. Sykes, *Christ, Faith and History* (Cambridge University Press, 1972).

Roy D. Morrison II (Ph.D., Chicago) is Professor of Philosophical Theology and Black Philosophy at Wesley Theological Seminary, Washington, D.C.

Victor L. Nuovo (Ph.D., Columbia) is Professor of Philosophy and Chairman of the Division of Humanities at Middlebury College, Middlebury, Vermont. A past president of the North American Paul Tillich Society, he also translated Tillich's two dissertations on Schelling, published by the Bucknell University Press in 1974.

H. Frederick Reisz, Jr. (Ph.D., Chicago) is Senior Pastor of the University Lutheran Church in Harvard Square, Cambridge, and Lutheran Denominational Counselor at Harvard Divinity School.

Robert R. N. Ross (Ph.D., Harvard) formerly taught Philosophy at Skidmore College, Saratoga Springs, New York.

Robert P. Scharlemann (Ph.D, Heidelberg) is Commonwealth Professor of Religion at the University of Virginia. He has published *Reflection and Doubt in the Thought of Paul Tillich* (Yale University Press, 1969) and *The Being of God* (Seabury, 1981). He is a past president of the North American Paul Tillich Society.

Joel R. Smith (Ph.D., Vanderbilt) formerly taught Philosophy at Lynchburg College, Lynchburg, Virginia.

Jerome A. Stone (Ph.D., Chicago) is Professor of Philosophy and Religion at William Rainey Harper College, Palatine, Illinois.

John R. Stumme (Ph.D., Columbia) is Professor of Systematic Theology at the Instituto Superior Evangelico de Estudios Teologicos in Buenos Aires, Argentina. He has published *Socialism in Theological Perspective: A Study of Paul Tillich, 1918-1933* (Scholars Press, 1978).

John Heywood Thomas (S.T.M., Union Seminary in New York) is Professor and Chairman of the Department of Theology at the University of Nottingham in England. He has published *Paul Tillich: An Appraisal* (Westminster, 1963) and *Paul Tillich* (Lutterworth, 1965).

Donald R. Weisbaker (Ph.D., Chicago) is Professor of Philosophy and Religion at the University of Tennessee at Chattanooga.

Paul Wiebe (Ph.D., Chicago) is Associate Professor of Religion at Wichita State University in Wichita, Kansas, and has recently completed a translation of Tillich's *Das System Der Wissenschaften*.